THE HIGH-PURPOSE COMPANY

THE *TRULY* RESPONSIBLE—AND HIGHLY PROFITABLE—

FIRMS THAT ARE CHANGING BUSINESS NOW

CHRISTINE ARENA

Collins

An Imprint of HarperCollinsPublishers

For my MBA research team at McGill University—
and inspired students of business everywhere

HarperCollins books may be purchased for educational, business, or sales promotional use. For information, please write to: Special Markets Department, HarperCollins Publishers, 10 East 53rd Street, New York, NY 10022.

Designed by Mary Austin Speaker

Library of Congress Cataloging-in-Publication Data

Arena, Christine.
    The High-purpose company : The truly responsible—and highly profitable—firms that are changing business now / Christine Arena.
        p.   cm.
    Includes bibliographical references and index.
    Contents: The context—The concept—The pitfalls—The progression.
    ISBN: 978-0-06-085207-8
    ISBN-10: 0-06-085207-0
        1. Social responsibility of business.   2. Corporate governance.   I. Title.
HD60.A75 2006
658.408—dc22

                                                                        2006049054

07 08 09 10 11 WBC/RRD 10 9 8 7 6 5 4 3 2 1

contents

MEMBERS OF *THE HIGH-PURPOSE COMPANY* RESEARCH TEAM ASSEMBLED FOR TEAM MEETING, MARCH 2006

Back row: *(left to right) Catherine Tang, Jamie Wald, Stephanie Vanness, Louis Dagenais, Professor David M. Lank*
Front row: *(left to right) Francie Dudeck, Ruchy Khurana, Joy Bennett, Jan Gora, Michelle Leggat, Stephanie Berger*

acknowledgments

I am tremendously grateful for the contributions made by others, without which this book would certainly not exist. First and foremost, I would like to extend my deepest appreciation to the extraordinary members of the research team. Ten MBA students from the McGill University Desautels Faculty of Management worked for two consecutive semesters to help put this project together. The research team contributed thousands of hours of hard work and set the highest standards for me and for themselves. Their critical thinking, business acumen, and passion lead me to pursue this endeavor with far more academic rigor and intellectual depth than I originally would have. I can only hope that the final output is worthy of their tremendous efforts and skills, which came in the form of individual and group analysis as well as intense classroom debates. More than providing the quality research necessary to complete this task, each team member represents a spirit and skill set that I believe will come to embody the future of business leadership, which is why this book is a tribute to both their vision and potential.

MEMBERS OF THE RESEARCH TEAM FOR
The High-Purpose Company:

Joy Bennett	Francie Dudeck	Catherine Tang
Stephanie Berger	Jan Gora	Stephanie Vanness
Louis Dagenais	Ruchy Khurana	Jamie Wald
	Michelle Leggatt	

I would also like to acknowledge the special efforts of Stephanie Berger, valiant student leader of the research team, as well as Professor David

M. Lank, who oversaw the entire process. Both were instrumental in helping me to recruit the very best graduate students, keeping things on-track and making the project a great success. I am particularly indebted to Stephanie who, delicately over wine and cheese, would encourage me to face the cold, hard truth about my early analysis and approach, which evidently stood to be improved. Along these lines, Stephanie helped immensely.

I was equally fortunate to engage participation from some of the greatest thinkers in the corporate responsibility community—most notably, Paul Hawken, Bill McDonough, Amory Lovins, Joel Makower, Gil Friend, and Mats Lederhausen. Through their striking new ideas, each of these leaders has contributed immeasurably to the field of corporate responsibilty. In many ways, this book measures the social, environmental, and economic conditions that they both predicted decades ago and helped to create.

In addition to the experts above—as well as the many consumers and activists who took part in this project—numerous people from inside corporations, not-for-profits, academic institutions, and consulting organizations were kind enough to provide me with key information as well as endure in-depth interviews and follow-up conversations. To each of the following people, I would like to express my deepest thanks: Kelly Costa of the Natural Capital Institute; Michelle J. McCulloch of Innovest Strategic Value Advisors; Dr. Gurkirpal Singh of Stanford University; Dr. Marcia Angell of Harvard University; John Mack of *Pharma Marketing News;* Barbara Enloe Hadsell of Hadsell & Stormer; Pratap Chatterjee of CorpWatch; Dave Taylor of Intuitive Systems; Alex Winslow of Texas Watch; Steve Cloutier of Bovis Lend Lease; Frederick Bermudez of Pacific Company New Mexico; Sheri Woodruff and Eric Pillmore of Tyco; Eric H. Israel of KPMG; Alice Tepper Marlin and Lisa Bernstein of Social Accountability International; Melissa O'Brien, Jason Jackson and Ray Cox of Wal-Mart; Larry Smith and Mark Weightman of the Montreal Alouettes; Jill

Zenger and Hannah Jones of Nike; Andy Fouché of Starbucks; Craig Minowa of the Organic Consumers Association; Nicole Chettero of TransFair USA; Pearse Edwards and Pamela Passman of Microsoft; Michelle Reardon and Dawn Rittenhouse of DuPont; Amaya Gorosti-aga of General Electric; Petrell Ozbay, Dave Long and Scott Johnson of SC Johnson; Brian Balwin of JetBlue; Jo Natale and Mary Ellen Burris of Wegmans Food Market; Steven Young and Robert Glassman of Wainwright Bank and Trust; Eve Bould of Patagonia; Susan Schor and Kathy D'Angelo of Eileen Fisher; and Tom Arnold of Terra Pass.

I would like to make special note of the supportive team at Collins, including Marion Maneker, Ethan Friedman, and Alex Scordelis; and also Mark Martucci as my talented graphics consultant; Lisa Hagan as my loyal agent; Lynn Harris as my research associate; and Herb Schaff-ner, who enthusiastically believed in and supported this book from the moment he learned of it.

I am so very fortunate to be married to Michael Donner. After months of hiding away in my office like a monk, Michael continues to tolerate my propensity for becoming all consumed with projects such as this and encourages me to focus on what really matters. In review-ing the manuscript, Michael's was the opinion that I valued the most. Not only is he my most helpful critic, but he is also my chief collabora-tor as he pushes me to venture further in my studies. A spouse's en-couragement is the ultimate mark of love and respect and owing to his I know that I am one lucky woman.

On an equally personal note, I view my passion for the major themes conveyed in this book as a reflection of where I come from. There are many on both sides of my family who have dedicated themselves to the pursuit of ethical business—including my parents, Angelo and Alice Arena, and in-laws, Conrad and Sandra Donner—but few have made more of an impression on me than my late grandfather, Simon Arena.

Simon lived to be one hundred years of age. He passed away in May 2006, the month I completed this manuscript. Simon had worked for

General Electric his entire career—from 1925 to 1967. Before he died, we used to visit together in his kitchen, which was decorated with nothing but GE appliances. He received no discount on the GE appliances, although he purchased them just the same. GE was an integral part of his life. It meant more to him than any other company, so he stayed true to it until the end.

At his kitchen table, Simon would tell me stories about how during the depression he and his fellow GE employees watched each other's backs like a tightly knit community and were equally vigilant about helping the company to stabilize during a time of economic turmoil. In response, I would tell him stories about Jeff Immelt's new vision of eco-friendly economic opportunity and how it was changing the face of GE and making the company invaluable to communities. Interestingly, the moral to both stories is identical: it's people who make the business, not the other way around. I will always remember that.

an explanatory note

What is corporate responsibility? Some regard the practice as a form of philanthropy, or marketing. But most experts in the field broadly define it as "the efforts companies make above and beyond regulation to balance the needs of stakeholders with the need to make a profit."[1]

Given these characterizations, it's no wonder why skepticism remains, or why the movement is only now gaining traction. Corporate responsibility is not really a practice about balance or trade-offs, since the scales are inevitably tipped. After all, given the choice, what company would opt to serve society *instead of* serving shareholders? Few that I know, or would invest in. Financial motives will always prevail in publicly traded corporations, so it makes little sense to posit otherwise.

This book pays homage to the reality of corporate responsibility, not the dream of it. I don't stress doing good for goodness' sake, the morality of the issues involved, or my own particular notion of what it means to be a corporate citizen in the twenty-first century. Instead, I focus on the simple idea of *market opportunity*—what it means with respect to corporate responsibility, where it can be found, and what companies are seizing it best.

The central findings of my research can be distilled in the following way: *superficiality fails* whereas *authenticity prevails*. Companies that falsely approach corporate responsibility as a form of marketing, public relations, or even philanthropy don't produce the most meaningful results. In fact, they often waste their money and create additional liabilities. Conversely, companies that truly approach the practice of corporate responsibility as a fully-integrated business strategy, wisely investing in profitable solutions to meet unmet social and environmental needs and problems find their performance greatly enhanced. The deeper and more strategic the investment, the better the overall result. Shareholder interests lead, not follow, effective corporate responsibility strategy.

Despite my findings, public discourse surrounding the merits of corporate responsibility continues to spin in circles. Critics like *The Wall Street Journal* and the *Economist* take pot shots at the concept, while advocates vigorously defend their beliefs. For this reason, we start off with a bird's eye view of the current state of the debate. The prologue presents readers with a context that frames the issues, and more important, refutes the misconceptions and myths that have dominated the practice of corporate responsibility for too long.

Once we've reviewed the historical and present-day context, we discuss what makes a High-Purpose Company, why they succeed by every available measure, and examine the unique process through which they are born. In subsequent chapters, we take a tour of this developmental process, starting with the lower rungs on the responsibility ladder where mistakes are often made, then climbing up to levels where the best market opportunities and results reside.

We conclude with some of the most compelling proofs of how and why corporate responsibility succeeds. Chapters 5, and particularly 6 and 7, demonstrate how some of the world's most successful corporations have leveraged corporate responsibility as a direct means of increasing their worth—and *worthiness*.

Implicit on every page is a simple question that I ask readers to answer for themselves: Besides make money, what in the world is your company here to do? The evidence from my research shows that answering this question, discovering and deciphering a higher purpose, is a significant part of the process of achieving organizational excellence. Companies that offer people something that's vital and substantive are more inclined to prevail. In this way, corporate responsibility pays. In this way, the strategies contained herein echo common sense.

CHRISTINE ARENA

PART 1: The Context

Prologue:
It's Not What (or Who) You Think

Those who are in love with practice without knowledge are like the sailor who gets into a ship without rudder or compass and who never can be certain whether he is going.

—LEONARDO DA VINCI

"There is something stirring unlike anything else I've seen in the past twenty years," says Paul Hawken, the controversial author, activist, entrepreneur, and founder of eco-friendly retail company Smith & Hawken. "There is original thinking going on."

Original thinking, Hawken believes, is the one key to triple bottom-line success. It's what separates the winners from the losers—the truly remarkable and innovative companies from the masses of others that adopt popular terminology like "socially responsible," "sustainable," and "green" without a genuine commitment to these concepts or an understanding of what they mean to a company's operations in the present and future. Original thinking requires the ability to see the bigger picture, to face the truth, to establish intent. Original thinking leads to brilliant business, social, and environmental results *only* when accompanied by the will and ability to transform accordingly.

"Real corporate responsibility involves systemic change," says Hawken. "It requires a business to carefully evaluate every aspect of itself, and very few want to do that." At the Natural Capital Institute (NCI), a source point for Hawken's principles and an organization that researches matters of economy, ecology, and social justice, projects are regularly produced that help people to embrace a new logic. Some of NCI's projects help investors to finally distinguish between the truly responsible companies that embrace necessary systemic change, and "the pretenders," as Hawken calls them, that reject or ignore fundamental transformative steps.

In June 2003, NCI undertook a large-scale project that caused quite a stir. The project targeted the $2.16 trillion[1] socially responsible investment (SRI) industry. The organization's team looked into over six hundred SRI mutual funds around the world in order to determine which publicly traded companies they invested in and whether those companies, based on their socially responsible activities, rightfully belonged in an SRI fund after all.

The NCI research team noticed straightaway that even though socially responsible funds are enormously popular in the United States, growing at a rate 40 percent faster than other professionally managed assets,[2] there are few common screening standards, definitions, or codes of practice for the SRI industry as a whole. They observed that, because of this, different SRI fund managers had different definitions of "socially responsible" and few if any investors had a firm grasp of what the term meant. This situation bothered Hawken. "SRI (qualification) can be determined by what is called a negative screen, i.e., if you don't do something, you qualify. Or if you say you do something even though you really don't (such as screening for environmental responsibility) you also qualify," he says. "The analogy would be a gang member who is a mugger. If the gang member says he will stop mugging senior citizens over 65, he now qualifies as a socially responsible gang member. By creating an industry that is identified by specific exclusions or inclusions, key information and criteria are conveniently overlooked."[3]

It also bothered Hawken to find that, at the time the study was conducted, some SRI firms did not openly disclose their screening criteria, research, or data to the public, while others did not reveal the names of each company contained in their portfolios to potential investors. It frustrated him further to see that the loose and clandestine standards employed by some fund managers enabled them to include virtually *any* Fortune 500 company—be it Raytheon, Halliburton, or Monsanto—in their SRI fund, and that such additions seem to be at least partially motivated by the manager's need to match or outperform the Standard & Poor 500. From where Hawken was sitting, here appeared a black box of an industry with little credibility, enforceability, or transparency. "To put it plainly, if the SRI industry were a corporation, it wouldn't qualify in a rigorously screened portfolio," said the NCI's scathing October 15, 2004, research report that summarized the findings of its yearlong study. "Either the industry has to reform *in toto*, or that portion of the industry that wants to maintain credibility has to break off from the pretenders."

Since the NCI's report was released, Hawken's positions and criticisms have not wavered. At the 2005 World Economic Forum in Davos, Switzerland, a list of the "100 Most Sustainable Companies in the World" was released by Canada-based Innovest Strategic Value Advisors, an environmental investment advisory firm that sells its analysis to the SRI mutual fund industry. Hawken publicly voiced serious concern over the list's exclusion of smaller companies with stellar environmental track records in favor of larger companies with questionable practices. For instance, Innovest's list included PepsiCo, a company that trails behind competitor Coca-Cola with respect to environmental issues and uses negligible recycled content in its plastic containers; ASEA Brown Boveri (ABB), a company that in 2004 settled a U.S. federal court action for bribery in Nigeria, Angola, and Kazakhstan, and continues to face ongoing corruption investigations; and Bristol-Myers Squibb, a company that recently paid over $670 million in fines to various states and the Federal Trade Commission to settle disputes over whether it had illegally blocked generic versions of Taxol, Platinol, and BuSpar from entering the market, thus allegedly costing patients and states billions of dollars.[4]

To be fair, Innovest is very candid about the criteria it used for selecting the 100 Most Sustainable Companies in the World. Innovest acknowledges that the title of its list is an overstatement designed to get it noticed. According to Innovest's director of client relations, Michelle McCulloch, the firm does not propose to present the world's most environmentally friendly companies per se, but rather the ones that are best positioned to profit from sustainability relative to their industry peers. "Whether Pepsi uses only 10 percent recycled content in their packaging or Bristol-Myers Squibb is facing legislative issues are small parts of a much larger focus," she says. "It's our opinion that these companies are in an excellent position to manage their sustainability-related risk opportunities going forward." McCulloch says that the firm's analysts selected Sustainable 100 winners based on how they performed across 120 "intangible" dimensions not considered under traditional financial analysis, such as the extent to which management is forward-looking, the degree to which a company has developed antennae and internal structures to identify new business opportunities, and the level of resources devoted to pursuing environmental technologies and solutions. Innovest starts with a list of two thousand companies from all over the world, then chooses the top performers in each sector, thus accounting for about 5 percent of their total sample and narrowing down to a selection of a final one hundred corporations. Although McCulloch says that the firm's selection process is methodical and rigorous, she concedes: "We don't simply downgrade or exclude companies for not being perfect."

Yet exactly what "perfect" or "sustainability" or "green" or "responsibility" means depends at least somewhat on whom you're asking, and subjective standards can lead to inconsistency and, Hawken insists, even deception. "SRI funds are misusing terminology to curry favor with progressive investors who truly want their money to make a difference," he says. "If they want to exploit broad definitions, that's fine, but let's not call it ethical investing."

THE STANDOFF

Hawken and the NCI have won few friends by pointing out alleged vast irregularities in the SRI industry or by insisting that the very industry that *sells* the value of values is as misguided as some of the more notorious businesses apparently included in certain SRI funds. Between the release of NCI's 2004 report and March 2005, multiple high-profile representatives from the SRI community launched counterattacks on Hawken's methodology, his findings, his tone, his proposed solutions, and even on him personally.

Weeks after NCI's report was released, executives from Pax World Funds posted a response on www.commongroundmag.com, arguing that Hawken's and NCI's emphasis on the industry's screening methods—or lack thereof—was unfair: "[His] approach is to isolate one aspect of socially responsible investing (SRI) and analyze it. Pax World and the other SRI mutual funds named in the [NCI report] utilize screening AND advocacy AND community investing. These are irrevocably intertwined strategies. To examine one without the others is like critiquing a house's architectural style when all you see is the basement."[5]

Others agreed. "Hawken is missing the concept," said Garvin Jabusch, director of sustainable investing for the Sierra Club. Jabusch was miffed by Hawken's scrutiny of the Sierra Club fund's practice of including companies like Outback Steakhouse and Estée Lauder in their SRI fund over smaller, more responsible companies. As Jabusch explained to the *Christian Science Monitor* in November 2004, this selection methodology is a matter of policy, as Sierra Club deliberately avoids choosing risky "microcaps" in favor of larger companies with established environmental and financial track records. While Jabusch conceded that Hawken made a few good points in his report, he said that "we disagree with his tenor and method." In the same article, Timothy Smith, chairman of the Social Investment Forum, characterized Hawken's proposed rating system for determining a company's true level of responsibility as "tiers of self-righteousness," while Doug Wheat, business development director of SRI World Group, acknowledged that Hawken opened a can of worms with his exposé, saying that "no one likes to have this kind of a discussion in public."[6]

Hawken deals with his detractors by calling attention to their defensive stance. He points out that since his opponents' fortunes are inextricably tied to their firms' reputations, they have something to protect and would rather sidestep constructive debate than confront a pervasive problem. He recently made this point in relaying a standoff he had with Terry Mollner, the cofounder of SRI company Calvert Group: "When I asked Terry how it was that two-thirds of the thousand largest corporations qualify as green, he asked me who did I think I was to say what was and what wasn't green?"[7] A few months later, in February 2005, Mollner fired back, accusing Hawken of using sensationalist tactics for his own public relations purposes. "[Hawken's] technique can comfortably be used by less mature people, people who believe that the end justifies the means. However, more mature people accurately see the process as the end," he says. "To perpetuate our more mature values, we must live them well instead of joining in this manipulative game."[8]

Skimming through SRI industry press, it's hard to miss the irony of the squabble between Hawken and a sizable group of his industry peers. The business icon and cofounder of the sustainability movement, the man who through his 1993 best-selling classic, *The Ecology of Commerce*, inspired countless executives to follow a more responsible business path, is today the industry's black sheep.

Is Hawken guilty of treason to the socially responsible investment and corporate responsibility movements? Is he, as so many of his colleagues and former friends insist, entirely off base with his accusations? And is it really his demeanor and method that angers people? Or is it that he hits a nerve of truth with his message?

Perhaps Hawken's research uncovered benign teething troubles or perhaps a genuine deficiency. In either case, this is *exactly* the kind of discussion that needs to happen in public. None of us needs to choose sides, though we must look deeper into the issue itself because what lies there is an opportunity too monumental to slight off.

THE END OF THE BEGINNING

Looking deeper, one might ask why things grew so muddled in the first place. I think the answer is fairly straightforward: rapid growth. The combination of increased regulatory scrutiny, corporate scandals, social and environmental crises, a twenty-four-hour news cycle, and technology-enabled information access drove a sudden demand for corporate responsibility, leading some to respond hastily through fragmented and low-quality approaches.

In general, people experience corporate greed more acutely today than ever before. As a result, they want more in the way of corporate integrity, transparency, and accountability, and are a lot less tolerant and trusting than they were five or ten years ago. For this reason, more companies see themselves as beholden not just to shareholders but to wider stakeholder groups, including employees, suppliers, consumers, and society at large. Many are beginning to answer to these demand shifts.

Some companies devise image-building advertising campaigns in an attempt to win the trust of consumers and investors. Other companies make more substantial progress by investing in solutions that are sustainable in every sense of the word: socially, environmentally, *and* financially. In any case, this plenitude of both definition and approach leads to a kind of industry-wide chaos, and the chaos leads to the current debate over what really works, which companies are doing it right, and whether or not corporate responsibility (CR) is even a worthwhile endeavor.

Today, corporate responsibility seems to be approached by some businesses with the same zeal and haste as was the dot-com movement during the mid-1990s. In recent years, most big companies have scrambled to respond to the trend by assembling CR departments, CR officers, CR Web pages, and CR reports. Everyone wants in on the "most ethical," "most responsible" who's who lists published by *Fortune* and *Business Ethics*, and when proud firms do make the cut, they are quick to send out press releases heralding their accomplishments. Such press releases typically include a well-crafted comment attributed to the organization's man or woman in charge that reads something like: "At X company, integrity is the key to our success, and every day we work to ensure that we operate in the most ethical manner possible." Pick up an annual report—any annual report—and you are likely to read something about how seriously the company takes social and environmental issues.

In 2005, Big Four consulting firm KPMG published a study entitled *International Survey of Corporate Responsibility Reporting*, which showed that 64 percent of the world's 250 largest companies issued either a separate corporate responsibility report or devoted a section to CR in their annual reports, up from 45 percent only a few years earlier. The study also revealed that 74 percent of executives were driven by "economic considerations," while only 27 percent selected "brand reputation" as the most important motivating factor for CR reporting. The KPMG study concluded that ethical issues are taken more seriously by a growing number of companies around the world.

A different 2005 study issued by Oracle Corporation and the Economist Intelligence Unit, entitled *The Importance of Corporate Responsibility*, reported similar findings. This report said that 85 percent of executives and investors believed that corporate responsibility was a "central" or "important" factor in their business and investment decision making, compared to roughly 42 percent only five years before. It also noted that 84 percent of respondents indicated that today they view corporate responsibility practices as potentially having a positive impact on a company's bottom line.

Despite the flurry of data supporting CR, critics like business news magazine the *Economist*—which, oddly enough, is part of the Economist Intelligence Unit, the same unit that published the *Importance of Corporate Responsibility* study—continue to poke holes in the legitimacy of the concept. They don't see the burgeoning interest in this practice area as a win-win for communities and companies alike. On the contrary, they view the development as nothing more than a fleeting fad, a temporary blip on the radar screen. Corporate responsibility, they argue, is a superficial, self-serving tactic at best and a waste of time and money at worst. "Better that CR be undertaken as a cosmetic exercise than as a serious surgery to fix what doesn't need fixing," said the *Economist*'s Clive Crook in his infamous January 2005 article, "The Good Company," in which he boldly proposed that capitalism is perfect just the way it is. Crook goes so far as to suggest that too much of a focus on ethics may in fact be unethical, as executives are accountable to shareholders above all else. "CR may encroach on corporate decision making in ways that seriously reduce welfare,"[9] he claims.

The University of California, Berkeley, Haas School of Business's David Vogel also asserts that there is little proof that CR is a safe or practical investment. "Unfortunately, there's not much basis for the claim that CR systematically pays . . . There is a market for virtue, but it is a niche market," he says. "CR is best understood as a business strategy that, like any business strategy, makes sense for a subset of companies under specific circumstances."[10]

The battle of corporate responsibility ideas continues. On one end of the spectrum, there is a group of truly innovative companies defying industry traditions and walking the corporate responsibility walk *profitably*. In the middle are mainstream corporations talking the talk but nothing more, then puzzling over why the corporate responsibility talk doesn't produce stellar business results or a better return on investment. And on the other end of the spectrum are critics ignoring or assailing nearly every aspect of the CR movement, focusing on the mistakes made by the many in the middle, thus making some excellent points in the process. Who is winning the battle of ideas?

The answer is: nobody, because too many of us look at the CR movement the wrong way.

As Hawken affirms, the term *corporate responsibility* has been coopted and manipulated to mean just about anything to anyone. Different sides have different notions of the concept, and each side executes and evaluates CR based on its particular and sometimes arbitrary interpretations and standards. So, at least a portion of the CR debate is futile. If we can't agree about what we're arguing about, then why in the world are we arguing?

What if, rather than focus on semantics, both advocates and skeptics stepped away from this issue for a moment. What if, instead of aiming for CR as an ultimate goal, companies reframed CR as a pleasant side effect of something equally if not more important, and yet often overlooked: *corporate health.*

What if we devised business strategies and initiatives that aimed to make our companies healthier—that is, more benign, resilient, enduring, and balanced? Specifically, what if rather than accept the harm produced for stakeholders and the earth as acceptable business costs, companies committed to creating safe and renewing work environments, processes, and products? What if companies invested in the world problems that their stakeholders face—to the point where the company's own success depended on the ability to find the right solutions? What if people within companies dedicated themselves to one meaningful, shared vision? And what if, instead of putting the bulk of corporate responsibility efforts and dollars into me-too approaches and counting chickens through exhaustive CR reports, companies concentrated on using their greatest strengths to hatch original ideas and enterprising solutions instead?

We are at the end of the beginning of the CR movement. We are in the midst of a refinement period where weaker approaches are being outperformed or replaced by stronger new approaches, and where consumers and investors are getting far better at distinguishing between the two. The market is adjusting itself, and if we want to stay competitive, we have to move with it. To do this, we must first reject the old ideas that hold us back.

SIX TIRED MYTHS

- **Myth 1: CR is about doing the right thing.** This favored definition of CR is found all over the Web, in books, and in press releases, but really, it is an incomplete thought. We need to answer the questions: what is "the right thing," and who gets to decide? Good CR is not, for example, so much about prioritizing the environment over shareholder interests as much as it is about solving environmental problems in a way that serves shareholder interests. Without the links that bind these separate interests together, the solutions themselves are not viable over the long term. Companies can't afford to throw good money after bad at programs that don't work and don't serve them. And without viable, long-term solutions, our biggest social and environmental problems will remain unsolved. No, CR is not about doing the right thing for one cause over another as much as it is about engaging in a continuous cycle of corporate self-improvement. When companies search for basic principles of corporate health, they necessarily begin to address their weaknesses. They start to examine all aspects of the company—from employee pay and benefits to work conditions, trade relationships, manufacturing techniques, product quality, and customer service—and to address whatever negative social and environmental issues affect their success within each of these areas. CR is increasingly about fiduciary duty, as failing to address these crucial areas and take necessary steps in time can put a company at a serious disadvantage.

- **Myth 2: Making the world a better place is the top priority of CR.** Many companies expend much time and money "giving back" to the community, when really they should *first* focus on eliminating the damage they create through their most basic business activities. Some of the best CR programs presented in this book and throughout the industry work to benefit society and the environment so well because they primarily target business inefficiencies and risks. For instance, without Gap's efforts to improve labor standards, the company would remain a target for watchdog groups, lawsuits, and negative publicity. Without Tyco's comprehensive ethical housecleaning, it would remain an SEC target and suffer from a dysfunctional internal corporate culture. Without DuPont's commitment to become a zero waste, zero emissions, and zero accidents organization, the company would face substantial liabilities produced by pollution costs and workplace fatalities and injuries—not to mention miss out on $2 billion in saved overhead costs. By both minimizing the practices that create business vulnerabilities and maximizing approaches that work to reverse related social and environmental problems, certain companies have become great examples of high-performance CR. Therefore, the first question for business leaders to ask themselves isn't necessarily, How can we better serve society? but rather, Where and how are we most vulnerable to the risks produced by social and environmental inefficiencies? By answering question two, companies naturally answer question one.

- **Myth 3: Competitive distinction is the top benefit of CR**. Many advocates tell companies to invest in CR because it can set their brand apart. This claim leads one to ask the valid question: If everyone else in my sector is doing it, then why should I? The fact is that brand differentiation is absolutely not the top benefit of CR. Innovation is. As the companies featured throughout this book prove, outstanding CR leads to higher-quality products, services, business models, management policies, operational innovations, and other advancements that can revitalize a company and catapult it forward. The advantages gleaned by a slightly better brand position alone pale in comparison.

- **Myth 4: CR is relevant only to niche businesses**. Narrowly (and erroneously) defining CR as a marketing ploy for liberal brands is a huge mistake, since there are very few if any companies for which CR is not totally fundamental. The routine acts of manufacturing products, using natural resources, trading in foreign nations, and managing stakeholder relations create both consequences and opportunities for wider society. The real issue is not whether CR is relevant, but whether or not companies choose to ignore or strategically manage the results they create.

- **Myth 5: CR doesn't always pay**. Actually, this is true—although not for the reasons that people often think. The chief reason why so many CR initiatives fail to produce tangible business rewards is that they were not designed to do so in the first place. Many companies approach CR in a superficial and compartmentalized way. CR is often used as a public relations ploy, an element of a company's branding, or as a mode of compliance with regulatory or industry standards. Such programs are generally defensive and narrow, not offensive or comprehensive in nature. They are often not created in order to help the company grow healthier or reach its ultimate business goals and are therefore not seen as "mission critical" by the senior executives leading the organization. Thus, it is no surprise that few companies devote substantial resources to the area or profit from those investments. The bottom line is that if a company wants CR to pay, then it has to design it to. It also needs to be patient enough to wait for the bigger rewards to accrue over the long term, as such rewards rarely surface immediately.

- **Myth 6: Increased CR reporting signifies improved CR performance.** While the current emphasis on CR reporting does indicate a shift toward corporate transparency, it does not necessarily mean that more companies are approaching CR strategically. Measuring the intangible social and environmental impact of a given company is only half the battle. The other half is optimizing the initiatives that create that impact in a way that improves social, environmental, and financial performance. It would be ideal if companies spent less time and money tracking and advertising their accomplishments, and more time and money actually accomplishing great things.

Rethinking old myths helps us apply fresh perspective to our own business approaches and the marketplace in general. If the new mode in CR is about change vs. charity, as this book suggests, then we need to reframe the classic strategic priorities. If the most useful tool for achieving this necessary change is indeed original thinking vs. conformity, then many CR consultants who teach companies how to catch up with competitors or comply with regulations might need to adjust their approach. In addition, if the best CR programs work to produce *healthier* companies, not just highly regarded companies, then some of our all-time favorite case studies may no longer serve as prime examples.

Ask yourself:
Which of these two companies is the more responsible?

- **Ben & Jerry's**, which built its brand on 1960s generation peaceful values but sells a product that may contribute to obesity, diabetes, heart disease, and other illnesses, or

- **Medtronic**, a company whose medical technology products offer lifesaving benefits for people with diabetes, heart disease, and other disorders, but which allegedly offered doctors kickbacks to boost sales in 2005.[11]

Which of these companies is the more sustainable?

- **Chevron**, which asks consumers to conserve energy through its $50 million "Will You Join Us?" environmental advertising campaign, yet tells shareholders that it plans to increase supply and control of oil in coming years and makes minimal or no investment in alternative energy sources like solar and wind technologies, or

- **Ford**, which currently has the EPA's rating of worst-performing fleet of vehicles on the road, yet, spent $2 billion dollars renovating its Rouge Center manufacturing facility into an ecological marvel, and pledges to produce 250,000 hybrid Escape SUVs, and use gas-electric hybrid engines in more than half of all Ford, Lincoln, and Mercury vehicles by 2010.

Which of these companies is the better corporate citizen?

- **Merck**, a company that was listed as a "best citizen" for years and spent $2.5 billion on drug research in 2004, but which denied all allegations that it improperly handled the marketing and recall of Vioxx even after several juries found it liable, 11,500 additional plaintiffs filed lawsuits, and the *New England Journal of Medicine* said the company withheld information about the drug's dangers from an article,[12] or

- **Tyco**, whose name was synonymous with accounting scandals and corporate greed, but which, following the indictment of some of its senior management, acknowledged wrongdoing in a hundred-page Form 8-K report filed with the SEC, and then conducted one of the most extensive ethical makeovers ever undertaken by a major corporation.

The answers to these questions aren't necessarily obvious, and reading through the following chapters, you may very well disagree with some of my or my research group's analysis. In fact, you may vehemently disagree. But that's precisely the point. There are not necessarily right or wrong answers to the interpretive questions above, just as there are no perfect or evil companies. One thing, however, is certain. To execute corporate responsibility more adeptly, we need to look beyond the superficial and the categorical. We need to evaluate old problems in a new light and search for great examples where we previously did not. Some of the most effective corporate responsibility initiatives reside in unlikely places, so it is essential that we keep an open mind and realize that while good public relations does not constitute good corporate responsibility, neither does blind idealism.

Like any investment, corporate responsibility is not a mindless game. It is not a fixed slot machine that automatically generates returns for all stakeholders, least of all investors and shareholders. The old argument over whether or not corporate responsibility yields consistent business returns is an arbitrary one given that this particular practice is interpreted and executed countless different ways, sometimes with little or no foresight. Right now, the key question is not, Does corporate responsibility work? but rather, How does it work? Why does it work? and Under what specific conditions does it work the best? These are the issues that formed the original basis for my research and for this book.

The High-Purpose Company is a book about making the kinds of corporate responsibility investments that generate maximum returns for all stakeholders. It is a book about escalating strategy and value. Owing to this, it contains a worldview that runs contrary to the one portrayed by detractors who simply see corporate responsibility as one of the business world's most liberal and misguided quests.

As you read this book, observe how the companies most deeply invested in corporate responsibility are not all hippy, do-gooder brands. Most are classic capitalist institutions. Take special note of their investment strategies. The ones generating the best returns don't allocate the majority of their corporate responsibility dollars to advertising and reputation management initiatives. Instead, they splurge on eco-effective technology and product development innovations designed to help the company compete better in the future. They also invest in socially and environmentally sound operational, supply chain, and management-related improvements, as well as in philanthropic programs with a definitive business edge. If you visit their Web sites, you will notice how the companies generating the best triple bottom-line returns also happen to supply metrics that prove exactly how and where they are making a marked difference in the world by, for instance, minimizing their strain on the earth's resources or maximizing their contributions to stakeholder communities. You will see how each stays paces ahead of industry regulations by proactively setting higher and higher goals for itself every year and by meeting those goals year after year. Collectively, what does this say? Could it mean that indeed corporate responsibility is not a cosmetic exercise at all, but rather the way business is changing?

A seismic shift is unfolding all around us. "It's as if the future hinted at by trend forecasters, scientists, and environmentalists has come hazily into view," concedes Hawken. "It's no longer a bunch of CR advocates wringing their hands, but a widespread realization that change is imperative for the health of every company and the world in which they operate."

This book examines the intricate nature of this shift and provides a blueprint for all businesses moving through it. Through solid evidence and in-depth analysis, it supports the claim that purpose is a driving force for corporate transformation, optimal CR performance, and corporate health. It reveals what High-Purpose Companies are, why they tend to succeed by most available measures and, just as importantly, how they are born, or reborn as the case may be. While the next chapter describes key principles, the progression chapters reveal a specific, step-by-step developmental process, and provide guidance and tips that help enable those who want to create and maintain High-Purpose Companies to begin to do so. The significance of purpose is therefore where we will start.

PART 2: The Concept

1:

Passing the Litmus Test

Why on earth would you settle for creating something mediocre that does little more than make money, when you can create something outstanding that makes a lasting contribution as well?

—JIM COLLINS, *BUILT TO LAST*

When author Jim Collins asked the question quoted above to his readers in the author's note of his best-selling paperback *Built to Last* in 2002, he perhaps unknowingly cut to the heart of the corporate responsibility debate and nailed the one thing that businesspeople need to know about it. The firms featured in his book are unique in a variety of ways. But the single variable that enables them to succeed, as Collins so eloquently noted, is *worthiness*.

The companies featured in *Built to Last* are worthy of lasting. They endure because without them, society would be worse off. These businesses grew invaluable to people because each stands for a purpose that is greater than the products it sells or the money it generates for shareholders. Each embodies something that is meaningful, substantive, and necessary. Whatever that particular something is, it drives most everything the *Built to Last* companies do and will do over decades, perhaps even centuries to come. For instance, Walt Disney's purpose of "using our imagination to bring happiness to millions" transformed that company from a rinky-dink cartoon maker into an entertainment monolith.[1] Though the world has changed drastically since the company's purpose was first identified, "using our imagination to bring happiness to millions" never tires. It continues to sustain the Walt Disney Company and to inspire it to inspire others. Conversely, lacking its clear sense of purpose, this and other companies that Collins highlights would have difficulty competing in the marketplace. They would, in a real sense, be crippled—utterly drained of creative life force—without it.

The distinction that Collins makes presents a litmus test of sorts which, when applied to the bewildering universe of corporate responsibility, helps to draw a tidy line in the sand. Although many companies claim to be dedicated to a purpose that serves the common good, surprisingly few of those companies actually absorb and reflect that purpose the way Disney has, especially during its formative years.

For instance, consider the juxtaposition between the words and actions of some oil companies that commandingly pose as leaders in the environmental arena. Several of the world's largest oil firms wage multimillion-dollar advertising campaigns designed to promote their support of energy conservation and renewable sources of energy. Meanwhile, in these same companies, business and growth strategies rely primarily on increased oil demand, supply, and control. Theoretically, widespread energy conservation or a widespread shift to alternative sources of energy would mean a diminished need for their most profitable product. Thus, without substantially investing in renewable sources of energy or in technologies that promote energy conservation, such companies leave a gap between their words and their actions. Not only could they just as easily survive without their decreed purpose, they actually benefit by undermining it. They have no vested interest in their cause, no business incentive to serve their purpose. Therefore, their extravagant language tends not to be enough to convince savvy stakeholders—thus creating backlash—while the money they do spend on "environmental" campaigns generates little in the way of a triple bottom-line return. Such companies fail the litmus test and also miss out on a great opportunity to make substantive environmental progress. While these companies may present a charitable facade to the public, they do not approach this particular aspect of corporate responsibility *authentically.* Chapter 2 of this book is filled with examples of such companies and provides a thorough explanation of why such companies fail the test, where they go wrong, and how they might approach these issues more constructively.

THE LITMUS TEST: IS PURPOSE *INVALUABLE* TO THE COMPANY?

At the opposite end of the spectrum are High-Purpose Companies. High-Purpose Companies are driven by purpose to the extent where purpose becomes a dominant force for corporate performance and development. In such companies, the concept of a higher purpose—of somehow serving society or protecting the environment—is so integral to the fabric of the organization that if you removed that thread, the company would start to unravel. Without their higher purpose, these firms would have difficulty competing in the marketplace, or even surviving.

High-Purpose Companies exist to serve the kinds of fundamental human needs that corporate responsibility advocates take so seriously, such as the need to stop environmental degradation; to end poverty; to promote equality; or to create health, security, happiness, and peace of mind. In contrast with the superficial needs catered to by so many other companies, the needs serviced by High-Purpose Companies tend to be deeply rooted throughout society. Thus, they are substantial enough to spur innovation and nourish the business over time.

General Electric's higher purpose of "providing imaginative answers to [the] mounting challenges to our ecosystem" or, "ecomagination,"[2] resulted not just in lip service, but in the creation of a revised corporate vision, which led to the development of environmentally friendly advanced materials, profitable new products, and major infrastructure and operational changes that are still under way. On the product front alone, ecomagination exists in the form of things ranging from energy-saving dishwashers to compact fluorescent lighting and fuel-efficient jet engines. So far, ecomagination products and services have generated $10 billion in revenue for GE. They are expected to generate $20 billion in revenue by 2010. Therefore, GE CEO Jeffrey Immelt doesn't regard ecomagination as a philanthropic endeavor any more than his shareholders do. But he is serious about environmentalism. "We're launching ecomagination not because it's trendy or moral, but because it will accelerate our growth and make us more competitive."[3] Green, Immelt concluded, is green. The company made the necessary connection. The more ingeniously GE goes about "providing imaginative answers to the mounting challenges to our ecosystem," the more precious it becomes to society and the better it performs overall. If GE were to suddenly abandon ecomagination, its market position, growth, and business strategies would be seriously undermined. The company's purpose and performance are fundamentally intertwined and therefore, while the company is certainly not flawless, GE is highly responsive to changing market conditions and environmental realities. It is authentic in its approach to environmental innovation. GE passes the litmus test.

In evaluating and carrying out corporate responsibility strategies, we are better off overlooking the subjective questions, like, Is company X intrinsically good or bad? Instead, we're better off asking, Has company X passed the point of no return? Companies pass the point of no return the moment when purpose becomes invaluable to the organization and the company and its contributions, in turn, become invaluable to society. They pass the point of no return when lofty rhetoric about bettering the world turns into actual rewards for *all* stakeholders.

> ## HIGHER PURPOSE = CORPORATE VALUES + DAILY PRACTICE

Many people have asked me to define the difference between values and purpose. My answer is simple. A company's higher purpose is the sum of its values put into action. Unless ideals translate into purpose, they are nothing but nice words on pretty paper. After all, Enron made a big deal of its values. It touted them on its Web site, in its press releases and advertisements, and most especially, in its comprehensive code of ethics manual. But these values were not internalized or operationalized. The company never made them *real*. In its 2000 annual report, Enron claimed that it stood for "open communication, respect" and "integrity,"[4] even though, at the same time, the company was deceiving analysts, government officials, customers, employees, and shareholders on a daily basis. Deception, as it turns out, was the strategy that Enron used to beat the market and maintain its unusually strong financial performance. If Enron had translated its values into purpose or turned its cunning tagline, "Ask Why," on itself and honestly addressed questions about how exactly it made money, then things might have turned out differently. Whether or not a company has a higher purpose depends entirely on how seriously it takes its values.

Most of you are familiar with your company's core values. But take those values steps further. Ask yourself: Why do we exist? What makes us invaluable to people and *worthy* of lasting? What is our *Ultimate Value Proposition*? A higher purpose is interminable and generative. It determines "who" a company is, what it does, and what it doesn't do over time. It keeps the company on a steady course, guiding it like a compass through the most brutal of storms. It powers creative sparks that give birth to countless possibilities, opportunities, and permutations. For any company, a higher purpose is a big thing, not a little thing.

BEHIND THE THEORY

Between the completion of my first book, *Cause for Success*, which introduces the concept of High-Purpose Companies, and the undertaking of this book, which explores the phenomena in much more depth, I thought a great deal about why this particular breed of business is so exceptional. High-Purpose Companies are unique, I realize, not just for their traits, but also for the developmental process they undergo—and for the results that the developmental process creates for all stakeholders.

In observing the most distinctive variables that sets these firms apart, and in examining how High-Purpose Companies embody these traits, I realized something. The companies that had the fifth trait *had* to have the first, second, third, and fourth traits as well. What revealed itself wasn't just a list of attributes, because the attributes had a sequence. It was a process, a progression, or continuum. Real High-Purpose Companies advanced or matured on a scale of sorts. And owing to this, there weren't just ten or twenty companies that qualified as good examples of some elite and distant class. There were potentially hundreds, even thousands of companies somewhere in the midst of these developmental stages.

With this idea in hand, I assembled a team of ten sharp MBAs from the McGill University Desautels Faculty of Management to put my theory to the test, refine it further, and determine what, if any, significant implications existed for the corporate responsibility and business communities as a whole. Each member of *The High-Purpose Company* research team contributed 250 hours of research time over two semesters—for a total of 2,500 hours of student analysis on this issue.

One of our first tasks was to identify a list of seventy-five companies from major industries—including retailing and consumer products, food and beverage, energy and utilities, technology, telecommunications, travel, pharmaceuticals, automotive, insurance and financial services—that actively promoted their commitment to ethics and responsibility through advertisements, press releases, annual reports, corporate responsibility (CR) reports, and other corporate-sponsored communications. We reasoned that these companies were good candidates for our study because, while some were controversial and others weren't, *all* had invested significant financial resources and effort into positioning themselves as good corporate citizens.

We then analyzed the CR-related actions of each company on our list. We dug through recent news articles, public records, company-issued reports, and other secondary information to assemble a picture of where each one was with respect to its level of CR authenticity. We also interviewed stakeholders inside and outside the companies—including executives, employees, consumers, shareholders, watchdog groups and NGO (nongovernmental organization) representatives, industry experts, activists, and other relevant parties. During our research, we were careful to look for gaps in conscience. For instance, a company's public claim that it "treats employees as family" coupled with expressed employee discontent and a class action lawsuit for discrimination or unfair treatment signifies the potential for such a gap.

> **WE DEFINED THE *QUALITY* OF CORPORATE RESPONSIBILITY IN TERMS OF THE TRIPLE BOTTOM-LINE RETURNS PRODUCED.**

In each case, our goal was to evaluate the *quality* of corporate responsibility initiatives, or the overall level of CR *effectiveness*. In other words, we sought to examine not only the sorts of CR investments that

THE ORIGINAL SET OF SEVENTY-FIVE COMPANIES*

⬆ Wainwright Bank & Trust Co.

⬆ Tom's of Maine, Ltd.

⬆ Aveda Corp.

⬆ Eileen Fisher Inc.

⬆ Patagonia, Inc.

⬆ Inter IKEA Systems

⬆ TerraPass Inc.

⬆ S.C. Johnson & Son, Inc.

⬆ General Electric Company

⬆ Wegmans Food Markets, Inc.

⬆ Montréal Alouettes

⬆ Toyota Motor Corp.

⬆ DuPont

⬆ Deere & Co.

⬆ JetBlue Airways

⬆ Southwest Airlines Co.

➡ Makivik Corp.

➡ Hydro-Québec

➡ BT Group PLC

➡ Henkel Group

➡ Ben & Jerry's (Unilever)

➡ Nike, Inc.

➡ Bank of America, N.A.

➡ McDonald's Corp.

➡ FedEx Corp.

➡ Starbucks Coffee Company

➡ Dell Inc.

➡ Cisco Systems, Inc.

➡ Microsoft Corp.

➡ Target Corp.

➡ HSBC Bank, PLC

➡ Odwalla (The Coca-Cola Company)

➡ Office Depot, Inc.

➡ eBay Inc.

➡ Ford Motor Company

➡ United Parcel Service, Inc.

➡ Procter & Gamble Co.

➡ General Mills, Inc.

➡ The Gillette Company

➡ Anheuser-Busch Companies, Inc.

➡ The Home Depot, Inc.

➡ Wal-Mart Stores, Inc.

➡ Public Service New Mexico

➡ Tyco International, Ltd.

➡ Gap Inc.

➡ Levi Strauss & Co.

➡ JP Morgan Chase & Co.

➡ Medtronic, Inc.

➡ Seiko Epson Corp.

➡ The Walt Disney Company

➡ Fluor Corporation

➡ Polaroid Corporation

➡ AOL Time Warner

➡ Pacific Lumber Company

➡ Abitibi Consolidated

➡ Kimberly-Clark Corp.

⇨ CVS Corp.

⇨ Bovis Lend Lease Ltd.

⇨ Mattel, Inc.

⇨ American Airlines (AMR Corp.)

⇨ De Beers Group

⇩ Bed, Bath & Beyond Inc.

⇩ Cingular Wireless, LLC

⇩ Goodyear Tire & Rubber Co.

⇩ U.S. Bancorp

⇩ MCI (Verizon Communications, Inc.)

⇩ Merck & Co., Inc.

⇩ GlaxoSmithKline, PLC

⇩ Altria Group, Inc.

⇩ Chevron Corporation

⇩ Allstate Insurance Co.

⇩ McKesson Corporation

⇩ Exxon Mobil Corp.

⇩ Monsanto Company

⇩ Halliburton Company

*Company rankings are based on our in-depth assessment.

Symbol key:
 ⇧ Passed the litmus test
 ⇨ Poised to pass the litmus test
 ⇩ Failed the litmus test

companies made, but how well those investments appeared to work in generating business, social, and environmental returns. Thus, we looked into the degree to which each company was approaching CR strategically. Where were the company's CR dollars going? Were the CR programs reactive or proactive in nature? Did they leverage the company's core strengths? Did they address prevalent and relevant societal and environmental needs? Had they won the full support of senior leadership? Did they target areas of strategic weakness or, better yet, optimize the potential for future growth? Did they generate social, environmental, and financial returns that could be measured and reported, and were the returns substantial enough to warrant continual reinvestment? What impressions did key stakeholders have about the company's approach? Next, we applied our high-purpose litmus test to each of our seventy-five companies to determine, in our view, which ones passed, which were on the road to passing, and which ones failed. Again, the key question asked was: Is purpose invaluable to the organization, and, therefore, is the organization invaluable to society?

We found that through a combination of primary and secondary analysis and back-and-forth debate, we were able to develop a real sense of how close each company was to passing the point of no return—that is, to reaching the stage where higher purpose becomes priceless and too precious to let go of. A fair portion of the companies on our original list, fourteen to be exact, appeared to be nowhere near this point. The group's general consensus was that many of these companies preached about their values, but didn't translate them into action or daily practice as well as they could have. In addition, their CR investments, which collectively amounted to *hundreds of millions of dollars* annually, generated relatively weak triple bottom-line returns and, we calculated, even increased business risks and created financial liabilities amounting to *billions of dollars more* in a few cases. For these reasons, such companies either fell off our scale or ended up in chapter 2.

We then turned our attentions to the remaining sixty-one companies, which either appeared to be on the right track or passed the litmus test. We analyzed these companies further by conducting additional personal interviews and by more closely examining the data that was publicly available regarding their activities. From this second round of analysis, we were able to revise the phases in the High-Purpose Progression and map each company along our continuum. We were also able to better examine the correlation between each company's higher purpose and its overall corporate health, and make some surprising conclusions that hold significance for every company invested in CR.

Here, then, is a summary of our progression and a preview of what's to come in the rest of this book (see illustration page 33). Think of the progression as a spiral series of cognitive and behavioral skills that need be mastered should companies wish to become high-purpose organizations. What's presented here is a change sequence of little corrective steps followed by big creative leaps, and divided into three broad stages: *realization*, *integration*, and *transformation*. Although different companies take different paths, there are normally no shortcuts. Each stage relies on the fulfillment of the previous stage, as learning from the former stage must generally be incorporated into the next in order for a company to advance up the spiral.

At stage one, companies develop a new level of awareness and adopt a higher mind-set. As a result, they begin to evaluate their business performance in new ways and integrate social and environmental insights into their business decision-making. At stage two, companies incorporate advanced strategic techniques. They become committed to making social and environmental progress and grow more adept at connecting their corporate responsibility and business strategies. As a result, such companies often start to experience significant business benefits, such as lower operating costs, improved efficiency, positive publicity, and higher levels of stakeholder loyalty. At stage three, companies center themselves around their higher purpose and become reliant on it. Their higher purpose informs most everything they do— from the way they engineer and manufacture their products to the way they treat their people and the planet. At this level, organizations pass the litmus test and transform into High-Purpose Companies. High-Purpose Companies experience major business benefits associated with the fulfillment of purpose, including a measurable surge in innovation, growth, and profit—in addition to lower operating costs, improved efficiency, positive publicity, unswerving stakeholder relationships, and overall corporate well-being.

Within this 1-2-3 (*realization*, *integration*, and *transformation*) sequence are a number of key concepts, shown below.

See the Bigger Picture: The environment, society, and business don't exist in isolation. Rather, they are three parts of an interconnected system. Business is joined to the environment because nature's

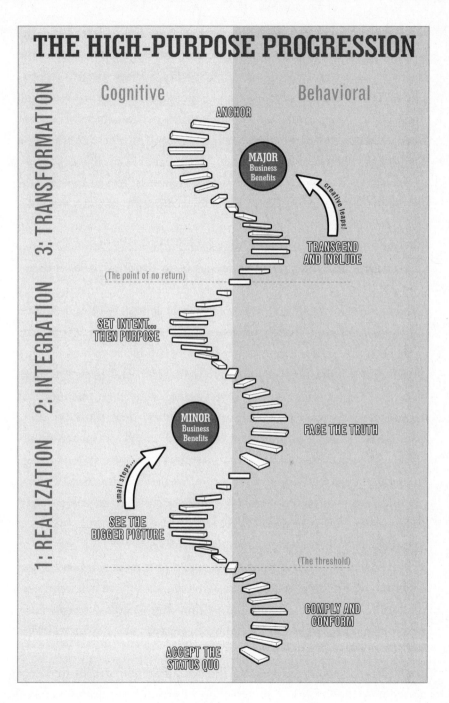

resources provide the raw materials that drive commerce. Thus, the faster companies plow through nature's already depleted resources, the more they undermine their long-term viability. Society sustains companies as well. When the communities that companies rely on are failing or struggling, then companies themselves can become unstable and insecure. Companies that "see the bigger picture" put these overarching connections together and understand that it makes no business sense to voluntarily damage critical support systems just to yield unsustainable, short-term returns. The full-blown realization of the bigger picture sets a context for future CR-related activities. It is a mandatory first step for any firm that approaches CR authentically.

Face the Truth: Lots of companies lie to the public and to themselves. Rather than acknowledge their shortcomings or mistakes, they hide behind rehearsed press statements and legalese. Although it is no doubt easier to avoid direct confrontation when controversy strikes or when an industry is under fire, it's also less conducive to a company's future health. Evidence shows that stakeholders tend to be far more forgiving of the companies that say, "We're sorry," than the ones that don't. In addition, a crisis can serve as crucial turning point. By taking a cold, hard look in the mirror and accepting, not shirking, responsibility, companies are able to more constructively resolve serious issues, strengthen their vulnerabilities, access breakthroughs, and improve overall. The act of facing the truth is a rite of passage that allows companies to better target their CR-related initiatives in the areas that need the most attention and advance to the next level.

Set Intent . . . Then Purpose: Companies don't reach their highest goals by accident. Instead, they get there consciously and by moving beyond ordinary procedures and limited thinking. Once a company faces the problems it contributes to and the pressing issues that affect its stakeholders, it can dig deeper to determine what potential it has and how—if at all—it wants to use that potential to develop solutions that reverse the tides and make a positive contribution to society. Not every company can or should be a High-Purpose Company, but the path to becoming one requires the establishment of the right kind of intentions. What ideal results does the company wish to create in the world? And using its greatest strengths, how can it effectively do so? At this phase, companies often signal their desires and ambitions to take a revised business course through bold public announcements. Internally, they begin to define their higher purpose and then experiment with it. Novel ideas trickle up or down throughout the company, and the ones that serve both shareholder and societal interests stick, while the ones that don't fade away or are refined. The key for companies moving beyond this phase in the progression is to let such emergent corporate-responsibility strategy transform into deliberate strategy, thus leading into a full-blown cycle of change and potentially to the company's most meaningful accomplishments over the rest of its lifespan.

Transcend and Include: Companies that successfully reach this stage in the progression officially pass the litmus test because a critical mass of their growth-enabling products, services, technologies, and management policies are responsively designed to fulfill a higher purpose. Keeping shareholder expectations squarely in mind and without scrapping their existing systems all at once, High-Purpose Companies engineer novel and profitable solutions that meet deep societal needs. In doing so, they enter into a continual cycle of self-improvement, where the better their solutions work, the higher the triple bottom-line returns produced, and as a result, more money is invested back into purposeful solutions. Companies at this stage lock into a pattern of good growth. High-Purpose Companies frequently stumble upon breakthroughs or creative leaps that hurl them toward their goals and also cause category disruption. Such breakthroughs are like wormholes moving a company from point A to point G. Although not every company at this stage makes dramatic creative leaps, all begin to live by new rules and experience improved corporate health on multiple, measurable levels.

Anchor: At this stage, companies "become" their higher purpose. Stakeholders inside and outside of the organization perceive the higher purpose and the corporate identity as indistinguishable. The higher purpose grows to be like an anchor in that it holds the company's place, and like the eye of a hurricane in that everything the company does revolves around it and is energized by it. Without the anchor or the eye, the company might drift off course, become weakened, or perhaps even fall apart. Anchored High-Purpose Companies are self-governing organizations. They do not often worry about regulatory standards because they far exceed them, just as they do not pander to public interest groups, public opinion, or the press because they remain true to their core. They have no need for extraneous rules, policies, or rigid corporate hierarchies because their ethics are autonomous, while purpose is completely ingrained throughout their culture. Such firms set their own superior pace. These are among the healthiest, most significant, and *worthy* companies around.

NATURE'S INFLUENCE

I had just unveiled my initial concept of the progression to the research team at McGill University, when a skeptical student named Stephanie asked: "How do you know you're right? I mean, are these necessarily the right steps in the right order?" It's a great question, and I was glad she posed it, because immediately the team started to debate about change, the way it unfolds, and whether a specific order or organizing structure was evident within the best business cases we could recall. Over the course of the next year, debates like this would immeasurably improve both my own train of thought and the insights revealed in the following pages.

Stephanie's question was helpful for another reason. It got me thinking about the quality of this book. So many business books are filled with prescriptive formulas that authors claim lead to success.

And although some of them may, the truth is that I can't stand strict formulas. I rarely stick with structured programs, and I generally dislike following the rules.

This is not a step-by-step program. This book contains no sure-fire recipe that the business world needs to follow. Though the High-Purpose Progression might be original in its application to business, the fundamental sequence it is based on surely is not. As Paul Hawken and others insist, true corporate responsibility involves systemic change. And systemic change—or evolution—tends to follow a particular pattern, no matter where it unfolds.

In the process of writing this book, I was greatly influenced by the works of brilliant theorists that I admire, and if you closely observe my spiral model, you will see traces of Dr. Abraham Maslow's hierarchy of needs, Jim Collins's *Good to Great* flywheel, Don Beck's Spiral Dynamics map, and Ken Wilber's fulcrum model. Also, if you step back and examine all of these models as a set, you will notice that they have a lot in common. That's because each model more or less stems from the universal change sequence found in nature.

According to nature, or Charles Darwin's process of natural selection, healthy species confront new conditions, alter aspects of themselves to ensure their survival, and eventually evolve into new and improved species. Similarly, in Maslow's self-needs hierarchy, psychologically healthy people endeavor to determine their worth, take repeated actions based on their sense of worth, and finally become their worth. In Collins's flywheel model of *Good to Great* companies, people or leaders see things anew by confronting the brutal facts and committing to being "the best in the world," then gradually behave in congruent ways, thus budding into enduring great companies. In philosopher Wilber's fulcrum model, developing humans and cultures identify with higher levels of awareness, disidentify or separate themselves from lower levels, and ultimately integrate with the new, higher levels. Even religions like Buddhism embody this 1-2-3 sequence, where spiritually healthy beings resolve to see past their negative habits (karma), enter a cycle of birth and rebirth (samsara), and end up enlightened (nirvana).

HOW THE HIGH-PURPOSE PROGRESSION'S 1-2-3 SEQUENCE LINES UP

Basic Level	High-Purpose Progression	Science (Darwin)	Psychology (Maslow)	Business (Collins)	Philosophy (Wilber)	Religion (Buddhism)
1	Realization	New condition	Self-esteem	Disciplined thought	Identification	Karma
2	Integration	Adaptation	Self-exploration	Disciplined action	Differentiation	Samsara
3	Transformation	Evolution	Self-actualization	Great company	Inclusion	Nirvana

In general, most dynamic and healthy systems follow this common sequence, and business is no exception. The High-Purpose Progression reflects an age-old cycle of change that relates to corporate responsibility, but that is not limited to it. So, to answer Stephanie's question: How do I really know that this is a valid concept that can stand the test of time? It already has.

You will need to decide for yourself whether any of the ideas or conclusions presented in this book apply to your business and if evolution is necessary or possible in your organization. I encourage you to wrestle with each notion presented, pose new questions, debate with your colleagues, reject or ignore the concepts that don't seem right for you, and embrace the ones that do.

The ultimate goal of this book is not to turn corporate responsibility into some trite, formulaic process. Quite the contrary—it is meant to help end the confusion and carelessness that undercuts progress and optimal corporate performance by putting things in perspective and presenting you with a challenge that's worth taking. So by all means, be an active participant in this intellectual journey.

But before getting started, you might find it helpful to take heed of the potential pitfalls and cautionary tales that, my research team and I concluded, help demonstrate what *not* to do. New market conditions render some widely used corporate responsibility tactics ineffective and even counterproductive. This is what the next chapter is all about.

PART 3: The Pitfalls

2:

Avoiding Old Mistakes

No ad campaign, no celebrity, no glorious blandishment can compensate for a lack of trust and the sense that this is all a scam and a sham, for the feeling that one is being fooled and fobbed off.

—LAURA PENNY IN *YOUR CALL IS IMPORTANT TO US*

Four recent studies typify the public faith in big business and signal the backlash against corporations that attempt to woo stakeholders through superficial or artificial corporate-responsibility gestures. In a Roper poll conducted in July 2005, for instance, 72 percent of surveyed adults said they believed that corporate wrongdoing was rampant and that executives are bent on "destroying the environment, cooking the books and lining their own pockets."[1] This ratio was up from 66 percent in 2004. Additionally, just 2 percent of Roper's 2005 survey respondents considered today's CEOs to be "very trustworthy," down from 3 percent in 2004, while only 9 percent of respondents indicated that they had full trust in financial services institutions, down from 14 percent in 2004.

A second survey conducted by Harris Interactive and the Reputation Institute initially asked six thousand respondents to name two companies with the best reputations and two companies with the worst. Some twenty thousand people were then asked to rate the companies on attributes such as emotional appeal, social responsibility, and vision and leadership.[2] The study resulted in a list of sixty companies, with the top portion representing companies with perceived good reputations. Companies in industries that were perceived to be irresponsible—such as pharmaceuticals, tobacco, and oil—ended up at the bottom of the pile. For instance, Merck ranked forty-fifth, Altria Group ranked fiftieth, Chevron ranked forty-seventh, Exxon ranked fifty-third, and Halliburton ranked fifty-seventh. The previous year's study showed similar results, as three-quarters of the 2004 survey respondents graded the image of big corporations in notorious industries as either "not good" or "terrible."

A third 2005 survey, called the Edelman Trust Barometer, reveals the same doubting trend, only this survey engages a different audience, so its findings are in a way more worrisome. The Edelman survey, which drew from interviews with 1,500 global opinion leaders from eight key markets around the world, reported that most view outside experts, academics, employees, nongovernmental organization (NGO) representatives, and "an average person like me" as the most trusted spokespersons for a company, while fewer than three in every ten people consider corporate CEOs or CFOs to be reliable sources of information. The Edelman survey also found that nine out of ten opinion leaders across all markets consider blogs and news stories to be more persuasive than corporate-generated communications, which Edelman says were perceived to be biased.

In light of this apparent "trust deficit," a phrase coined by Edelman, we found this fourth piece of research from the Center for Corporate Citizenship at Boston College to be revealing and a little disheartening. That organization's *State of Corporate Citizenship in the U.S.: Business Perspectives in 2005* report shows that, although more corporate executives pay homage to the concept of corporate citizenship, many acknowledge that actions lag behind words. While 81 percent of respondents agreed that corporate responsibility needs to be a priority, only 60 percent would go so far as to say that they integrate internal priorities with obligations to do right by society. In other words, fussing about how seriously a company takes its commitment to the world at large is something that most companies are willing to do through words, symbols, and remedial gestures. But doing something constructive about those postures—well, perhaps that's something else.

The evidence is clear. As Edelman's end analysis concludes: you can't buy trust through advertising. And yet, that is only as far as some executives indicate they are willing to go. Notably, the companies and industries that, according to these studies, consumers and opinion leaders trusted and admired the *least* spend enormous amounts of money every year on corporate communications campaigns designed to make them appear to be good Samaritans. Several of these companies were in our study.

During our analysis, we determined that although these organizations are among the world's best-equipped and financially successful, a substantial portion of our base of seventy-five companies tended to launch corporate responsibility outreach programs with the chips stacked against them. Several seemed to overlook highly relevant market conditions and, often, realities with respect to the way they run their businesses.

THE WEB OF ACCOUNTABILITY

The public is only getting better at distinguishing between reality and rhetoric. As the statistics show, people are growing more frustrated because they sense a widening disparity between what companies say and what they do. The statistics above are the results of not just one or two isolated events or conditions, like the Enron scandal or the surge in oil prices, but rather, of a steadily building tension brought on by a combination of factors. Americans are frustrated by bad customer service, bad health care, bad prescription drug coverage, bad work environments, bad environmental policies, unjust social policies, and so forth. They are fed up with bad corporate experiences in general. Too many companies tell them one thing and then do or sell something else entirely.

John Q. Public has been burned. And although many people in the business world grapple to present their own theories regarding precisely when, why, and how things went wrong, the fact is that here we are. This is the way it is. Public distrust is a constant. It is something that we can all rely on. It is one of several new market conditions explored in this book. Thus, to develop any form of corporate responsibility outreach as if this were not a prevailing condition risks wasting money, effort, and the opportunity for positive progress.

To win back the lost trust, we must first acknowledge that the trust has been lost.

Another new condition is the web of accountability that companies face. When companies issue campaigns and especially when the campaigns contain statements about the company's corporate responsibility accomplishments, those messages get filtered through layers of critiques and fact and background checks. Journalists, bloggers, watchdog groups, NGOs, and activists add their two cents and put the company's words to the test. Each of these individuals or groups has an incentive to find a discrepancy between what a company says and what it does with respect to corporate responsibility, because that's their job. Therefore, when they do find such a gap, they are quick to pounce. Consumers and shareholders, the intended end audience of the original corporate-generated communication, are also the intended end audience for these rogue stories as well, and as was evidenced with the survey statistics above, many find this information to be more compelling and convincing than that which was spun out of the corporate office. In many cases, it seems, they trust the points of view of journalists, bloggers, NGOs, and watchdog groups more than they do the brand.

No communication exists in isolation, and every campaign is interpreted in tandem with other corresponding news or events surrounding it. Today, the public is more informed about corporate track records than ever before. They have instant access to information and look out for inconsistencies. As a result, companies are more quickly caught in their own deceptions. They are held more accountable to their public relations claims, and they have to work a great deal harder to win back lost trust.

Despite what some think, corporate responsibility outreach is not like brand advertising. The same rules do not apply. In brand advertising, exaggeration, and occasional fabrication are accepted tools that enable marketers to produce a more saleable image. This is because on their own merits, product attributes are often boring. They need a context, a new dimension, or added personality to make them seem more desirable and interesting. Because they need a layer that does not inherently exist, it is the marketers' job to invent such a layer. With corporate responsibility outreach, however, it is essential that no such extraneous layer be invented. Hyperbole can seriously backfire, causing a company to lose face with key stakeholders, diminishing its credibility and even creating risk—and financial liability—in certain circumstances. The next eight cases will demonstrate how this can happen.

We will start with the evaluation of two of the most expensive and highest-profile corporate responsibility–related campaigns in our study: Merck's $20 million "Where Patients Come First" campaign and Chevron's $50 million "Will You Join Us?" campaign.

In evaluating both campaigns, we were chiefly interested in how the campaigns were interpreted by the web of accountability just discussed. We wanted to know what impact the campaigns seemed to have on the company's perceived corporate reputation. Therefore, we reached out to stakeholders within the web, including consumers, industry experts, watchdog and NGO representatives, former company representatives, and even plaintiff attorneys. We also gathered secondary evidence from shareholders, concerned citizens, bloggers, Web site users, journalists, and other key stakeholder groups. Our objective was not to judge these companies as good or evil, because that kind of judgment is arbitrary and irrelevant to our study, but rather to analyze each company's approach to responsible communications: Did the campaigns respond to the new market conditions? More important, did the campaigns respond to the legal or trust problems that currently face the businesses? We were also looking for the triple bottom-line returns generated on the back end of these rather large corporate responsibility investments. Were there any? For triple bottom-line returns to be substantial, the corporate responsibility claims themselves needed to be substantiated. We did some digging.

PUTTING PEOPLE BEFORE PROFITS

The toddler's big brown eyes sparkle innocently at the cameras lens. With adorable bewilderment, she tries to define terms that are foreign to her, such as "measles," "mumps," and "chicken pox." A motherly voiceover interjects: "Most kids don't have a clue about diseases adults remember, thanks to Merck's scientists. We've invested billions to research heart disease and asthma. Now we're trying to make Alzheimer's, diabetes, and cancer history, too." Enter the company's slogan: "Merck. Where Patients Come First."

This advertisement was part of a national campaign that, before it expires, will have reached 90 percent of Americans with the message that Merck puts their interests ahead of its own. As a matter of fact, Merck spends billions of dollars every year trying to discover cures to insidious diseases. In 2004 alone, Merck spent $2.5 billion on drug research, provided free medicine to third-world communities and U.S. citizens with no health care coverage, and issued various discounts to senior citizens crippled by sky-high prescription costs. Merck is clearly calling attention to its strong suits, and on its Web site, it reminds shareholders of its founder's vision of establishing Merck as a purpose-driven organization: "Our commitments as a company have long been guided by the vision of our modern-day founder, George W. Merck, who said, 'We try never to forget that medicine is for the people. It is not for the profits. The profits follow, and if we have remembered that, they have never failed to appear' "[3]

The problem we identified is not that Merck's campaign is baseless. The problem is the milieu. Merck's "Patients Come First" advertising message coincides with what's been called the worst drug disaster in history. In August 2005, as Merck's ad campaign was in full swing, a Texas jury found Merck liable for the death of a man who took the COX-2 painkiller Vioxx. They awarded his widow $253.4 million. Evidence presented during that and several subsequent trials convinced jury members that Merck not only heavily marketed a drug that dramatically increases the risk of heart attacks in some patients, but that it stifled information that could have better warned the public, and in the Texas case, Robert Ernst, about the drug's potential dangers. The Texas case is just the tip of the iceberg for Merck, as it represents just one of 11,500 lawsuits filed against the company by former patients and widows—each of whom insists that Merck did anything but put patients first.

In December 2005, as the ad campaign played on, the *New England Journal of Medicine* issued a statement accusing Merck representatives of deliberately withholding information from an article relating to Vioxx's dangers. According to the journal, had that data been reported, it would have shown that Vioxx increased patients' risk of heart attacks fivefold:

On October 5th, 2004, days after Vioxx was removed from the market, Journal editors had examined a computer diskette that had been submitted along with the paper manuscript. It showed

details about heart attacks and other cardiovascular problems
were deleted two days before the publication received the manu-
script on May 18, 2000. The diskette also indicated that the com-
puter used to delete that information was owned by Merck.[4]

In the process of our analysis, we could not help wanting to pick up the phone and talk to experts who played a role in the alleged research suppression story. While we knew that we might never discover the whole truth about Merck and Vioxx, we also knew that it would be impossible to fairly evaluate the validity of Merck's "Patients Come First" campaign without doing some homework in this area. Can Merck honestly say that it puts patients first? Furthermore, given that both the new market conditions and ongoing ethical scandal exist, does saying that Merck puts patients first actually make Merck look worse in stakeholders' eyes, rather than better?

To answer the first question, we called on Dr. Gurkirpal Singh, adjunct clinical professor of medicine at Stanford University School of Medicine and chief science officer at the Institute of Clinical Outcomes Research and Education. Dr. Singh was hired by Merck to promote Vioxx in May 1998. As a physician with an excellent reputation at the Food and Drug Administration, expertise in arthritic conditions, and relationships with potential institutional buyers, Singh originally appeared to be an ideal spokesperson for Vioxx. He promoted Vioxx through a series of lectures to other physicians, medical schools, and universities around the country.

Not too far into the lecture program, Singh told us, he and his Stanford University research team evaluated a study conducted by Merck scientists in 2000 and drew conclusions that differed from those made by the company. Singh's team interpreted the results to read exactly what the *New England Journal of Medicine* suggested—that Vioxx increased patients' risk of heart attacks four- to fivefold. "I wanted to know exactly how many people had this problem, how many had hypertension, how many had strokes, how many had heart attacks, what the blood pressure readings were," Singh said.

According to testimony Singh gave to the Senate Finance Committee in November 2004, which was later reported by the *New York Times* and other sources, Merck was allegedly unresponsive and later hostile to his repeated questions about the drug's potential dangers. "I was warned that if I continued in this fashion there would be serious consequences for me."[5] Following the Senate committee hearings, National Public Radio (NPR) interviewed Singh and ran a June 2005 story called "Documents Suggest Merck Tried to Censor Vioxx Critics." In NPR's story, a senior business director for Merck's San Francisco office allegedly sent an e-mail that read: "The one thing I am pretty sure of is that Dr. Singh could impact us negatively if he chose to do so . . . I would recommend that we handle this very carefully . . . I just don't think canceling all the [lecture] programs and walking away completely will serve us well in the long term."[6]

Other media entities broadcast portions of different e-mails and memos that surfaced during the Vioxx trials. One such memo, which was allegedly sent by a senior executive at Merck to Merck sales personnel in 2000, was excerpted by both *Brandweek* and *Mediaweek*. The memo allegedly read: "Our sales force needs to STOP defending Vioxx against outrageous claims from our competitors and START offensively selling the core benefit of this product . . . efficacy."[7]

Vioxx was a blockbuster, $2 billion drug for Merck, and marketing around the drug was aggressive. Aggressive marketing is not unethical. But by the time Merck voluntarily withdrew Vioxx in September 2004, many patients are believed to have suffered serious complications and the press had tracked the scandal relentlessly. "At that point the pressure against the company was very strong," says Singh.

All along, Merck has insisted that it broke no laws and acted conscientiously and correctly in the way it developed and sold the drug. Perhaps it did. Perhaps it didn't break any laws. But did it put patients first?

The company has certainly used its marketing muscle to convince people that the answer to this question is a resounding "yes." After the scandal broke, the company placed full-page advertisements in the *Wall Street Journal* and other select newspapers, denying any wrongdoing. "When we obtain data from our clinical studies, we promptly disclose them," the ads read. But this and other of Merck's promotional tactics didn't sit well with the FDA, which reportedly sent a warning letter to the company in 2001 encouraging it to stop engaging in "false or misleading promotional activities" and presenting information that "minimizes the potentially serious cardiovascular findings" about Vioxx.[8] Here, the company's aggressive marketing approach actually caused additional liabilities, making it look defensive and even perhaps tagging on a new fine or two.

NOT BUYING IT ENTIRELY

In a recent interview with marketing magazine *PRWeek*, Merck's marketing director, Len Tacconi, indicated that "We're suffering from a lot of misconceptions and concerns that are related to a lack of information," and that the "Patients Come First" campaign is "not self-serving in any way."[9] The central issue is not whether or not Merck's "Patients Come First" campaign was designed to be self-serving. The central issue is that, in light of the Vioxx scandal, it *looks* self-serving, at least to a small but well-informed group of stakeholders that we surveyed.

Since the "Patients Come First" campaign was ongoing as we conducted our research, and as it received so much publicity, it was fresh in people's minds. Thus, we engaged a few industry insiders to get a sense of what they thought about the message's authenticity: What did the experts think about Merck telling people that it puts patients first? "In my view, all the big drug companies are much alike in not walking their talk. Merck is no different," says Dr. Marcia Angell, senior lecturer in the Department of Social Medicine at Harvard Medical School and author of *The Truth About the Drug Companies*. "As for the slogan, what else would you expect from them?" Angell's overall critique of Merck's campaign was aloof. She clearly wasn't buying it, yet she wasn't particularly irritated by it. Others were.

"The veracity of Merck's claim of 'Putting Patients First' may be on par with other infamous slogans such as 'War is Peace' or 'Work Makes You Free' . . . They should hold off on the doublespeak and ad agency dribble," said *Pharma Marketing News* publisher John Mack on his blog (http://pharmamkting.blogspot.com/). We found those to be particularly harsh words, coming from someone inside the pharmaceutical industry, so we called on Mack for further clarification, to which he explained: "I would have avoided that tagline. If you know anything about the evidence or the trials, then you know that they weren't putting patients first. But if the public isn't following the news, then Merck might get away with it for the most part."

Mack's comment led us to want to talk to the public. Specifically, we wondered what an *informed* public, who knew about the Vioxx recall, would think about the campaign. How would the "Patients Come First" message affect their impressions of the company? Would it improve it or make it worse? We conducted a little experiment. We interviewed twenty-five adults who regularly bought prescription medications and knew about the Vioxx recall. First, we asked them to give us their take on the company and the Vioxx recall situation. Next, we showed them Merck's "Where Patients Come First" print ads, which highlight some of the good and socially responsible things the company does. After the respondents viewed the ads, we asked them to give us one word that best describes the kind of company they think Merck is.

Contrary to our hypothesis, the ads did work the way Merck planned. They made roughly half of our respondents feel better about the company. People who felt reasonably good about Merck to start with felt just as good about the company after viewing the ads. And the ads made some people feel even better about Merck. After viewing the ads, roughly half of the people we surveyed gave us words like "recovering," "proactive," "struggling," "research-driven," "committed," "child friendly," and "innovative." Some people clearly felt sorry for Merck and wanted to see the company get back on its feet.

However, the remaining half of the respondents had an existing negative perception about Merck. It is important to point out that these respondents knew about the Texas verdict, whereas the people in the first group had heard about the Vioxx recall but they were less knowledgeable about the specific details of the Texas case and other pending trials. The more informed individuals tended to view Merck in a more unfavorable light after seeing the ads. They gave us words such as "unjust," "untrustworthy," "scared," "manipulative," "reactive," "hypocritical," and "spin-controlling."

The ads seemed to antagonize even those individuals who were very informed about the pending 11,500 lawsuits. Antagonized consumers grew weary of Merck and viewed the ads as part of the company's cover-up efforts. One such respondent told us: "Merck's management of the recall was a corporate nightmare. There is no excuse for covering up or not immediately notifying the public once the connection between heart attacks and Vioxx users was made. This ad is hypocritical. One looks at the ad after we know how the company handled patient concern and it becomes more of an irritant."

While roughly half of the consumers that we talked to bought Merck's message, half did not. Ours was not a scientific study, but it does demonstrate an important qualitative finding. When corporations appear to minimize or block extreme transgressions by conveying an altruistic persona, educated and well-informed consumers tend to grow more suspicious and eventually, more outraged. Merck legitimately makes some wonderful contributions to society. But the timing and the context of "Where Patients Come First" seems, well, challenged, to say the least.

It is possible that Merck's strategic objectives might have been better served had the company's ads featured the views of credible third parties—such as doctors with no financial ties to the company, patients whose most desperate needs were fulfilled by Merck programs, non-profits with evidence of Merck's real impact on pressing social issues, or even employees who believe that the Merck they joined ten years ago still exists today. At least that might have been more believable. Better yet, if Merck *really* wanted to prove that it put patients first, then per-haps it could acknowledge the ten-thousand-pound gorilla in the room. Even if Merck insists that it did nothing wrong and made no mistakes in the past, then it could at least talk to patients about its research pro-cess and disclose exactly how ethics plays a part in that process. Subse-quently, it could demonstrate how it does business with patients' interests at heart so that people could understand a little better exactly what the company means when it says, "Patients Come First." Of course, that's just a suggestion.

What's a fact is that the charges do add up. Aside from costing Merck its reputation for ethical leadership, economists predict that the Vioxx debacle might also cost the company up to $18 billion in legal fees and liabilities. Add that number to a decline in share price (Merck's stock has fallen 25 percent since the Vioxx recall was announced), an-other $2.5 billion in lost annual sales from the drug, and more lost sales due to potentially diminished doctor loyalty. Lost trust is such a diffi-cult thing to rebuild. The very best idea, of course, is not to lose the trust in the first place.

THE PITFALLS

An altruistic slogan is not corporate responsibility. Neither is a green label slapped on an existing product with no real environmental or so-cial benefits. These superficialities or common pitfalls were briefly ex-plored in the prologue. What wasn't explored was the top reason why companies should avoid cursory measures. Several reasons exist, but the top business reason is that there is a good chance that such investments will turn out to be an utter waste of resources that don't convince stakeholders, or that even backfire and cost companies more money in the long run. Why take such a gamble?

There is a twist on the *Economist*'s argument that is accurate: *When* corporate responsibility is approached as a cosmetic exercise, then companies ought not invest at all. Ideally, companies ought to channel the superficially invested resources into areas that legitimately make a positive difference. However, in cases where companies are *only* willing to invest at a superficial level, then they might as well distribute the change back into shareholders' pockets, because when a company has little to no substance behind its corporate responsibility position, or worse, when a company takes a position that runs in stark opposition to shareholder interests, then it's not corporate responsibility at all. It's marketing. So just call it that.

On this admittedly pessimistic, yet realistic note, let's take a look at another high-profile campaign: Chevron's "Will You Join Us?"

In Chevron's "Will You Join Us?" the company acknowledges that "easy oil" has ended and warns of serious, resulting ramifications for those of us who've grown quite attached to our current modes of efficiency, power, and transportation. Each of these dependencies, the company says through print, television, outdoor, and online ads and a promotional Web site, www.WillYouJoinUs.com, will have to change soon:

Many of the world's oil and gas fields are maturing. And new energy discoveries are mainly occurring in places where resources are difficult to extract—physically, technically, economically, and politically. When growing demand meets tighter supplies, the result is more competition for the same resources.

We can wait until a crisis forces us to do something. Or we can commit to working together, and start by asking the tough questions: How do we meet the energy needs of the developing

*world and those of industrialized nations? What role will
renewables and alternative energies play? What is the best way
to protect our environment? How do we accelerate our conservation efforts? Whatever actions we take, we must look not just
to next year, but to the next 50 years.*

*At Chevron, we believe that innovation, collaboration and
conservation are the cornerstones on which to build this new
world. But we can't do it alone. Corporations, governments
and every citizen of this planet must be part of the solution as
surely as they are part of the problem.*[10]

For decades, big oil companies have refused to acknowledge that
we're running out of their chief product and the massive implications
of that. In an attempt to position itself as an environmental leader,
Chevron does so. Through its promotional Web site, the company invites people to "join the discussion" about challenging environmental
and energy-related issues. To be sure, this campaign reflects a new attitude for the once aloof company. Chevron talks its talk exceedingly
well. But does the talk also reflect a change in policy? Is the company
constructively addressing its role in contributing to the energy problems it highlights, and, given this, how is the campaign settling in with
Chevron's web of accountability?

Once again, we asked the experts: do Chevron's actions match its
words? "That remains to be seen," says sustainable business expert
and consultant Joel Makower. "So far, I don't see Chevron making
any concrete business changes. But I can't imagine an oil company
going out on a limb in this day and age without having something
substantive behind it. I will be as shocked and outraged as anyone if
this campaign turns out to be pure cover." In his green marketplace
Web log, http://makower.typepad.com/joel_makower/, Mackower
tells people: "I'll watch ChevronTexaco's current campaign with high

interest to see where it goes—and how much change is apparent in the company's actions, including its commitment to mitigating climate change."

WORDS VERSUS INTERESTS

Makower is onto something. While Chevron's consumer-targeted Web site talks to the public about the importance of "innovation, collaboration and conservation," the company's investor-targeted Web site sings a different tune. That site, in addition to the company's annual report, demonstrates only minimal investments in technologies that promote conservation and even promises shareholders an increase in oil supply and control—as evidenced in part by the company's aggressive $17 billion bid for Unocal—as well as in continued soaring profits brought on by rising oil and gas prices. When "Will You Join Us?" launched, Chevron claimed to invest $100 million a year on "renewable energies, alternative fuels, and improving efficiency." However, we noted that Chevron is a $150.9 billion company, and since only $100 million was diverted into environmental technologies, whereas $50 million was spent on environmental advertising—and since the future growth and profitability of the company hedges on increased oil supply and control plus rising oil and gas prices, then it would appear that Chevron's core strategies and economic policies hadn't yet caught up with its corporate responsibility positions. Others within Chevron's web of accountability noticed this, too. The company's shareholders, they point out, stand to gain a great deal from the end of oil.

"Oil prices are going through the roof. We're going to see $100 barrels within the next couple of years, which means windfall profits for oil companies," says Pratap Chatterjee, executive director of CorpWatch, an organization that holds companies accountable by monitoring the discrepancies between their promises and actions. Chatterjee has been tracking the oil industry for over a decade. More than once, he has been a thorn in the side of multinationals like Halliburton, Shell, Chevron, and others. Chatterjee says that companies like Chevron, which brand themselves as environmentally responsible, are sophisticated marketers but nothing more. "Whatever they've said within the past couple of years about being more environmentally sustainable is going to go out the window because they're going to realize that they can sell their gas for $5 a gallon."

Profit motives aside, it appears that consumers were frustrated by Chevron's "Will You Join Us?" campaign as well, although for different reasons. As mentioned, one key aspect of the campaign was an online "Join the Discussion" message board, in which users were encouraged to contribute their own thoughts about energy issues. However, some users concluded that Chevron appeared determined to edit any critical statements from that message board, keeping the "debate" screened and fairly promotional. One Web-savvy consumer complained: "Chevron moderators censored a post of mine from a discussion about what should be done to prepare civilization for the end of cheap oil. The moderators cited 'community guidelines' as the reason, which usually means they objected to some racial fact that was included in the text of the censored post. But there was no racial information in this particular post." Another user grumbled: "My post said there were better sites on the net [than Chevron's] about oil depletion and suggested that people use the search engine of their choice to look for 'peak oil.' It was a perfectly civil post that never made it to their 'discussion board,' plus I got NO feedback from them about it one way or other." Another noted: "When I click on 'Join the Discussion,' I can't join the discussion. It's a primitive discussion forum for all the pretty design. I'm having a hard time grasping what this Web site actually means."[11] There are many posts across the Web from people reporting similar results.

As for the media, it is important to point out that not every outlet perceived Chevron's "Will You Join Us?" campaign as unconvincing or superficial. The campaign received a relatively warm reception by various news organizations and Web entities such as TriplePundit.com, *Sacramento News & Review*, the *Japan Times*, and a few others. They characterized the campaign as an "interesting twist" for a major oil firm and more or less praised Chevron for dealing with a serious energy issue. But clearly, there is a great deal of suspicion and hostility brewing in the minds of other stakeholders who feel swindled by big oil. Thus, when a campaign launches with apparent bias or with questionable substance behind it, the company responsible for the campaign can reasonably expect critical reaction to follow. Indeed, in Chevron's case, this is precisely what happened. Along these lines, perhaps the most telling commentary comes not from media sources but from concerned citizens: "Most oil experts agree that Peak Oil will happen and Chevron wants to appear to be the oil company to act for the public good by informing people that we are indeed running out of oil," says Dr. Shepherd Bliss, a professor at the University of Hawai'i at Hilo, in a message board generated by concerned citizens in response to Chevron's campaign. "Chevron seems more greedy than green. The same Madison Avenue firm that put together Bush's TV ads in 2004 and the army's 'Be All You Can Be!' campaign prepared these ads,"[12] he commented, suggesting that in his view, the same exaggerative esthetic shows through.

As with Merck's campaign, Chevron's "Will You Join Us?" campaign launched on the heels of three separate ethical scandals that also helped to dwarf the company's message and encourage an overall cynical response, especially among industry experts, journalists, watchdog groups, and concerned citizens. In addition to the surge in oil and gas prices, these three scandals included the November 2005 US Senate hearings, in which oil chiefs were pressed to account for their high profits and it was alleged that companies including Chevron gave "detailed energy policy recommendations" to President Bush's task force; a class action environmental suit, in which Chevron faces charges relating to alleged environmental misconduct in Ecuador; and a human rights suit, in which a Chevron subsidiary is accused of human rights abuses associated with its Niger delta operations.

In the Ecuador case, local officials dubbed the suit the "trial of the century." More than thirty thousand Ecuadorian plaintiffs allege that Chevron drilled for oil without adequate safeguards and dumped 18.5 billion gallons of unremediated waste and other sources of oil contamination into unlined pits, streams, rivers, swamps, and pristine rain-forest land.[13] Two separate shareholder resolutions were filed asking Chevron's management to better report on how it was dealing with the Ecuador situation, indicating that liability is potentially severe and that the company has been slow to respond on its own volition. According to Barbara Enloe Hadsell, one of the lawyers for the plaintiffs involved in the Niger delta case, two separate incidents took place that allegedly left at least two villagers dead and multiple others injured after villagers protested against Chevron's activities in the region. "These people are basically begging for some sort of compensation for what has happened to their lifestyle and environment," she says.

Since the Niger delta and Ecuador stories broke, each case has been covered incessantly by media entities and watchdog groups, including ABC News, the *Economist*, SFGate.com (Web site connected with the *San Francisco Chronicle*), the *Seattle Post-Intelligencer*, the *Sacramento Bee*, the *Village Voice*, MSN Money, MarketWatch, Truthout, AlterNet, Amnesty International, CorpWatch, SocialFunds.com, Advocacy.net, Multinationalmonitor.org, Globeinvestor.com, Business-humanrights .org, Amazonwatch.org—in addition to two Web sites, Chevrontoxico .com and Texicorainforest.org, specifically devoted to tracking these scandals. The stories and commentaries ran concurrently with the "Will You Join Us?" campaign, presenting a most incongruous backdrop for Chevron's caring message.

With respect to the Ecuador and Niger delta cases, Chevron insists that it broke no laws and has admitted no wrongdoing. Again, there is no way for us to know with total confidence what happened in either instance. What we do know is that for the time being, although the company has acknowledged the problem of "end of oil," the solutions "innovation, collaboration and conservation" do not appear to be a significant part of Chevron's core strategy. In 2006, Chevron increased its renewable energy investments to $300 million annually. Still, though, given the company's $15 to $16 billion budget for exploring and producing fossil fuels, it appears that today, increased oil prices and supply and control remain the chief means of revenue and growth at Chevron, while a pattern of environmental and social transgressions blemish the company's character. Thus, when Chevron asks, "Will You Join Us?" well-informed stakeholders feel inclined to ask back: "Join You Where?"

AD NAUSEAM

Chevron's and Merck's campaigns are by no means unique. Corporations spend millions annually on corporate responsibility–related advertising designed to sway public opinion. Most of the time, the central goal of those campaigns is to minimize significant social and environmental problems by positioning the company as a social or environmental leader. As we have seen, however, the public increasingly seems to be unwilling to buy what these companies are determined to sell. Savvy stakeholders have built up an immunity to such campaigns, particularly to companies that they suspect have something to hide. With greater frequency, the public calls foul or tunes those messages out, for even the slightest reason.

Agrochemicals giant Monsanto learned this the hard way after it tried to bend European public opposition to both its brand and its genetically modified foods with a series of seven full-page advertisements that read: "Food technology is a matter of opinions. Monsanto believes you should hear them all." The campaign essentially flopped on a technicality. In it, Monsanto tried to convince sophisticated Europeans that genetically modified foods are better for them and the environment be-cause they are "grown in a more environmentally sustainable way, less dependent on the earth's scarce mineral resources." The ads implied that the company had been testing GM foods for twenty years, and that such crops were approved for sale in over twenty countries. While Monsanto's ad campaign did get a lot of press in the UK, it wasn't for the reasons the company had hoped.

Watchdog organizations in the UK like the Advertising Standards Authority (ASA), GeneWatch, and the Soil Association have called Monsanto's campaign false and misleading. They pointed out that GM foods like the tomatoes and potatoes pictured in the ads were not ap-proved for use in Europe. They also found that the company had in fact *not* conducted twenty years of research on the topic. These discrepan-cies lead to the filing of eighty-one complaints with the ASA from inde-pendent pressure groups such as the Soil Association, as well as from concerned citizens, prompting Monsanto to pull the campaign.[14] Shortly after the company did pull the campaign, a Monsanto representative apologetically explained to BBC News: "We perhaps did not take suffi-ciently into account the difference in culture between the UK and the U.S.A. in the way some of this information is presented."[15] This state-ment irritated some further, as it suggested that Americans are more easily hoodwinked than their British counterparts.

On its Web site, Monsanto poses as the friendly neighbor next door. It gushes over the benefits of biotechnology and claims its methods are "opening the doors to new possibilities." It commits itself to "stake in the ground" honesty and decency, and asserts: "integrity is the founda-tion of everything we do." That's not a bad thing. The real problem, in our view, is this statement: "What the world sees when it looks at Mon-santo is a solid, successful, and socially responsible company."[16]

Vocal individuals and groups, including the Center for Food Safety, Amnesty International, CorpWatch, Willie Nelson, and a band of in-fluential small family farmers don't quite see things the Monsanto way.

They devote substantial energy to disproving everything Monsanto says on its Web site and through its other communications. These detractors insist that Monsanto effectively bulldozes environmental and health concerns about any of the products it sells, and guarantees that it will effectively own patents to everything that consumers eat and farmers grow.

To make matters worse, in what has been called a classic David and Goliath struggle, seventy-five-year-old family farmer Percy Schmeiser is entangled in a legal battle in Canada's federal courts. Schmeiser has been growing canola on his farm in Saskatchewan for more than forty-five years, and in 2002, he found what he describes as a "large infestation" affecting more than 320 hectares of his land now "contaminated" by Monsanto's herbicide-resistant Roundup Ready canola, a GM variety of the oilseed. Schmeiser's theory is that the company's seed could have easily blown onto his soil from passing canola-laden trucks. "I never put those plants on my land," he claims.[17] Monsanto says that whether or not Schmeiser planted Monsanto's canola seeds, he owes the company a $15 per acre fee for the privilege of bearing their GM canola, and wants additional damages totaling $400,000 and legal fees on top. That would ruin Schmeiser financially, so in protest of a "grave injustice," he launched a Web site (http://www.percyschmeiser.com) so that he could rally other farmers and communities around the world, and also filed a $10 million countersuit against Monsanto for libel, trespass, and property damage.

Word eventually gets around. According to Greenpeace, Monsanto takes its intention to control the world's foodstuffs far beyond canola and the patenting of seed technologies. In 2005, Amnesty International officials claimed to have discovered an application that Monsanto allegedly filed with the World Intellectual Property Organization (WIPO) to patent both methods of pig breeding and actual herds of pigs as well as their offspring. In objection, Greenpeace posted a mock-up advertisement for the company on its Web site (www.greenpeace.org), featuring an image of a squealing pig and reading: "The Earth is flat, pigs were invented by Monsanto, and genetically modified organisms are safe. Right." Similarly, in June 2005, the Organic Consumers Association (OCA) rallied farmers and consumers to sign a "Stop Monsanto" petition. In asking people to sign the petition, the OCA mentioned: "If you're talking about PCBs, Agent Orange, Bovine Growth Hormone, water privatization, biopiracy, untested/unlabeled genetically engineered organisms, or persecuting small family farmers, you're talking about the Monsanto Corporation." According to the OCA, over one million people signed the petition.

There are bad public perceptions, and then there are *bad* public perceptions. Thus, when Monsanto says: "What the world sees when it looks at Monsanto is a solid, successful, and socially responsible company," how does that statement make Monsanto seem?

Another firm involved in the GM debate is Altria Group, the parent corporation of the companies that bring us Virginia Slims, Velveeta, and Miracle Whip. Altria does not set forth opinion the way Monsanto does. Rather, the company tries to distance itself from controversial GM- and tobacco-related issues and takes a neutral approach to corporate responsibility overall. One could say, a tad too neutral. One of Altria's 2005 print ads depicts an image of an lush green tree and reads: "Meeting the expectations of shareholders, customers, regulators and wider society is simply the only path to our future." Altria's ad doesn't say what those expectations are or how the company is meeting them but instead presents these deep thoughts: "For a company as newsworthy as ours, it can be hard to see the forest for the trees. But to look beyond immediate challenges and position our company for long-term success, we have to keep the whole forest squarely in sight. And that's a vision we feel is worth sharing. Our name is Altria Group." Altria leaves people its name but neglects to give them an indication of what its corporate vision is or why it's remotely worth sharing.

Critics have a generally mordant response to this and other of

Altria's ads showing similar trees and random, deep thoughts. "[They] should have shown hideously deformed 'Franken-trees' instead," said WireTap's Michael Gaworecki. Gaworecki contends that Altria Group's Kraft, Inc., is one of the nation's largest users of GM ingredients and, as such, contributes to the health and environmental problems alleg- edly caused by GM. "Think about that the next time you go out of your way to eat organic instead of Taco Bell taco shells, Post cereals, or Jell-O pudding," he says.[18]

Many firms today use the "we are a good, honest company" sales pitch to appeal to conscientious consumers, but that pitch generally doesn't work because people need to determine such things for them- selves, through experience. Just because a company thinks highly of itself and feels compelled to tell consumers about it doesn't mean that consumers will embrace the company's point of view. Smart people don't have to tell us they're smart. Cool people don't have to tell us they're cool. And good companies don't have to tell us they're good. If they do, then it's a clue to their darker side. Most people construe cor- porate gloating as conceited and clumsy. Even nauseating. For example, with charges of war profiteering, bribery, fraud, and mismanagement[19] battering Halliburton's corporate reputation, its 2004, $1.4 million "Halliburton Proud" advertising campaign never stood much of a chance of convincing many "liberal" thinkers of anything other than the com- pany's self-infatuation.

Halliburton's ads, according to a company spokesperson, attempted to "educate those who didn't know what to think about all the charges"[20] that the company faced. At the time the campaign was launched, the plaintiffs in one lawsuit against Halliburton in U.S. District Court in Riverside, California, alleged that the company enticed employees to work in Iraq with false claims that the jobs were safe. The "Halliburton Pride" ads recast this ruse by featuring patriotic Halliburton employees who were proud to work for the company on behalf of "American free- dom." One ad included an Iraq-based worker saying, "I helped move containerized housing units into the camps, helped hook up running water, power, and sewage so that the soldiers could have a decent place to come back to at the end of the day. . . . We got 80,000 troops out of the sand in three months. It was awesome. No other company could have done that."

Halliburton's employee-centric "Pride" campaign happened to launch after it filed a suit against former workers who publicly complained that Halliburton canceled their hard-earned pensions and health insurance benefits. In its hometown newspaper, the *Houston Chronicle*, Halliburton was ridiculed for making a hostile move to silence retirees at a time when the company vied to position itself as a Good Samaritan: "It was a blunder on a par with the cattle industry's decision to sue Oprah Winfrey, or Fox News's lawsuit against author and liberal talk radio host Al Franken for using 'fair and balanced' in the title of his latest book," the *Chronicle* wrote in 2004. "Halliburton really didn't need this self-generated hit."[21]

Despite the need to improve their image, self-generated hits are clearly the best that some companies can muster, since their practices lead few outsiders to offer any flattering. Insurance companies are notorious examples of this phenomenon. So many wield buoyant taglines like, "You're in Good Hands," "We Live Where You Live," "We Get You Back Where You Belong," or "You Can Rely on Us" to lure new customers in, and then allegedly deny coverage to policy holders for legitimate claims. On its Web site, Allstate Insurance Company says that it's rooted in a history of "serving our customers by providing peace of mind and enriching their quality of life through our partnership in the management of the risks they face." The company reaffirmed this commitment in its 2005 "Our Stand" advertising campaign. According to the company, the campaign "takes a strong stand for consumers' interests by delivering a simple, straightforward message that highlights the many benefits of having insurance protection from

Allstate."[22] One of these spots featured a fictional couple named Kate and Howard, who were sued after a car accident and found themselves in a jam when their liability coverage didn't pay for all the damages ordered by the court. Heartbroken and undone, the two had no choice but to sell their home. Better to be "in good hands" with Allstate, the ad suggested.

Shortly after that ad aired, the company received a cease and desist letter from the Texas attorney general's office. That letter called the spot "false, deceptive and misleading."[23] Apparently, the Texas constitution prohibits insurance companies from forcing consumers to sell their homes except under certain specific conditions, none of which were illustrated in the ad. Though this was another technicality, and Allstate did agree to pull the Kate and Howard spot off the air, it remains to be seen whether or not the company knowingly violated deceptive trade practice laws and the insurance code with its ad in the first place. Either way, the situation conveys how eager stakeholders are to jump on companies the moment they spot an opportunity. "I think the attorney general's action should send a message to insurance companies that if you're going to do business in Texas and you're going to advertise on our airwaves, you need to be forthright with your policy holders," says Alex Winslow, executive director of consumer advocate group Texas Watch in response to Allstate's decision to pull the ad.

What's noteworthy about Allstate's failed advertisement is that it ran just before Hurricanes Katrina and Rita ravaged Louisiana, Mississippi, and parts of Texas, causing Allstate policyholders to file thousands of claims with the insurance carrier. Allstate was one of the five named defendants in the Mississippi attorney general's 2005 suit against insurance carriers for allegedly defrauding policyholders by requiring them to sign a form stating that their property damage was caused by flooding, not hundred-mile-an-hour winds before they were able to receive the living expense checks that were payable under their policies.[24] "In exchange for a small amount of money upfront, people were having to sign away their ability to get a full claim down the road since flooding is not covered," says Winslow. He asserts that the Mississippi suit prompted his organization to ask the attorney general and insurance commissioner to issue warnings to Texans, and specifically to Allstate insurance holders, after Hurricane Rita, as well as to generate press coverage about the situation. "We're trying to get out in front of them before they have the opportunity to do the same thing here," Winslow told us.

ALL THE RAGE

Alex Winslow represents a growing trend. The little guy, be it a local official or an individual consumer, is rising up and taking matters into his own hands. Due to the general sentiment that fleecing is a way of doing business for many industries of scale, more people feel as if they've been left with no other choice. The realization that one is being cheated or maneuvered creates a level of hostility that carries over from one brand experience to the next. In time, isolated negative incidents start to blur together, and people start to think, "All airlines try to cheat me out of my rewards. All hotels try to cheat me on my bill. All cellular companies try to get me through unfair contract terms. All banks try to impose hidden fees. No one is looking out for me. It's me versus them. I have to defend myself." Pessimistic thought patterns are reinforced by future instances, and the outcome of this mental programming leads to the trust deficit statistics previously cited. The deficit, in turn, leads to brand disloyalty, employee turnover, quality control issues, and a range of other business headaches.

But what happens when people get pushed over the edge to the offensive end, like Percy Schmeiser from Saskatchewan or Alex Winslow from Texas Watch? It's one thing to be weary of corporate interests, but quite another to wage war against them. Yet, every day, more people feel prompted to do exactly this. A 2005 survey conducted by the Customer Care Alliance found that 90 percent of respondents were unsatisfied with how organizations treated them, while 64 percent reported feeling "rage" against companies with which they had particularly bad experiences. The survey also found that more than half of all respondents who had bad experiences decided to take their business elsewhere, while *90 percent* shared their war stories with friends or others.

By the time Eric Stoffers decided that U.S. Bancorp's pledge to "operate with a tradition of uncompromising honesty and integrity"[25] was inconsistent with the way the company had treated him, he was furious enough to create http://www.usbanksucks.com, a Web site that has attracted more than 375,000 unique visitors since it launched in March 2003. There, Stoffers describes his "horror story" about the organization and encourages other disgruntled customers and bank employees to do the same. "It's incredible what U.S. Bank has put me through," he states. The user postings on Stoffers's site reflect accounts of alleged bungled transactions, disappearing deposits, exorbitant fees, uncompensated worker overtime, and even employee and customer discrimination. The site also tracks various lawsuits filed against the bank and points users in the direction of five other Web forums dedicated to achieving the same anti-U.S. Bancorp goals. "U.S. Bank has always had the capability to make me shut up and go away," claims Stoffer. "All they had to do all along was correct their mistakes. Instead, they have consistently chosen to escalate the matter and act in an increasingly outrageous manner." Stoffers's latest posts describe U.S. Bank's reputed legal efforts to force him to dismantle the Web site. This, says Stoffers, only adds more fire to his cause. He tells people: "You decide who the real maniacs are."

Increasingly, put-off customers like Stoffers don't just get mad, they get even. They take their score settling to cyberspace, where they can control the circumstances. It's a therapeutic means of getting stuff off their chest and doing something about the lack of personal service and respect that, with the switch to automation, a great many companies cease to provide. The cyber-rage phenomenon is growing. More sites like www.usbanksucks.com get posted every day, as more companies alienate their stakeholders.

Cingular and AT&T, the two entities that combined in 2004 to form one of America's largest wireless phone companies, represent another business in the customer hot seat. In addition to sharing a balance sheet, the two also rank poorly in their industry with respect to customer satisfaction. Complaint data obtained by Consumers Union, publisher of *Consumer Reports* magazine, indicate that the two companies had more filed customer complaints in 2004 than any other providers. A simple Web search led us to over thirty separate customer-hosted and regularly updated complaint sites, blogs, and chat rooms about the pair, including a Yahoo! Finance group called Cingular Sucks (http://finance.groups.yahoo.com/group/cingular-sucks2/).

Featuring an artistic impression of the Cingular logo being sucked down a toilet, this group is dedicated to trashing the company's reputation by "making public our common negative experiences with Cingular and helping to inform potential customers of their unethical practices." Further, the site's hosts intend to "Help stop companies such as Cingular from utilizing financially-motivated guerrilla tactics such as simlocking and termed service agreements that financially force customers to remain with the service." On a weekly basis, this site is updated with fresh material that Cingular's policies ostensibly provide.

Browsing through a jungle of similar sites—and there are many out there—one thing becomes crystal clear. Forums like these have an enormous influence on the way people view corporate responsibility. Because they merge firsthand experiences with the power of word of mouth and the Web, they arguably have more pull, more quickly on a firm's corporate reputation any other "touch point" possibly could. So, rather than try to intimidate hosts and shut them down, thus inflaming the situation further, smarter companies will start to utilize the unfiltered feedback. These sites contain valuable market intelligence. They serve as a barometer for how well a corporation is doing reputation-wise. Forget focus groups or surveys. By simply conducting a Google search for terms that average consumers use, such as "[your company name] + sucks" or "I hate [your company name]," companies can get a fairly accurate sense of how they fare.

In conducting their searches, companies should carefully observe the nature of customer complaints. From the types of stories told, they can better determine exactly what it is they are doing that's making people feel jilted. Companies should also take note of the number of results that pop up and just how many sites are exclusively dedicated to lambasting their organizations. For instance, as of March 2006, the term "U.S. Bank sucks" generated 617 results, whereas "I hate Cingular" generated 1,010, indicating that indignation toward both companies is fairly widespread.

THE WATCHDOGS

Watchdog groups are another force on the rise, and they are featured intermittently throughout this book. Whereas watchdogs were once considered off-the-wall, anticorporate renegades, they are now credible and influential resources. They spur major news stories, generate public outcry, and force corporate accountability. Many of them, though not all, have a great deal of information and research at their disposal and are therefore used as sources for journalists gathering information. A growing number of groups target the activities of specific companies.

There are specialized organizations like Wal-Mart Watch, Halliburton Watch, and Jumpstart Ford—each with a full-time staff dedicated to tracking and critiquing the practices of their particular corporate focus. And there are also generalists like the previously mentioned Organic Consumers Association, the Public Interest Research Group, CorpWatch, and Amnesty International, which track industries like food and oil, or that monitor global corporations overall.

Watchdog groups have essentially become the corporate world's equivalent of paparazzi. They come with the territory of being big and powerful, or even up-and-coming. Companies that come up against them and refuse to deal with them constructively, snub them off, demean them, or treat them like the enemy find that oftentimes, the groups only come back with a vengeance. Several watchdog groups, like Wal-Mart Watch, for instance, are run by former political operatives who have a great deal of experience running national campaigns and stirring public emotions. In their communications, these groups are increasingly organized, tactical, and brutal. They have connections on Capitol Hill, on the ground, and in Hollywood. Often, people find their campaigns to be highly convincing and emotive. Thus, the best corporate response is to seriously listen to their concerns and then try to deflate the tension. Corporations would do well to invite such groups to headquarters and address their chief concerns directly. Corporations should respond to the groups' tough questions and let them know exactly what the company is doing, what it is willing to do in the future, and why. If this open dialogue occurred, then most major conflicts might be resolved. But some corporations caught up with watchdog groups are unwilling to meet eye to eye. Based on the conversations we had with watchdog group representatives, including people at CorpWatch, Wal-Mart Watch, the Organic Consumers Association, and others, the general sentiment is that corporate executives from certain routinely targeted companies are primarily interested in addressing the facts that they want to convey to watchdog groups, and not the issues that watchdog groups want the company to acknowledge.

When it comes to everything from consumer-directed corporate responsibility outreach to managing watchdog relations, sincerity, openness, and two-way interaction simply works better as a tactic than impenetrability or ambiguity. Watchdog groups may well tone it down once they feel they've been heard and, better still, that the company is actually doing something productive to improve its ways. Obviously, the key is that the company is in fact willing to (a) listen to criticisms, (b) improve its behavior, rather than systematically deny wrongdoing, and (c) acknowledge that any progress can be made and that progress is worth making.

Ultimately, the very best thing that any company can do to deflate tension with outside groups is to stop spending frivolously on reactive publicity bonanzas and invest in developing better policies instead. After all, if Chevron had put its $50 million "Will You Join Us?" advertising budget where its mouth was, it could have increased its initial environmental technologies investments by 50 percent.

In any case, no company is immune to the potential of organized backlash, as watchdog groups go after corporations of all sorts, not just the usual suspects. For example, CorpWatch and the Global Alliance for Incinerator Alternatives (GAIA) recently disparaged Seiko Epson, an otherwise decent performer, shortly after the company issued a seemingly benign September 2004 press release announcing its FundingFactory "recycling" program. In its press release, the company stated that the program "allows schools and nonprofits nationwide to return ink cartridges for rewards that can boost fundraising efforts and help the environment . . . The cartridges will be converted to energy through an environmentally sound incineration process at a licensed waste-to-energy recycling facility." This latter statement waved a red flag to environmentalists, who immediately drew a distinction.

"Burning is not recycling!" said CorpWatch and GAIA in a call to action that ultimately encouraged hundreds of consumers to write complaint letters to Epson vice president John Dillender. Both organizations argued that incineration is inherently polluting, wasteful, and threatening to human health. They accused Epson of deceiving teachers, students, and the public through a fake recycling program and further encouraged it to take steps to begin turning its empty print cartridges into new cartridges the way several of its competitors were.

Although GAIA spokesperson Monica Wilson says that she never got a straight answer from Epson as to why they used the term "recycling" in the first place, she gives the company the benefit of the doubt: "I think that perhaps they didn't realize that combustion wasn't recycling. A lot of incineration companies market themselves as recyclers, which is totally bogus. The National Recycling Coalition is very clear about the fact that when you incinerate something, that's definitely not recycling." Interestingly, Epson's European subsidiary seems to understand the meaning of the term perfectly well, as they do recycle, not burn, ink cartridges collected in the UK and elsewhere under a similar program. Wilson says that following Epson's press release, GAIA took the opportunity to educate the company's U.S. headquarters about recycling and offered a few tips. "What's happened so far is that Epson has been trying to deal with the problem," she says, "but they haven't come up with any solid solution yet." The noise made by GAIA and CorpWatch on this issue caused a little commotion in the environmental community, which has followed the company until today. "We are actually just about to write Epson another letter asking them for an update on what they are doing," says Wilson. Although she didn't come out and say it, we suspect Wilson and others involved would like to send a loud and clear message to this and other corporations invested in environmental programs, which is: don't promise anything unless you know what you mean and you mean what you say.

MOVING FORWARD

In this chapter, we explored challenging territory. We looked at one part of the changing business landscape—the surge in stakeholder activism—and how different companies are struggling to respond through their communications. We learned that consumers, shareholders, employees, bloggers, journalists, watchdogs, and other influencers are not the recipients of a company's CR outreach. Rather, they are participants in that outreach.

In the next chapter, we will open our lens wider still. We will attempt to define the whole new business landscape in its multiple dimensions. Through the eyes of renowned experts, we will observe how the landscape is changing, how certain companies are starting to cope with that change, and most importantly, what the changes mean to the future of business.

To move forward into the progression, one simply has to take a step back—way back—from the clutter. Before one can advance, it is helpful to first attempt to think as broadly as possible about the deepest issues that plague companies, our planet, and our civilization. Within these problems are answers and strategic possibilities. Conversely, without adequately considering such problems, businesses risk missing such opportunities and again running into problems.

If companies truly want to make a positive difference, if they desire to be perceived by their stakeholders as good citizens, then let them first become prepared. Let them see the bigger picture: the good, the bad, and the ugly—and how it all relates.

THE PITFALLS

Top Mistakes	Optimal Approach
Ignoring the trust deficit.	Give stakeholders a legitimate reason to trust and believe.
Communicating without regard to what else people hear.	Assume that every audience is well informed.
Using standard clichés and rhetoric.	Develop the company's unique, authentic story.
Standing for something that runs contrary to the interests of company shareholders.	Either financially get behind what the company claims to stand for or don't take the position at all.
Telling the audience how they view the corporation.	Let the audience be the judge.
Making vague statements or gloating and self-praising.	If the company can't discuss concrete accomplishments, then address what future goals are and how the company plans to achieve them.
Exaggerating CR positions or distorting the facts.	Stick to the facts. Do not distort the facts in any way, shape, or form.
Systematically denying any wrongdoing.	No company is perfect. Every company makes mistakes. From time to time, it's okay to admit that an error was made and even productive to a company's future. See chapter 4.

PART 4: The Progession

3:

See the Bigger Picture

The whole problem *is* the machine—not simply the grinding gears of a global-
izing economic system but an entire way of thinking.

—ELIZABETH DEBOLD, "THE BUSINESS OF

SAVING THE WORLD"

In her March 2005 *What Is Enlightenment?* magazine article, "The
Business of Saving the World," journalist Elizabeth Debold posed a provocative question to thirty of the most progressive change makers in
business today. She asked: What would happen if corporations, filled
with the creative potential of thousands of human beings, were to wake
up to the true interconnectivity among themselves, the planet, and its
people?[1] In other words, what if corporate decision makers finally recognized that there is no division between business, society, and the environment; that each of these spheres of influence is part of the same
living system; that results in one sphere creates results for the other two;
and that if society or the environment fails, then business fails?

Remarkably, each person who answered Debold's question, from Whole Foods Market's Walter Robb to McDonald's Mats Lederhausen, Nike's Darcy Winslow, author Meg Wheatley, systems expert Peter Senge, and leadership expert Richard Barrett, had the same answer: If corporations were to suddenly see the bigger picture and then conduct business with the understanding that business, society, and the environment are not three independent concepts but one unified, organic construct—they might change the world in unprecedented ways, creating totally new conditions. Debold and her legion of experts concluded that the understanding of systemic interconnectedness is a key to the long-term survival of the planet and every single living thing on it, including corporations. The issue, they said, was not whether or not businesspeople had the ability or tools to see and respond to the bigger picture, but rather, whether they had the desire. "World-transforming change *is* possible, but only if we are willing," Debold says. "And that big 'if' will determine what kind of future we have—or whether we will have any future at all."[2]

Companies operating in the modern world have some monumental choices to make, whereas the will that Debold touches on has several sides to it. First, there is the will to see the bigger picture—to understand *why* change is necessary—or to remain in the dark, so to speak. Next, there is the will to respond to the bigger picture—to *change*—or to remain the same. While subsequent chapters will deal extensively with the change side of the equation, this chapter primarily deals with outlook. When companies choose to see the bigger picture, they get why they need to substantiate their claims of corporate responsibility. Seeing the bigger picture typically causes an urge to take action, but at first, most companies respond by drawing basic new conclusions and connections, as well as by taking small but significant steps.

There is a growing wave of businesses with the will to look beyond the balance sheet to grapple with the multilayered complexities affecting them. As the following stories demonstrate, it is critical that companies begin to use a new lens—to broaden the traditional, linear approach to problem solving so long relied upon and incorporate wider social and environmental realities in their business decision-making. While the firms below are at the start of a much longer journey, they are signals that the system is stirring.

The first step in the progression is a new way of thinking, of seeing older problems in a new light, and the following four firms are doing just this. For example, multinational construction firm Bovis Lend Lease used to view fatalities and workplace injuries the way the rest of its industry did—as a serious liability. Over the past twenty-five years, 2,800 people have died working for Bovis and other construction companies through on-the-job accidents.[3] Today, however, Bovis regards worker safety another way, as "a choice and a basic human right." Bovis recently committed to operating incident and injury free wherever it has a presence.

"We were not satisfied with our prior performance," says Stephen Cloutier, director of environment, health, and safety in the Americas. Cloutier says that Bovis made the connection between worker safety and worker happiness, workplace morale, and productivity. Essentially, the company adopted a healthier attitude with respect to its people, which in turn enables the company to become healthier and attract motivated workers. "Now we feel it's a human right to go home at night the same way you came to work in the morning, and it's okay for people to stop work if they perceive an unsafe condition. We continue to push this message throughout the organization." Although no metrics are yet publicly available to indicate the company's improved performance in this area, Cloutier explains that Bovis is presently taking all levels of management and workers through an extensive safety-training program. "We're trying to change the mind-set of the organization, and we're committed to making this journey happen," he says.

Changing the mind-set of a huge organization that has been operating in a certain manner for decades is no easy task. But in order to remain competitive, more companies are coming to grips with social issues previously swept under the carpet. Diamond mining giant De Beers, for instance, was long accused of operating like a cartel, controlling up to 90 percent of the world's diamond trade. Literally hundreds of articles and thousands of online posts track allegations about the company's dark history. Recently, the Motley Fool's Lawrence Meyers summarized some of its key problems: "[Critics] claim that [De Beers's] century-old near-monopoly of diamond production and distribution artificially inflated the price of diamonds, resulting in economically driven African civil wars. Tens of thousands of innocent civilians were murdered, mutilated, and displaced in these battles."[4] More recently, Nicholas Howen, secretary-general of the International Commission of Jurists noted: "The De Beers group has admitted buying diamonds from rebels, knowing that this money funded these groups' military activities and serious violence against civilians. The South African Truth Commission documented how mining companies in South Africa under apartheid helped the Government create a discriminatory migrant labour system for their own advantage and how they called the police into factories to brutally disperse striking workers. These are just a few examples from many well-documented cases."[5]

Controversy caught up with De Beers. Until recently, it was barred from conducting retail business in the United States on the basis of price-fixing and other charges. Numerous activist groups around the world boycotted the firm. Today, however, De Beers seems to be re-evaluating. "Our new thinking [guides] us in how we partner with employees and this has inspired new and innovative thinking in mining diamonds more efficiently, protecting our environment and fostering a more focused approach to corporate social responsibility,"[6] the company says.

De Beers's new thinking might have also been responsible for the company's 2005 decision to pay $338 million to settle price-fixing lawsuits filed by U.S. consumers, retailers, and jewelry makers. It might additionally have played a role in the company's guilty plea to the separate 2004 price-fixing charge filed by U.S. prosecutors. De Beers faces multiple other suits alleging price-fixing as well, and although it has denied wrongdoing in these cases, it is finally paying attention to class action suits and wider complaints about its business practices. These are new moves for the company.

De Beers is now a supporter of the Kimberly Process, an attempt to remove diamonds from the market that are used to fund bloody conflicts in Africa. As of 2004, most of its operations were ISO 14001 certified, meaning that they operate with higher environmental management standards. De Beers also claims to have set aside natural diamond reserves several times the size of its mining footprint. On the social front, De Beers recently adopted diamond mining best practices to ensure higher professional, social, environmental, legal, and ethical standards, and also established joint venture partnerships with the governments of Namibia, Botswana, Tanzania, and India. According to De Beers, these partnerships help to temper regional conflicts and foster sustainable development. These small and calculated moves in the right direction exhibit the initial pace that mega-corporations follow during the first phase of transition.

Kimberly-Clark, the world's largest producer of tissue products and a company often blamed for creating environmental degradation, is also responding to criticisms made against it by incrementally improving performance. Recently, serious environmental issues have come to a head. In April 2005, protesters from Greenpeace and the Natural Resources Defense Council (NRDC) attended Kimberly-Clark's annual meeting to voice their concern over the company's logging practices. "Kimberly-Clark is wiping away ancient forests by using boreal tree fiber for disposable tissue products, including the Kleenex brand. They need to be a responsible corporate citizen and increase ecologically sound fiber in all their brands," said Pamela Wellner, senior Greenpeace forest campaigner, who attended the annual meeting.[7]

Canada's ancient boreal forest is where logging companies are accused of clear cutting. Kimberly-Clark buys pulp from several of these companies, including the Neenah Paper pulp mill. In November 2005, Greenpeace and the NRDC ran a full-page ad in the *New York Times*, calling for an end to Kimberly-Clark's "destructive" environmental practices. According to Greenpeace, over forty thousand consumers were activated through this campaign, resulting in local boycotts and letters of protest.

Greenpeace says that between 15 and 30 percent of Kimberly-Clark tissue products originated from fiber derived from the Canadian boreal forest and that Kimberly-Clark used about 2.5 million tons of virgin tree pulp to make its tissue products in 2004. That year, less than 19 percent of Kimberly-Clark's fiber allegedly came from recycled sources while the other 81 percent, or 3.3 million tons, came from forests.[8] In the consumer products category, the industry average for recycled fiber use is 60 percent, which places Kimberly-Clark behind its competitors, especially smaller brands like Cascades and Seventh Generation.

However, Kimberly-Clark recently signaled the start of its new environmental mentality. "It is vital that Kimberly-Clark manage the natural resources we use and the environmental footprint we leave behind in a way that will enable both our business and future generations to prosper," says Kenneth Strassner, vice-president of environment and energy. "This is our strategy for environmental stewardship—and sustainability thinking." As of 2005, all of Kimberly-Clark suppliers were certified by one of five internationally recognized forestry groups, including the Forest Stewardship Council, which employs a management and certification system that encourages responsible forestry practices. In addition to improving standards for its suppliers, Kimberly-Clark's sustainability thinking also led the company to increasingly rely on the forestry woodlands that it owns: "Our forestlands are managed in a continuing cycle during which we plant, nurture and harvest trees and then start over again by replanting harvested areas. During this process, Kimberly-Clark plants about two trees for every one we use, ensuring that our woodlands are managed as sustainable resources," the company says.[9] While Greenpeace is not satisfied with the company's new forestry policies and Kimberly-Clark itself admits that there is still much environmental progress to be made, the company does set improved forestry goals each year. This indicates that it is seeing things differently and not totally insensitive to the problems that it faces.

Another company in the midst of reevaluating old approaches is American Airlines. Like most major air carriers, American is struggling financially due to rising fuel prices and pressure from low cost airlines. As recently as 2004, it was on the brink of bankruptcy. Post 9/11, the company responded to its financial difficulties much the way other major airlines did: by slashing labor costs. This created intense employee strife.

More recently, however, American began *listening*. In 2005, American's management asked employees for help. American needed to save about $500 million annually but did not want to interrupt quality, eliminate jobs, or institute pay cuts. It was a tall order, but as it turns out, employees were more than happy to assist management. One solution came from two mechanics who determined that they shouldn't have to throw away $200 drill bits after only a few uses. The duo rigged up a drill bit sharpener made from a secondhand motor and an old vacuum cleaner belt. Their invention, dubbed "Thumping Ralph," saved American as much as $300,000 a year. Another tip came from a maintenance crew engineer who discovered a way to save 90 percent on restroom mirrors by designing them on-site from less expensive materials on hand rather than special ordering them from an outside source. Yet another idea came from a group of pilots who discovered they could taxi into arrival gates just as effectively and safely using one engine instead of two, thus saving fuel.

Ideas from all areas of the company continue to trickle up to American's management, and in July 2005, the company announced its first profit in five years. Although American's stronger financial performance is not entirely due to employee innovations, it is to some degree, and the program itself displays the positive effect that good relationships can have on a company's ability to perform. "Communication lines were suddenly open," says Justin Fuller, an American engineer in Tulsa, Oklahoma. "Before, people had ideas, but they didn't know where to take them. They also thought it wouldn't make any difference if they did. Now, the groundwork has been laid so people know where to take their ideas and how to get them implemented."[10] By becoming more receptive to its own people, American learned that it could perform a little better. In turn, American's people grew more supportive of their organization. Though the lesson itself cost the airline nothing out of pocket to execute, the learning gained was arguably priceless.

American Airlines, Kimberly-Clark, De Beers, and Bovis Lend Lease represent the changing tides. These companies are better poised today than they once were because of their understanding of how larger connections work—that is, how environmental and social issues can influence business performance. They have become more responsive to stakeholder concerns and needs, rather than remaining impervious to them.

To fully leverage the skill of big-picture thinking, and to maximize the business benefits of this and future phases, it is necessary to acknowledge the underlying forces that affect today's companies. It is helpful to consider the magnitude of those underlying forces and where they stem from. The argument, or *need* for corporate responsibility, is not just a humanitarian one. The argument is not only a matter of our planet's survival, as Debold suggests. There is, as the following section will attempt to briefly outline, a compelling business case, too. Therefore, it matters not whether any of us choose to define ourselves as altruists, survivalists, radicals, conservatives, or egocentrists. The bigger picture concerns us all, equally.

THE PRESENT

We are at the intersection of two conflicting management paradigms. One is reflected by business decision-makers who embrace what Debold refers to in her *What Is Enlightenment?* article as the "corporate mechanistic mind-set." These are managers ruled by traditional greed: the balance sheet and short-sighted business strategies. They perceive trade-offs among optimal financial, environmental, and social performance or are unwilling to consider that their companies' performance is inextricably linked to broader social and environmental contexts. Therefore, they often make decisions that create negative stakeholder results. By instilling loose supply chain standards, for instance, a great number of executives knowingly or unknowingly help to perpetuate world poverty and child labor. Certain cost-cutting management measures also often work to demoralize a company's own employees, thus potentially creating hostile work environments, interrupting productivity, and alienating customers. Measures such as these save money in the short term, but also harm businesses by disrupting quality in all forms—quality of work, quality of product, quality of experience, quality of reputation, quality of life, and so forth.

In truth, businesses cannot succeed if their communities are struggling or failing. It makes little sense to deliberately damage the critical support systems that allow a business to function properly. Perpetuating policies that either cause stakeholders harm or that cause them to feel disloyal and resentful toward a company is more reckless than rational.

In her description of the ongoing shift to an advanced mind-set that will ideally guide how business is conducted over the next century, Debold says:

> *The first step is a new way of thinking—a new consciousness or worldview that enables us to recognize how everything is interdependent and how connection to a larger purpose is critical for personal and professional success. . . . The machine is*

*not simply a metaphor. It is a state of consciousness. A new
creativity can be released when leaders reach beyond the numbers and controls to find out what moves the human beings inside organizations.*[11]

Mechanistic thinking relies on simple chains of cause and effect
and thus does not account for wider results, nor does it allow for the
most innovative solutions. Is it more opportune to drill for oil in Alaska's Arctic slope or invest in renewables? Is it more worthwhile to sell
drugs that cure malaria in third-world countries or male pattern bald-
ness in wealthy countries? Is it less costly to invest in effective environmental management systems or pay fines for exceeding pollution
standards? The answers, Debold indicates, depend on our outlook.

Many of us are trained to devise business strategies based on nu-
merical analysis and cases histories—or the past. But what we need to
do more than anything else right now, both with respect to corporate
responsibility and overall business decision-making, is concentrate on
the present. We need to get our heads out of the "machine," take a
look around, and recognize that, for some years now, the way that we
have been going about certain things is out of sync with what is truly
necessary.

The fact is, too many people don't believe that the company they
work for cares for them. Conversely, too many don't feel passionately in
what they do for a living or feel as if it serves any fundamental purpose.
Many people work in environments where the pressure to perform is
driven by the need to consistently turn in short-term profits rather than
produce long-term prosperity and seize future potential. In these environments, corporate responsibility initiatives are often approached reac-
tively rather than proactively. If a problem occurs, only then is it fixed.
When vast quantities of waste are being produced, only then is waste reduced. When scandals arise, only sometimes does a company deal with
the underlying issues that caused things to go awry in the first place.

When corporate responsibility departments within large corporations set out to develop social programs, oftentimes the aim of many of those programs is to minimize or offset the social injustice done by the corporation, rather than strengthen communities. Leading edge thinkers in the field of environmental performance and sustainability have long concluded that most companies are concerned with making the wrong types of products and processes more efficient, rather than designing the right kinds of things from the start. There is a growing tension between the "corporate machine" mentality Debold describes and the modern age, calling for change.

The world has grown infinitely more complex and demanding since the industrial revolution, with the rise of technology and the surge of social and environmental problems facing our civilization. Old boundaries of location, culture, ideology, religion, and national affiliation blur, and most of the planet is networked, allowing people in all areas of the world to know more about how companies really operate in foreign nations and those in foreign nations to make their voices heard. Modern advances have led to the doubling of life expectancy, and they have also led to spikes in population and other serious problems like our diminishing oil, natural gas, and water supplies, just to name a few. In general, people have totally different needs, lifestyles, and expectations than they did one hundred years ago.

In response to these and other changes, however, many see that the business world has only grown more competitive, cluttered, and less differentiated. "The large company of today has reached the end of a defining period," says Mats Lederhausen, who in addition to serving as managing director of McDonald's Ventures also serves as chairman of the board for nonprofit group Business for Social Responsibility. "Fifty or more years ago, companies invested in a business model that was new and unique in the sense that it solved human needs in very different ways. Since then, companies have expanded that business model using every conceivable permutation. They've expanded their business geographically, they've lowered costs, they've adopted new distribution channels, they've expanded into other vertical markets. Now, they've simply run out of ways to improve on the old."

Innovation is the way for companies to press forward, and that means moving with the market or just ahead of it. Moving ahead of market forces requires letting go of the past as a guidepost for future activities. "We need a blank sheet," says Lederhausen. "What we need to do right now is break free from that reliance on the status quo." The place to start is by opening one's mind to new ideas and possibilities: a practice that takes time. But once people do reach a higher mind-set, then it becomes extremely uncomfortable for them to make or contribute to the wrong kinds of rudimentary business decisions, Lederhausen indicates, so they are less inclined to do so and the system changes for the better. That's how real corporate responsibility, or systemic change, commences. People, not policies, reports, or regulations, ultimately make it work.

A practical example of this people-driven shift is the surge of business executives passionately and hurriedly working to improve their companys' environmental performance. Last year, when I interviewed Ray Anderson, chairman of Interface Inc., the world's largest manufacturer of commercial carpet, he recalled his personal epiphany: "[I realized] my business was a culprit and I was a plunderer of the earth . . . The economy is a wholly owned subsidiary of the environment. It's not the other way around." Anderson had quite suddenly realized that the biosphere is in decline, that every living system on the planet is experiencing a downward spiral, and that, due in part to the activities of businesses like his, evolution is moving in reverse for the first time in 3.5 billion years. He saw that even though natural resources from water to wood and petroleum drove his product cycle, Interface's actions were damaging to the quality and quantity of these resources. Moreover, they were hugely damaging to the wider environment, thus producing an enormous societal and ecological burden. Anderson got it. He understood that although Interface was profitable from a one-dimensional balance sheet perspective, it was by no means successful or healthy. The company's way of doing business was not sustainable from a long-term financial or environmental point of view. "We realized that our old business approach was upside down," he said.

Through its natural resources, the earth provides $33 trillion worth of value to the global economy.[12] But for the most part, the value of these resources are not factored into market prices. Nor are the ecological and social consequences produced by economic development, known as "externalities." However, although businesses do not currently pay for these things, they are accounted for. People pay the price when they get lung disease from breathing in the "externalities" we pump into the atmosphere. Supplier communities pay the price when commercial exploitation tears apart their cultural and economic way of life. Employees pay the price when the companies they work for instill such loose health and safety standards that they are injured or killed in preventable accidents. Both insurance companies and consumers pay the price when insurance claims and, therefore, premiums escalate due to a rise in incidents or illnesses caused by corporate activities. Perhaps someday in the future, the companies contributing to global problems like climate change will have to pay, too, much the way tobacco and asbestos companies were held liable for the damage caused by their products.

Somehow, though, these things just don't seem to factor in for many of those making counterproductive decisions. Or if they do, then perhaps individual leaders just don't care enough. Or if they do care enough, then perhaps they're subject to enough outside pressure to force them to make decisions that run contrary to their instincts, but that seem necessary for short-term financial reasons. In any event, by means of a primitive form of risk analysis, many corporations and government leaders conclude that responsibility is not their responsibility, or that it is cheaper to pay fines and legal fees that stem from externalities rather than adjust their processes so as not to produce the costs in the first place. Of course, none of these conclusions are entirely accurate. Nor is any such situation so simple.

What does seem to be true is that our economy is built on some terribly irrational premises, such as the notion that nature's resources are free and unlimited and that external costs that businesses produce for society and the environment don't count. The problem with basing a system of any kind on irrational premises is that the system itself becomes irrational. If we want our companies to embody the resiliency that evolution naturally demonstrates, then we must base our companies on similar principles. To prosper in the future, companies need to become more like nature in the sense of nurturing support systems rather than undermining them, and adjusting to new conditions rather than continuing to operate in a vacuum.

In the book *Cradle to Cradle*, coauthors William McDonough and Michael Braungart ask: "Why not challenge the belief that human industry must damage the natural world? In fact, why not take nature itself as our model for making things?"[13] Indeed, why not? And also, what are the business risks of not doing so?

MARKET PULL

Executives owe it to their stakeholders to be responsible. When they choose not to, they hedge the first rule in capitalism. "The bottom line is that executives and boards of directors risk violating their fiduciary duty to shareholders by failing to pay attention to the changing expectations in the marketplace, to the changing responses in the global climatic system and to the new reality that their companies face," says Gil Friend, CEO of Natural Logic, a California-based sustainability consulting firm. "By sticking with this Old World notion of assuming 'trade-offs' between social, environmental, and economic well-being, they're actually leaving money on the table and sacrificing the economic health of their company as well as the health of us all and the living systems that support us."

Friend is adamant that companies need not decide between doing well and doing good. In fact, he's quite sure that it's the other way around. By ignoring social and environmental variables, companies increase risk, detract from their financial value, and undermine their long-term viability. "The challenge is to understand where the market is moving and move there before the market gets there. Companies that wait for regulations are frankly going to be playing catch-up forever," says Friend. "We actually tell our clients to ignore regulations. Businesspeople don't want to run their companies by state or federal mandates. They want the freedom to set their own priorities and run their companies in a way that meets the needs of the market today and in the future. Now, if they do that well and smart, and if they do that guided by the laws of nature, their companies will run much cleaner than any regulator expects of them. They're automatically going to be in compliance with the law."

More companies are catching on. A report issued in 2005 by the Carbon Disclosure Project (CDP) showed a marked increase in climate change awareness among U.S. businesses, and also found that 63 percent of the world's largest companies were starting to take proactive steps to mitigate the financial risks of climate change to their business. While this is good news, Friend notes that a 37 percent failure rate is unacceptable. His advice to every firm grappling with environmental issues is to break free of the outmoded herd mentality, and fast. "Invest your money in designers and engineers instead of lawyers or lobbyists, leapfrog your competitors, be cleaner than your government expects, and take market share."

Right now, one key question to ask is: Who takes the lead? Which countries or regions set the pace? Remarkably, many eyes are on China at the moment, one of the most polluted nations in the world. That country has pledged to spend $85 billion on environmental projects and to source 10 percent of its energy from clean and renewable sources like wind power by 2010. That makes its environmental agenda significantly more progressive than that of the United States. On this note, President Hu Jintao of China stated the following at the APEC CEO 2004 summit, sending a clear message to U.S. companies and the Bush administration:

Mankind's history shows that development must not be achieved by squandering resources and destroying the environment. Acting otherwise will result in paying a heavy price, even costing the very development we sought to achieve. Therefore, development should be pursued on the basis of high technology content, good economic returns, low resource consumption level, minimum pollution of the environment, and fullest play of human potential.

We should optimize the economic structure; change the way of achieving economic growth; pay closer attention to the conservation and comprehensive utilization of resources; advocate an environment-friendly way of production, life, and consumption; and bring about a virtuous cycle in both our ecological and socioeconomic systems. We should put in place a conservation-oriented management system throughout the process of exploitation, processing, distribution, and consumption of resources with a view to building a resource-effective national economy and a resource-effective society.[14]

Many say that the environmental sustainability game will be won or lost in China, and more enterprising American firms are moving money there. In subsequent chapters, several Fortune 100 companies doing immense business with China are featured, along with their corporate responsibility–related rationale for securing trade relationships with that nation.

Friend points to Europe for leadership. In the summer of 2005, the European Union instituted one directive on the restriction of Waste Electrical and Electronic Equipment (WEEE). The WEEE directive requires all electronics manufacturers operating in Europe to take back and properly recycle equipment at the end of its lifespan at no cost to consumers. Later, in 2006, the EU also required that toxic and hazardous substances, including lead, mercury, cadmium, and bromated flame retardants be eliminated from electronic equipment sold in Europe. This is a perfect example of executives and boards risking an element of their fiduciary duty to shareholders. Friend notes that *40 percent* of the global electronics industry was not ready for these regulatory mandates. "They saw it coming for four years, but they embraced the outmoded way of thinking and assumed that the EU's proposal would just go away," says Friend. "But of course it did not. It passed into law. Electronic executives' decision to not proactively respond is ludicrous when you consider the fact that Europe represents a third of the electronics market. So now you have nearly half of the global electronics industry with a third of their revenue at stake."

Europe's lead doesn't stop with the electronics sector, and neither does the gap between progressive policy and slow business response. In 2007, the EU has promised to require higher energy efficiency standards, and in 2008, they will insist that all chemical substances be tested and registered for environmental and health risks before they can enter the market. Rather than leave it up to individual corporations, a new European Chemicals Agency will disseminate information to the public. "As you can imagine, many pharmaceutical and chemical companies aren't too thrilled about this," says Friend. "There is major lobbying going on, but that's the direction in which Europeans are moving and overall, an example of market pull. We're talking about a market of over 400 million people saying, 'this is what I will buy and this is what I will not buy.' And that *will* get the attention of the global industry."

APTITUDE

Corporate responsibility involves foresight. Foresight, or big-picture thinking, is the enabler of effective corporate responsibility. It is impossible to respond to the problems in the world, let alone to emerging market conditions, if we can't see past our own nose. We must look beyond the bottom line and the next quarter if we are to prepare ourselves for what's ahead. We must think in systemic terms. Big-picture thinking is not only a necessary business skill, but also a survival skill.

As you read the rest of this book, notice how the corporate leaders who express their views about change grow increasingly prolific. Notice how their explanations and conclusions grow more impassioned and how they are increasingly able to draw systemic connections. This is because the degree of big-picture thinking corresponds with the level of strategic corporate responsibility within the company. The more fluid the thinking, the more committed the individual tends to be, and the more committed the individual, the more advanced the company's CR mode likely is—and vice versa. The more advanced the company's CR mode, the higher the probability that there are enlightened people involved. Corporate responsibility is not black or white, nor is big-picture thinking. It is all about varying degrees. There are most definitely skill levels involved.

This preliminary "seeing" phase in the progression is critical, and companies can spend months or years mastering its concepts. Again, this is just the first small step and part of a much longer journey toward improved corporate health. The second, more monumental "doing" step unfolds when a company's newfound understanding, policies, and goals are put to the test, as they often are.

THE BIGGER PICTURE

PAST EMPHASIS	FUTURE EMPHASIS
The industrial age	The conceptual age
Left-brain logic	Right-brain creativity
Linear thinking	Systems thinking
The status quo	A liberated frame of mind
Accounting models	Nature models
Decisions based on past experience	Decisions based on future potential
Organizational hierarchy	Organizational fluidity
Authoritative leadership	Adaptive leadership
Teaching organizations	Learning organizations
Relentless growth	Organic growth
Short-term profits	Long-term prosperity
Reactive corporate responsibility	Proactive corporate responsibility
Minimizing environmental damage	Maximizing environmental repair
Reducing social injustice	Strengthening communities
Limited self-interest	Higher purpose
RESULT = **DESTRUCTIVE ECONOMY**	**RESULT =** **CONSTRUCTIVE ECONOMY**

4:

Face the Truth

Truth indeed rather alleviates than hurts, and will always bear up against falsehood, as oil does above water.

—MIGUEL DE CERVANTES

When a commodity is in scarce supply, it becomes all the more valuable. Frederick Bermudez, director of corporate communications for utility company Public Service Company of New Mexico (PNM), learned this for sure after a hole smaller than the size of a grain of rice led to a gas main explosion that ripped apart an office building, shattered the windows of nearby buses and cars, trapped one person under rubble for nearly ninety minutes, and left two people seriously injured.

"That tiny 1 millimeter by 1.8 millimeter hole turned our business upside down," says Bermudez. "It changed the way we approach media relations in a crisis situation, the way management tackles tough ethical issues, and the way we run our operations."

PNM is the largest utility company in the state of New Mexico, serving over one million customers statewide. The explosion occurred on April 25, 2001, at the Northern Insurance building located on Santa Fe's busiest street. Immediately, it set off a local media frenzy and prompted reporters and state officials to start asking serious public safety questions. Networks gave the incident 130 minutes of live coverage, while cameras and helicopters swarmed above the wreckage and honed in as one victim was pulled from the debris and another who suffered burns was carted off in an ambulance.

"The stakes were high for the company," says Bermudez, who joined PNM months after the incident and was involved in helping to explain what caused the explosion a year later. PNM faced potentially huge liability from personal injury, business interruption, and auto damage resulting from the accident, not to mention an undermined reputation in a very tightly knit community. "The last thing we needed were panicked customers or angry state regulators. Fortunately, there were key people in the company who were very disturbed by the incident. They took it personally because it happened under their watch." That integrity, he explains, was PNM's saving grace.

Corporations that directly or indirectly cause catastrophic scenarios sometimes withhold information, shift blame, censor or denigrate whistleblowers, reinterpret the events, or let lawyers take control of the aftermath. To its credit, PNM did none of the above. Within one hour of the explosion, before the company even knew for sure whether it was caused by a gas leak or another problem within the building, PNM personnel were out in front of news cameras making the statement: "We think the incident may have been a result of a natural gas leak. We're starting to investigate, and we *will* get to the bottom of this."

Away from the scene, other key PNM personnel followed victims to the hospital to offer support, cover expenses, and help make necessary arrangements. "PNM basically extended ourselves to the point where we offered to kennel their dogs and fly relatives in from out of town," says

Bermudez. "We let them know that we suspected that the explosion was caused by a gas leak and that we were serious about making sure they had everything they needed."

The next morning, as newspaper headlines read: "Ground Zero," "Devastating Blast," "Massive Explosion," and "Blown to Smithereens," PNM hosted a joint news conference with the mayor as well as fire and police officials to give the public a briefing on what was known at the time. As it was clear by then that a gas leak had caused the explosion, the company pledged to immediately replace the faulty pipe and launch an internal investigation in cooperation with outside agencies. In a subsequent meeting, spokesperson Melvin Christopher would announce: "We regret what happened. We regret that several families have gone through hardship as a result of the explosion. And we have committed to an action plan to ensure that this never happens again."

In the weeks and months following the incident, the company constructed its own extensive internal investigation, replaced and upgraded large sections of pipe throughout the city, and consistently expressed concern to the individuals affected by the accident. PNM settled every single claim filed in conjunction with the incident. "Our approach was to convey sincere compassion and aid for victims, regardless of the liability," says Bermudez.

A year later, when the company's internal report was released to the public, it presented conclusions that were totally consistent with those drawn by the state's Office of Pipeline Safety. What surfaced in both reports were lots of red flags—thirteen in total—that should have signaled a problem to PNM, but did not. Bermudez likens the experience of the company's internal investigation to that of peeling an onion. "The more layers we unwrapped internally, the more systemic problems we found within our company," he says. "Our own internal investigation revealed incredible violations of internal policies and state procedures as well as serious operational inefficiencies that required attention."

In its report, PNM acknowledged that its technicians knew that the seventy-year-old, carbon-steel pipe involved in the explosion was corroded and a potential problem, but failed to keep adequate records of that and other issues they found. Apparently, PNM personnel had also failed to make necessary repairs to that pipe and to other faulty pipes prior to gradually increasing gas pressure during a standard process known as "uprating." At the Northern Insurance location, that uprating process caused gas to leak out of the faulty pipe from a tiny, corrosion-caused hole. The gas migrated up through the walls of the building and under the pavement, and when an office worker stepped outside and lit a cigarette, the explosion ignited.

PNM thoroughly reviewed these findings in a press conference it held as soon as the report was released. "We walked reporters through the entire case step-by-step," says Bermudez. "We presented our findings and supplemented them with visual aids to give them a clear sense of what we were talking about. We had pieces of a pipe similar to the one that caused the accident. We had grains of rice and rulers so they could visualize just how small the hole was. We had examples of the new pipe we were laying down. We had gas monitoring systems, the mechanisms used to detect leaks, available. We showed them maps, photos, and plans that illustrated not just what we planned to do, but what we had done since the accident took place."

PNM spokesperson Melvin Christopher received few loaded questions from reporters that afternoon. The following day, when the results of PNM's report hit the airwaves, virtually none of the press coverage was negative. "Since the incident, PNM has taken numerous steps to avoid a similar accident and improve its system to ensure safe operation," reported *New Mexico Business Weekly*, while the *Albuquerque Tribune* told readers: "The company agreed with many recommendations made [by] the state and had already implemented some of them . . . and has also made changes in policies and is retraining its workers." A press release later issued by New Mexico's Public Regulation Commission (PRC) reflected a similar optimistic tone: "I'm very pleased with what is being proposed because it keeps us away from adversarial relationships," said PRC chairwoman Lynda Lovejoy in the release. "It would accelerate actual physical improvements to pipelines around the state and lead to greater public safety well beyond the community where problems were exposed."[1]

Reporters and state officials reported just what the company told them. They practically recited PNM's key messages and didn't feel compelled to dig deeper because it was clear that the company wasn't trying to hide anything. PNM essentially broke its own bad news, telling people, "our own internal investigation reached conclusions that were hard for us to accept. This incident was our fault and it could have been avoided." PNM candidly discussed its inadequate policy and operational failures and took full responsibility. So, the event was over. Done with. Frederick Bermudez says that PNM's reputation was actually better *after* the accident than it was prior: "The way we handled this took us a long way with key stakeholders, particularly the state." What could have been a public relations disaster turned into a demonstration of ethics in action. It positioned PNM as a trustworthy, concerned citizen.

PNM's proactive communications plan was executed—one could say flawlessly—from start to finish. "There was a strong internal commitment to doing the right thing, not just immediately following the accident, but after the report was issued as well," says Bermudez. More than just communicating well, the company acted well. It promised to address its findings and then did so. Following the accident, PNM dismissed the workers who ignored danger signals and kept inadequate records. In addition, it instilled stricter internal policies with respect to record keeping and maintenance, initiated a more rigorous safety-training program, and required constant communications between departments. The company also undertook systems upgrades that included the replacement of approximately sixty thousand feet of carbon-steel piping with practically indestructible polyethylene throughout New Mexico. This whole process cost PNM approximately $12 million, but Bermudez says it was money well spent. "Now our standards are far more stringent, our system is safer, and as a whole, we are a more functional organization—all because we admitted fault and faced serious flaws in our system."

TURNING POINTS

PNM's story is unusual because it deviates from the status quo. Too many corporations attempt to shadow the truth when caught in a tight spot, and in responding, they typically act rather slowly or grudgingly, if at all. The problem with this typical response, aside from the moral conundrum it presents, is that it can devastate a company's reputation more than the initial incident and be damaging to shareholder interests. Corporate irresponsibility—in the sense of refusing to take responsibility—increases potential liability. For instance, after the *Exxon Valdez* ran into Bligh Reef in Prince William Sound, Alaska, spilling an estimated 11 million gallons of crude oil across 1,300 miles of coastline, it took former CEO Lawrence Rawl *six days* to make a public statement. He didn't get around to visiting the scene of the accident until two weeks had passed. When the company did issue statements regarding damage in the area, it said things that ran contrary to public opinion, such as:

> It is ExxonMobil's position that there are now no species in Prince William Sound in trouble due to the impact of the 1989 oil spill . . . The environment in Prince William Sound is healthy, robust and thriving. That's evident to anyone who's been there, and it is also the conclusion of many scientists who have done extensive studies of the Prince William Sound ecosystem. The claim made by several environmental groups of

continuing "severe" ecological damage to the Sound is simply untrue. It is contradicted by hundreds of peer-reviewed scientific studies conducted by researchers from major independent scientific laboratories and academic institutions.[2]

The *Exxon Valdez* case represents one of the worst public relations incidents in corporate history, not just because the event itself had a negative impact on wildlife, the environment, and the financial and physical health of surrounding communities, but also because the company is believed to have responded poorly to the crisis. "Exxon and *Valdez* have become the sine qua non for the mishandling of both an environmental disaster response and the corporate communications surrounding it," says James E. Lukaszewski, a Fellow at the Public Relations Society of America (PRSA) in his article "Exxon Valdez: The Great Crisis Management Paradox."

Exxon's widely perceived lack of appreciation for the true scale of the problem coupled with its slow response signifies a possible operational deficiency stemming from ethical problems. It suggests an absence of empathy, caring, or compassion toward the communities hurt and shows a minimal understanding of the bigger picture and how vital support systems feed the business. That disregard came back to haunt Exxon.

Following the *Valdez* spill, Exxon not only voluntarily paid over $2 billion in clean-up efforts, but was also forced by the Alaska courts to pay an additional $1 billion in criminal charges, restitution, and punitive damages for the injuries caused to fish, wildlife, and land.[3] On top of this, after a class action suit was filed on behalf of thirty-two thousand Alaskan fishermen in Alaska courts in 1994, the jury awarded $5 billion in punitive damages to the plaintiffs in the case. Exxon vigorously appealed this decision on the grounds that the award was excessive, but on January 28, 2004, a U.S. District Court judge found that a punitive damages award of $4.5 billion plus $2.25 billion in interest was in accordance with Supreme Court authority.[4] Although the company appealed this decision as well, both cases send a clear signal. One can only speculate about how fishermen plaintiffs might have responded or how the Alaska courts might have ruled had Exxon and Rawl more convincingly and sincerely expressed emotional anguish, more fully acknowledged the extent of the damage, and better engaged with the people and groups affected by the accident.

Examples like this one abound throughout corporate history. Although it is certainly easier and more common to avoid facing the inferno immediately after a huge catastrophe sends a company's reputation up in flames, it is also much less constructive to a company's future health and reputation. Regardless of their history, how companies respond to their present transgressions and flaws sets the pace for future perceptions *and* performance. The renowned Warren Buffet, head of Berkshire Hathaway, knows a few things about building and maintaining corporate reputation. One of his more famous aphorisms is: "It takes twenty years to build a reputation, and five minutes to ruin it."

The moment a company willingly and publicly faces the truth by acknowledging its mistakes or weaknesses, it experiences a rite of passage. It graduates to a higher level of being, creating a self-generated momentum that encourages it to grow even further. It finds that it can't help but better its ways and turns proactive rather than reactive. People inside and outside the company keep watching and listening as the company is compelled to take swift action to remedy the identified problems. Company leaders, shareholders, and employees activate, organize, and help to guide the company forward. As people galvanize, the risk of future negative incidents begins to diminish, internal shortcomings start to transform, external groups tend to forgive, the public tends to forget, and the whole company, as Bermudez describes, becomes more "functional." It simply starts working better.

Right now, there are multiple corporations—large and small,

controversial and commonplace—engaged in this critical turning point. Like PNM, these firms demonstrate why the truest test of a company's character comes when things go wrong, and how when a company is well-managed, the test itself can serve as the basis for the most positive kind of organizational change.

BOLD MOVES

Tyco's lapse in corporate governance was among the most publicized in history. It posed Dennis Kozlowski and Mark Swartz as poster boys for chief executive arrogance, while the company brand itself became synonymous with an age of corruption and greed as further exemplified by WorldCom and Enron. The difference is that in Tyco's case, the company bounced back—and totally transformed.

Tyco's initial meltdown was in many ways more sensational than those at WorldCom and elsewhere. After gutting millions of Tyco's dollars through hiding, stealing, and lying, Kozlowski reportedly spent $2 million of the company's money on a Mediterranean island birthday party for his wife, featuring Jimmy Buffett, toga-clad waiters, an ice sculpture of Michelangelo's *David* urinating a stream of high-end vodka, and a cake in the shape of two enormous breasts. He also dipped into company coffers to purchase "accessories" for his Fifth Avenue apartment, including paintings by Monet and Renoir, a $15,000 dog-shaped umbrella stand, a $17,700 traveling toilette box, a $2,200 waste basket, $2,900 worth of coat hangers, and a $6,000 gold-embroidered shower curtain. These lavish items dominated headlines and were presented to jurors as evidence in Kozlowski's 2003 grand larceny trial. That, on top of Tyco losing $9 billion around the time of the scandal, proved to be extremely embarrassing for all of the company's stakeholders, particularly employees.

But the real story at Tyco is what's happened *since* the scandal took place. In the three years following, the company has made bold moves and done many things right. To begin with, after Kozlowski's indictment, Tyco launched an extensive internal investigation and filed a hundred-page Form 8-K report with the Securities and Exchange Commission (SEC). The report detailed what the company called "a pattern of improper and illegal activity" that included nearly $100 million in unauthorized payments to Tyco executives, including Kozlowski and fifty-one other employees. For the first time, Tyco disclosed the details surrounding its loan forgiveness program and other financial improprieties:

> [Under] the "TyCom Bonus" Misappropriation, Mr. Kozlowski caused Tyco to pay a special, unapproved bonus to 51 employees who had relocation loans with the Company. The bonus was calculated to forgive the relocation loans of 51 executives and employees, totaling $56,415,037, and to pay compensation sufficient to discharge all of the tax liability due as a result of the forgiveness of those loans. This action was purportedly related to the successful completion of the TyCom Initial Public Offering. The total gross wages paid by the Company in this mortgage forgiveness program were $95,962,000, of which amount Mr. Kozlowski received $32,976,000 and Mr. Swartz received $16,611,000. These benefits were not approved by, or disclosed to, the Compensation Committee or the Board of Directors. However, the employees who received these bonuses were led by Mr. Kozlowski to believe that they were part of a Board-approved program.[5]

The results of Tyco's internal investigation—many of which are freely accessible at the company's Web site, http://www.tyco.com/committment—detail a five-year pattern of illegal activity. Tyco notes just how widespread senior management misconduct was and how severely it harmed the company's reputation and credibility with investors, lenders, and other stakeholders. In the interest of restoring the company's reputation, Tyco said, its 2002 Form 8-K report went "beyond what the law requires, or what would ordinarily be disclosed in such a filing."[6]

Since Tyco filed its candid report with the SEC, it has totally gutted and redesigned itself in what *Business Ethics* magazine calls the most "exceptionally thorough and thoughtful ethical house-cleaning and the most effective corporate response to an ethics disaster ever seen."[7]

Between 2002 and 2003, Tyco made drastic managerial changes. Kozlowski was replaced by former Motorola president and chief operating officer Ed Breen, the entire board of directors was convinced to step down, and the company replaced 290 of its top 300 executives. Tyco also created significant new positions, like that of diversity vice president Lydia G. Mallett, PhD; environmental, health, and safety leader Bob Frantz; and senior vice president of corporate governance Eric Pillmore.

Upon stepping in, Pillmore's first mission at Tyco was to assess exactly why things went wrong. To do this, he and his team spent a fair amount of time looking for patterns in the chaos. They researched ethically challenged organizations and the types of people guiding them. "I wanted to know what caused the leaders of certain companies to go bad and what had caused the people *above* those leaders—specifically the board of directors—to miss the fact that things were going bad," explains Pillmore. "I thought that was a fascinating concept to consider because my belief is if you can understand this, then you can greatly reduce the chance that such problems will ever surface again."

Pillmore's evaluation of troubled leaders gleaned six valuable lessons for Tyco. Among these were the notions that it is absolutely essential to evaluate the character of senior management, as well as surround company leaders with an internal web of accountability. Hereafter, these lessons and others would cast Tyco's ethics strategy. The lesson on senior management character, for instance, prompted Tyco to stop obsessing about the public image of its leaders and better evaluate *who* these people really were. "We realized that in the past, we made the mistake of

focusing on the reputation of our leaders. We celebrated their reputations to the point where we almost set them up for disappointment," says
Pillmore. "What we needed to do going forward was dig in and better
understand the character of the individual. Then, in understanding that
individual's character, we needed to determine whether their behavior
was consistent with the company's values." Identifying corporate values,
Pillmore maintains, is not enough to succeed from an ethics or business
point of view. "Behavior is what counts," he says.

After researching the issue of problem leaders, Tyco isolated nine
ideal behaviors—including "demonstrating managerial courage" and
"championing integrity and trust"—that it wished to promote throughout the organization. Today, the performance of every Tyco employee
and leader is evaluated against these nine traits, thus creating a true
ethical mandate. In 2003, Tyco took its 250,000 employees through an
ethics-training program that allowed people to grasp how the broad
behaviors apply to their daily jobs. "You can define what it means to
be 'managerially courageous' for an individual contributor, a midlevel
manager, or a senior executive," says Pillmore. "It is about the idea
that if you're a contributor or manager in a meeting, for instance, and
you know in your heart of hearts that there are eight people sitting
around the table ready to make a decision that you think conflicts with
the company's policy, you need to have the courage to intervene and
say something. And for the senior executive, it's about establishing the
kind of environment where this sort of thing can take place."

Between 2003 and 2005, Tyco's senior management embodied several ideal qualities by instilling aggressive policy changes that served
company stakeholders and humbled them. One such change was the
decision to put a cap on executive bonuses. Another emerged when
they actively encouraged shareholders to vote yes on a resolution that
would require the company to take a closer look at its environmental
performance and management system. One more brave transition came

with the choice to formally establish the internal web of accountability that Pillmore previously recognized was necessary through his research. Today, Tyco's modified operational structure has its three senior leaders in the company answer to the board of directors, while all finance and legal personnel report to the chief financial officer and general counsel. "The idea is that if a significant irregularity were to occur in the future, we have the structure in place to ensure that it would be immediately apparent," explains Pillmore. "We've worked around the premise that leaders are going to fail. They're going to be tempted to do things that aren't necessarily in line with policies or the right thing to do from an ethics point of view. Therefore, we've designed our system around the fact that everyone has character flaws. There are no perfect people."

There are no perfect companies, either. But Tyco has focused on continual improvement, and transparency is a key to that improvement. As a means of providing further lucidity on its new philosophy, Tyco recently wrote a new "Guide to Corporate Ethics" and launched a corresponding mini Web site that clearly explains what its ethical standards are and how they are implemented and monitored across the organization. The mini site demonstrates how Tyco has significantly broadened its efforts to become a more forthright firm. Thus far, the company says that its ethics guide has been downloaded by stakeholders 99,000 times.

Further evidence that the new Tyco isn't afraid to face reality is the company's attendance at unlikely public forums, like the May 2004 Green Mountain Summit on Investor Responsibility. There, Pillmore gave a presentation entitled "Repairing Trust in a Broken World," in which he detailed what had gone wrong at Tyco and why, and also disclosed the wider morals of the story. Pillmore's mission to tell Tyco's true story and enable big-picture thinking across the business world frames Tyco as an illustration of fortitude, not a counterexample.

"The question is, are we just going to let this era of corporate wrong-doing pass by, or are we going to learn from our mistakes?" asks Pill-more. "There's only one way to prevent a recurrence, and that's to learn from the past. As a company, we had two choices. We could have gone into a cocoon and not told anybody what we found, or we could share what we know with people who might really benefit from the knowl-edge."

Tyco's decision to share its knowledge and learn from its mistakes formed a new atmosphere inside the company, an atmosphere where everyone is continually encouraged to face the truth. "One of the things I found in studying the businesses where leaders went bad is that in those businesses, employees came to work knowing that they couldn't speak up," Pillmore says. "My hope is that we've built an en-vironment where people can feel good about speaking up. My hope is that it's not going to take an auditor, an expensive consultant, or some other outside group to discover a problem at Tyco. But rather, that our new system ensures that whatever problems we have are continually uncovered and addressed by us." This, Pillmore explains, leads to a level of stability and resilience, as the company grows less susceptible to outside forces. "I believe pretty strongly that we are a healthier company today than we were in 2002. But again, that's not to say that we don't have issues. As company with 250,000 employees, we're go-ing to have issues."

Despite Tyco's imperfections, the fruits of the company's ethics-related labors are confirmed by independent outside sources. In De-cember 2002, research firm GovernanceMetrics International (GMI) gave Tyco a meager corporate accountability score of 1.5 on a scale of one to ten. By 2005, Tyco's GMI score had climbed to 9.0. Not bad for just a few years of hard work and determination in one of the world's largest corporations. Still, Pillmore concedes, his job isn't done yet: "We're still not a 10."

WHAT GETS MEASURED GETS MANAGED

Perfection is never achieved, as the saying goes. But in the best companies, it is a constant goal—and that means knowing where to focus and
what to measure. Corporate responsibility (CR) is not an *exact* science. It manifests on multiple levels and in multiple dimensions. Both
Tyco and PNM demonstrate that a distinct human element is involved.
That human element enables CR to resonate at the deepest levels of
an organization and, thus, to spread throughout it effectively. But it
doesn't necessarily take a catastrophe to prompt such a phenomenon.
Some companies adopt an integrated and wholehearted approach to
CR in response to results created by and for the business, and more are
quantifying the right kinds of things.

In the process of conducting our research, we scoured dozens of
corporate responsibility (CR) reports. We determined that a fair portion were essentially marketing pieces, not tools for genuine transparency or stakeholder engagement. The more superficial brochure reports
spoke volumes about the company's ambitions, beliefs, and values; depicted employees with smiling faces; and reported selective tidbits of
information about the company's most charitable deeds—but failed to
include the sorts of indicators that constitute real accountability.

In our process of comparing companies to one another, no company received extra credit for simply producing a CR report. What
mattered to us was the nature of the report and how information was
presented. For us, and we suspect for many of you, it isn't enough to
hear that a company is "committed to managing its impact on society
and the environment." We wanted to see the proof points, the data that
shows what the company's real impact is, and how the company is continually working to minimize the negative and maximize the positive.
As Pillmore says, it's not about values. It's about *behavior* and how
that behavior affects the organization and the outside world.

Of the seventy-five companies we reviewed, forty issued corporate responsibility reports in 2004 and 2005. While thirty of those reports included some metrics on such tangibles as employee satisfaction, turnover, and diversity; ethical sourcing; water and electricity usage; carbon dioxide emissions; and waste or recycled materials, there was little in the way of reporting consistency. For the most part, companies highlighted or minimized whatever they deemed appropriate. On the upside, ten of the reports we reviewed constructively addressed externalities, or serious costs the business creates for stakeholders and the planet. A closer look at a few of these cases reveals how addressing and monitoring such problems encourages more constructive policies and, overall, better business decision-making.

TRANSPARENCY AS RISK MANAGEMENT

Two of the most noteworthy CR reporting approaches we found reside at two European-headquartered companies that have evolved past the phase in the progression of facing the truth. These companies are British Telecom (BT), Europe's largest telecommunications provider, and HSBC, one of the largest banking organizations in the world. BT has been active in the field of corporate responsibility since the 1980s. At first, it focused mainly on philanthropy and assembling an environmental management system. But today, the company goes steps further by facilitating what it calls CR "health checks" and "risk registers."

In implementing CR health checks, BT regularly engages with shareholders, suppliers, NGOs, employees, and customers about how the company is meeting expectations. In its CR reports, BT reflects the findings from these surveys and tracks its performance along twelve corresponding nonfinancial indicators, such as carbon dioxide emissions, employee and customer dissatisfaction, health and safety incidents, and subpar supply chain standards. Using concrete targets and timetables in each of these areas, BT tracks and discloses both its performance highlights and lowlights. In 2004, for instance, BT's showed impressive performance highlights, such as the fact that the company is now the world's biggest corporate user of green energy, having sourced nearly all its electricity needs from hydro, wind, and combined heat and power plants. In terms of carbon dioxide emissions savings, BT's shift to green energy translates to a reduction of 325,000 tons each year, according to the company. BT met other impressive environmental and social targets in 2004 by reducing the amount of waste it produces by 8 percent and by improving its safety record by 23 percent. On the downside, however, the company undershot its employee diversity target by 0.3 percent and its customer dissatisfaction target by 2 percent.

What sets BT's approach to transparency apart is how the company calculates how much it could lose by underperforming corporate responsibility–wise. The company's CR risk registers assess how potential ethical or environmental problems could harm the business. In one such assessment, the company found that so-called rogue Internet dialers were causing a serious reputation problem. Rogue dialers are viruslike software programs that customers unknowingly download onto their computers. Once downloaded, these dialers instruct computers to make multiple premium-rate long distance calls at the customer's expense. Unfortunately, the company says, many of BT's customers don't realize they have the virus until they receive a whopping phone bill. And although the company has nothing to do with the virus scam, it found that customers associated the fraud with BT. Therefore, BT has recently invested in combating the problem and in developing services like Modem Protection and Early Warning Alerts. As of March 2005, the company says that around one million BT customers had signed up for one or more of these barring services. In addition, the company made the following announcement: "BT is doing everything in its power to stop this menace. We have taken the decision to block numbers suspected of being associated with dialers as soon as we are alerted to a problem. We have offered free premium rate barring to all customers, and a removable bar for premium rate and international calls for £1.75 a month. We have made it clear that we are not the ones profiteering from people's misfortune. In fact, we will continue to forgo our share of the call revenue generated by these disputed calls." In communicating about these and other risks—from worker safety to child labor and the excessive use of nonrecycled paper—BT has found that is better able to keep stakeholders happy. "Transparency in dealing with controversial issues is paramount. We will never satisfy everyone, so openness is key," says BT chief executive Ben Verwaayen.[8]

In addition to evaluating risks, BT also routinely assesses how much it stands to gain by improving its CR performance. "About one-third of our corporate reputation is driven by socially responsible endeavors," says Verwaayen in BT's 2004 CR report. Verwayeen knows this because the company's CR health checks constantly research reputation and other issues with customers, suppliers, and employees. A recent survey found that a 1 percent improvement in the public's perception of BT's CR activities translates to a 0.1 percent increase in the company's retail customer satisfaction figures. "I am convinced that being a responsible citizen brings us great business advantage," he says.[9] Overall, BT demonstrates how stakeholder engagement and a willingness to remain transparent can enhance a company's ability to stay in touch and be competitive.

Similarly, HSBC uses a strategic approach to transparency as a means of improving its overall performance. Like any huge multinational, HSBC is a company that faces its share of criticism. Among these are HSBC's alleged poor pay of employees at a time of record profits, its use of inflated charges and customer fees, and its role in contributing to environmental problems. Although the company's 2004 CR report did not tackle these issues head-on, several other noteworthy elements signal that the company is progressing toward total transparency. First, rather than set its own ethical standards, HSBC uses independent third-party auditing systems to assess and report its progress. These include the commonly used Global Reporting Initiative (GRI) guidelines, which help HSBC measure its relative sustainability against globally applicable standards, as well as ISO 14001–based environmental management system (EMS) principles, which enable HSBC to determine how it is reducing its environmental impact against internationally accepted criteria. Along these lines, HSBC reported substantial improvements in 2004, citing that 91 percent of its operations complied with the company's EMS in 2004, compared with 68 percent in 2003; that total environmental data quality was up to 7.7 on a scale of one to ten, compared with 5.2 in 2003; and that the company's per employee carbon dioxide emissions were 2.7 tons in 2004, compared with 3.7 tons in 2003.[10]

More notably, HSBC recently met an aggressive CR-related goal. In 2005, it set a benchmark for its sector by becoming the world's first major bank to go "carbon neutral"—meaning that *all* of its carbon dioxide emissions are reduced by the company or offset by its investments in environmentally friendly projects like wind farms and cogeneration plants. HSBC reached its carbon-neutral goal three months ahead of schedule. In addition, unlike HSBC's American competitors, this bank makes it abundantly clear where it stands on serious environmental issues such as global warming. "[C]limate change represents the largest single environmental challenge this century," said then–HSBC group chairman Sir John Bond in a 2004 speech he delivered at the Climate Group, an international NGO. "It will have an impact on all aspects of modern life. It is, therefore, a major issue for our customers and our staff, as well as for every organisation on the planet, no matter how large or how small."[11]

HSBC's 2004 CR report reflects a level of openness and big-picture thinking. The company clearly has a grasp of the issues it faces and evaluates the effectiveness of its CR initiatives in terms of how they impact shareholder value. It tells stakeholders:

We are clear about where our priority lies. Our number one objective is to ensure that our shareholders get a better return from HSBC than they would from investing in our financial service competitors. To achieve financial success over the long-term requires a sustainable approach and our strategy seeks to address the expectations of our customers, colleagues and those who represent the interests of various communities, the wider society and the environment . . . Banks may be liable for the environmental damage caused by the companies they finance, so we manage these risks carefully.[12]

Along the lines of liability, HSBC's CR report gives stakeholders an indication of how the bank determines which projects to finance and which to avoid. For instance, the bank purports to avoid dangerous businesses such as the manufacturing and sales of chemical weapons, persistent organic pollutants (POPs), and certain hazardous pesticides and industrial chemicals, as well as transactions that may be used to evade tax or launder earnings from crime. Also, for investment projects that fall outside of the no-go zone, HSBC says it weighs the potential environmental and social impact against the economic upside and makes decisions accordingly. However, it does not present a formula for this, leaving outside critics some room to question how far the bank takes its environmental positions.

In 2005, the London-based *Ethical Corporation* criticized HSBC's 2004 CR report, saying, "[An] issue that is not clear is exactly how HSBC has identified or prioritized the issues . . . Overall, HSBC's approach comes across as fragmented rather than strategic."[13] In reviewing that same report, our group had a very different take. Perhaps we missed something, but we determined that HSBC approaches CR as a necessary and fundamental vehicle for protecting and maintaining the overall health of the company. By taking steps to reduce its own energy use, to buy green electricity and trade carbon credits to cut carbon dioxode flows, HSBC sends the message that it understands and can compete in the emerging low-carbon economy. Similarly, HSBC's decision to screen finance projects on the basis of environmental and social costs versus economic gains signifies that the company is looking at its indirect impact on society and the environment, as well. Overall, these decisions show that there is a clear CR strategy in place at HSBC, even if it has yet to be fully executed across the business. This, we felt, is far more than can be said for most others in its sector, particularly in America.

EUROPE VERSUS AMERICA

Perhaps one reason that *Ethical Corporation* is so critical of HSBC is simply that Europeans have high standards and tend to be extremely demanding and critical of their peers. Of course, this is a stereotype, but it might be an accurate one nonetheless. Though American companies and businesspeople will hate to acknowledge this, in general, European business executives and, especially the European media, are more resistant to whitewashing or corporate spin compared to their mainstream American counterparts. They also tend to be more globally aware. This is clearly evident in the quality and nature of American versus European CR reporting styles.

Eric Israel, managing director of consulting company KPMG, which published the 2005 study *International Survey of Corporate Responsibility Reporting*, referred to in the prologue, and which helps corporations in both America and Europe to compile CR reports, agrees. He sees a gap not only in terms of reporting, but also in execution: "I would say that European multinationals continue to design and implement CR strategies and initiatives that are linked to their overall business strategies, whereas in the U.S., the focus is still primarily on understanding the concept and verifying the business case. European companies consider transparency issues to be vital to their global 'license to operate,' whereas American companies are generally more resistant to that concept."

In other words, the mainstream American attitude is that global markets are something to be seized, whereas in Europe, more companies feel they must *earn* the right to be a part of the global business community. "European companies have more peer pressure to initiate CR," says Israel. "They can't afford to focus too narrowly, and thus must address how their operations affect foreign markets." Israel says that in America CR standards, and especially CR reporting and transparency standards, *must* improve if corporations wish to remain successful on foreign soil. "The current Achilles heel for American companies is the CR measurement factor," says Israel. "But American companies are brilliantly innovative. If only they were to reverse this weakness and embrace transparency, they might even move ahead of their European counterparts."

Based on his experience and KPMG's research, Israel concludes that there are two types of U.S. businesses that take a leadership position in this area. The first group includes companies like PNM and Tyco that "walk the walk," implementing comprehensive programs and tracking and reporting real results. The second category, Israel maintains, includes companies with individual "heroes" or "first movers" who bravely embrace legal complexities and have the courage to bring difficult CR issues to the forefront of stakeholders' attention.

This second group is an interesting breed. In sticking their necks out to address industry challenges, such companies can become more of a target. There are risks related to taking strong CR positions in America, and as the previous examples have shown, transparency isn't an easy thing to create. Doing so necessarily means exposing weaknesses and mistakes for all to see and judge. That's a downright frightening prospect, particularly for those companies that tend to be the subject of frequent protests and lawsuits. However, more American companies are doing just this—and reaping rewards.

BARING IT ALL

Gap is no doubt one such company that sticks its neck out. After spending years at the top of anti-sweatshop activist lists, Gap acknowledged: "We believe that garment workers deserve better than the reality that many unfortunately face. We recognize and embrace our duty to take a leadership role."[14] In both 2003 and 2004, Gap released provocative CR reports with much fanfare. Both show a remarkable level of transparency around labor issues.

"In the days after we released our first CR report last year, it wasn't easy to read headlines like 'Gap Admits Factory Abuses,'" recalls Gap CEO Paul Pressler in the company's 2004 CR report, *Facing Challenges, Finding Opportunities*. Clearly, it was a challenging decision for Gap to come clean. But since the company did, it says stakeholders—including the media, shareholders, and employees—have been very supportive. Their encouragement reinforced Gap's commitment to setting higher standards for the retailing industry as a whole, Pressler says: "Over the past year, we've learned the power of collective engagement, and of open, honest discussion about the issues that we and many of our competitors face."[15]

The industry issues that Pressler talks about literally affect the lives of tens of millions of people throughout the world. As a $15.8 billion retailer with brands that include Old Navy, Banana Republic, and Forth & Towne, Gap Inc. sources from approximately 3,000 factories in fifty nations, including Guatemala, El Salvador, India, Egypt, Sri Lanka, Thailand, China, and Bangladesh. In Cambodia alone, for instance, making clothes for Gap Inc. and other leading retailers employs 220,000 people and accounts for one-third of the country's gross national product. Everything Gap does, directly or indirectly, in that and other regions throughout the world sends a wave through communities and the industry as a whole.

In its quantitative rating of the ethical compliance performance of the factories it uses, Gap shows that between 25 and 50 percent of its 423 factory partners in China enable child labor by using poor age documentation, that more than half of its 29 Persian Gulf–based factory partners impose work weeks in excess of sixty hours, and that up to half of its 351 Mexico and Central and South America–based factory partners pay workers below minimum wage. By supporting noncompliant factory owners financially, the company unwittingly helps to perpetuate a negative pattern of discrimination, human rights abuse, and poverty.

Conversely, when a company like Gap raises its hand or steps forward to *break* that negative pattern, the ripple effect is equally pronounced. In 2002, Gap made a move in this direction by joining Target, J. C. Penney Company, and twenty-one other retailers in settling a class action lawsuit that alleged sweatshop conditions in Saipan. Under terms of the settlement, each company made a one-time contribution to a $20 million fund that financed a monitoring program and compensated more than 30,000 Saipan workers for unpaid overtime. The basis and outcome of this lawsuit, confesses Gap on its Web site "highlights the need to refine and better articulate requirements for foreign contract garment workers."[16]

In light of this and other class action lawsuits filed against retailers on the basis of unfair working conditions, it's interesting to note that Gap's 2003 and 2004 CR Report disclosures raise more questions than answers. "We did not see significant changes in overall factory compliance levels between 2003 and 2004," the 2004 report says. "In fact, we would have been surprised if we had, given the ongoing changes in our supply base, new program procedures and the fact that remediation takes time." Gap says that it approved 349 new factories in 2004, but estimates that many of these factories will be "likely to have compliance problems, particularly in basic health and safety areas."[17]

In openly communicating that problems still exist, that it has yet to solve all of them, and that it will continue to work with noncomplying factories, Gap really pulls its guard down. That's hardly bland rhetoric and clearly not a decision made solely by the company's legal team as the company leaves itself vulnerable.

In 2003, Gap demonstrated its commitment to improving labor standards by joining NGO monitoring groups Social Accountability International (SAI) and Verité. Both groups promote human rights and fair labor conditions around the world. With encouragement and guidance from these groups, Gap adopted higher labor standards and also subjected itself to far more comprehensive auditing systems, like SAI's SA8000, which measures ethical workplace conditions throughout global supply chains. The net results of Gap's voluntary participation in these programs are significant. "Gap has been wonderfully responsive and enthusiastic," says Alice Tepper Marlin, president of SAI. "Since joining, they've been a part of every capacity-building research project that we've undertaken."

In conjunction with SAI and other key groups, Gap is now a part of a several-year-long project that trains and provides technical assistance to suppliers in Central America. This project, according to Marlin, is making real progress in improving labor conditions in factories throughout the country. Gap is also a leading participant in an initiative called the Joint Initiative in Corporate Responsibility and Workers' Rights, which seeks to improve supply-chain management practices through common codes, shared learning, and industry-wide collaboration.

In terms of dealing with its own internal issues, Marlin says that Gap has, at least in principle, taken on all of SAI's recommendations to buck up management, auditing and verification systems, stakeholder relations, capacity building, and overall transparency. The most notable of these improvements is the addition of a vendor scorecard, which gives both buyers and factory owners the business incentive to embrace Gap's new ethical supply chain goals. "In these scorecards, Gap rates all of its factories along five factors: cost, quality, speed to market, strategic capability, and social compliance," explains Marlin. "Buyers then use the scorecards in deciding where to place orders."

When Gap joined SAI a few years ago, it didn't have a single factory that was SAI certified. Today, twenty of its factories are certified, and the company says that its vendors are quite happy with the benefits that the SAI system has brought, not only in terms of improved conditions and higher quality, but especially, the larger orders placed as a result of an improved overall score. "This rewards system has really been a key to making Gap's overall program work," says Marlin. "Based on the company's constructive and savvy response to its own internal management and labor issues, I would say that they are setting the pace for the entire industry."

Other major retailers, like Levi Strauss & Co. (LS&CO.), are following Gap's lead. In 2005, LS&CO. voluntarily disclosed its list of factory suppliers that produce the company's Levi's, Dockers, and Levi Strauss Signature brands. The list, available on the company's corporate Web site, http://www.levistrauss.com, reflects 750 factories in countries including Turkey, Portugal, South Korea, Cambodia, Taiwan, and Vietnam. "We believe that greater transparency within the supply chain will provide additional momentum for our efforts to improve working conditions in apparel factories worldwide," said David Love, LS&CO.'s senior vice-president of global sourcing in the press release that announced the company's decision to make the list publicly available. "Our hope is that this level of transparency will become standard across the apparel sector, fostering greater collaboration among brands in shared factories. We believe that when brands are working together on issues of compliance with codes of conduct, factory monitoring will ultimately be more effective and less burdensome for suppliers, allowing them to focus time and resources on making improvements that benefit workers."[18]

In addition to publishing its supplier list, LS&CO. also makes the details of its responsible sourcing program readily available. On its Web site, the company highlights efforts to improve working conditions across its 750 factories and posts a seventy-page terms of engagement handbook, which details a range of policies that are instilled at the factory level. Among these policies are employment standards, such as: "We will not utilize or purchase materials from a business partner utilizing prison or forced labor" and "Workers can be no less than 15 years of age and not younger than the compulsory age to be in school." If you ask us, fifteen years of age is still too young for a tiny person to work forty hours a week or more in a cramped factory, but at least LS&CO. pledges to "Support the development of legitimate workplace apprenticeship programs for the educational benefit of younger people."

More compelling is that LS&CO. describes serious ethical violations found in various factories and provides explanation about what the company is doing to address the problems. For instance, the company's inspectors recently discovered that two factories in Bangladesh employed workers under the age of fifteen. This was an especially challenging issue for LS&CO. to resolve, since it is customary in Bangladesh that very young children work to support their families. Cutting off children under a certain age also means eliminating financial resources for the family members who depend on that child's wages. So rather than instruct the factory owners to simply dismiss underage workers, LS&CO. says it devised another solution. "[Our] managers and consultants met with the contractors to develop an agreement, [under which] the factories agreed to continue to pay the already employed underage workers their salaries and benefits while they attended school and offer them full-time jobs when they reached the legal working age. LS&CO. agreed to pay for the students' tuition and books. If there was no room in the nearby public school, LS&CO. and the factories would rent space and hire a teacher for the students."[19] According to the company, factory owners in Bangladesh agreed that in the future, they would require school certificates stating that a child is over fifteen before making any hiring decisions, while the Bangladesh Garment Manufacturers and Exporters Association along with other groups set aside approximately $1 million for the education of about 75,000 underage girls who previously worked in factories.

There are no easy answers when it comes to transparency in an industry like retailing, but one key to success in this matter is a company's willingness to be constructive. Marlin notes that labor problems like forced overtime are often perpetuated by unreasonably tight deadlines or other demands imposed by corporate buyers. "It's critical that in an effort to solve labor issues, companies look at their own management policies as well," she says. "I envision a day when consumers can walk into a store and access information that enables them to reward or reject companies based on their ethical decisions." In some ways, Marlin's vision is already coming to fruition as trails of leaked information tell compelling stories that inspire stakeholders to respond.

FORCED TRANSPARENCY

There are always elements of liability in being transparent or in accepting blame. However, there are even greater liabilities in *not* being transparent. This is because, while concealing problems inside a company can work for a while, it rarely works forever, as the previous section, Pitfalls, demonstrated. Internet technology, the independent media, and stakeholder demands force corporations to become more forthright.

Case in point: while conducting research for this chapter, we obtained a twenty-six-page Wal-Mart memo entitled: "Supplemental Benefits Documentation: Reviewing and Revising Wal-Mart's Benefits Strategy." The memo was submitted to Wal-Mart's board of directors by Susan Chambers, executive vice president of risk management and benefits administration, sometime in 2005. It is clearly marked "confidential," but we downloaded it off the Web after the *New York Times* embedded the link in a story it wrote about Wal-

Mart's health care position, thus effectively making it available to millions of Internet users. The *Times*, CNN, and other news channels that featured similar stories say that they initially obtained the memo from the watchdog group Wal-Mart Watch. In any case, what was once confidential and proprietary information is now public record, as everybody who cares to can get an in-depth, firsthand account of Wal-Mart's proposed health care plan. Critics of this memo are aggravated by its suggested strategy of trimming company health care costs by discouraging full-time, elderly, ill, and overweight associates from working at Wal-Mart.

"Growth in benefits costs is unacceptable and persistently driven by root causes (e.g., aging workforce, increasing average tenure)," says the memo. "Most troubling, the least healthy, least productive associates are more satisfied with their benefits than other segments and are interested in longer careers with Wal-Mart." In response to high health care costs, Chambers and her team recommend designing the company's health care plan around the needs of younger, healthy employees and designing all jobs to include physical activity, saying: "These moves would dissuade unhealthy people from coming to work at Wal-Mart." Chambers reports later in the memo that Wal-Mart's executive benefits steering committee "enthusiastically" received her recommendations and asked that they be presented to the board of directors for approval.[20]

Call it dumb luck or clever activist strategy, but the memo leak came on the heels of another brouhaha over the November 2005 national release of Robert Greenwald's film *Wal-Mart: The High Cost of Low Price*. In response, Wal-Mart countered with a communications approach that the *New York Times* likened to a war room and the *San Francisco Chronicle* described as "worthy of the final days before an election."[21] Just prior to the film's debut, Wal-Mart sent a ten-page press release to major news sources, condemning the movie as a "propaganda video." Although the leaked Chambers memo revealed Wal-Mart's intent to shift more associates to part-time status, Wal-Mart's release claimed: "We offer 1.2 million hard-working men and women not only jobs, but careers." It presented the company's opinion that "[Robert Greenwald's] narrow agenda is wrong for the working families of America" and mentioned, "The director should look into another line of work."[22] This response was not unusual, as in 2004, Wal-Mart launched a major public relations campaign that characterized various other criticisms made against it as "urban legends."

Wal-Mart is a company featured in the next chapter due to its significant movement on the environmental front and its response to Hurricane Katrina. But Wal-Mart's leaked memo and customary reaction to its detractors is also a good example of how corporate transparency works—and *doesn't* work. Corporate transparency works virally and by building trust and encouraging open dialogue. It doesn't work by creating more spin and further division.

Today, corporate transparency is a dynamic and unstoppable force. While it can no longer easily be avoided through cover-ups, mudslinging, or war room counterstrikes, it can be harnessed. PNM and Tyco show how acknowledging mistakes, volunteering information, and proactively addressing problems can effectively offset the damage done to a business after a crisis occurs. BT and HSBC show how tracking and reporting environmental and social underperformance can help to identify business opportunities and risks, leading to improved decision making. Gap and LS&CO. depict how honest communications can temper activist concerns and help set better standards across an industry like retailing.

Each of these companies has stronger stakeholder relationships today than it did prior to its truth-telling moves. As stakeholders have grown more trusting and supportive, each company has managed to grow in a healthier direction. But as expectations rise, so must a company's future actions. These firms now play by different rules and need to continue to walk on higher ground. Doing so requires the wherewithal to set the right kinds of priorities, intentions, and ultimately, reasons to succeed—bringing us to the next phase in our progression.

FACING THE TRUTH [23]

Company	Challenge	Response
PNM	Liability surrounding gas main explosion that left two people seriously injured.	"This incident was our fault and it could have been avoided."
Tyco	Scandal involving financial improprieties and former CEO Dennis Kozlowski.	"We made the mistake of focusing on reputation [vs.] the character of our leaders."
BT	Business risks resulting from CR issues, including "rogue dialers" and resulting customer dissatisfaction.	"We will continue to fight vigilantly and forgo our share of revenue generated by these disputed calls."
HSBC	Criticism about the bank's unwillingness to address CR issues like "indirect" environmental impact.	"[We agree] banks may be liable for the environmental damage caused by the companies they finance."
Gap	Activist concerns regarding unfair labor conditions in overseas factories.	"We believe that garment workers deserve better than the reality that many unfortunately face."
LS&CO.	Also dealt with activist concerns regarding unfair labor conditions in overseas factories.	"Transparency within the supply chain will provide additional momentum for our efforts to improve conditions."

5:

Set Intent . . . Then Purpose

A good intention clothes itself with sudden power.

—RALPH WALDO EMERSON

Rubber duckies symbolize what *Cradle to Cradle* author and architect Bill McDonough calls our "strategy of tragedy." The squeaky, nostalgic bath toy is made from toxic chemicals that have been linked to cancer, birth defects, and other reproductive problems. In a 2005 speech that he delivered to the Industrial Designers Society of America, McDonough boldly asked his colleagues: "What kind of society would make something like this to put in the mouths of children?" The room was silent. "Design is the first signal of human intention," he continued. "What is your intention?" It was another great question that cuts past nonsense to get to the heart of the corporate responsibility debate.

What kinds of intentions drive the ongoing creation of belching smokestacks, poisonous household products, carcinogenic sweeteners, fume-laden carpets, noxious computers, heavily polluting vehicles, or repressive urban centers? McDonough says that the inherent designs of these things are clues about our priorities as a civilization. If we mean to render our beautiful green-blue planet uninhabitable, then annually dumping billions of pounds of toxic junk into the environment is the right thing to do. But certainly, tragedy isn't the goal of even the worst corporate offenders—and if it isn't the goal, then McDonough insists we need another plan. Devising that plan requires that we ask the right questions at the onset of the strategic development process.

For companies of all varieties with shareholders motivated by even the most bullish Wall Street criteria, the questions of the day are not: Growth or no growth? Efficiency or inefficiency? But rather: What do we want to grow? And further, how can we grow the optimal things most effectively?

The businesses profiled in the coming pages are now asking themselves the right kinds of questions. Furthermore, each has answered the general question that indeed, Yes, we choose to start growing health versus disease, intelligence versus ignorance, and enrichment versus adversity. Subsequently, each is deciphering exactly *how* it will go about achieving these favorable ends. Every firm profiled here is in the midst of undertaking company-wide initiatives and most are even pondering, What will our larger role be in the world? What are we really here to do?

Not every company has answered these latter questions or succinctly crystalized its higher purpose, but each is undergoing a fascinating process of self-discovery, where its most meaningful ambitions, desires, and strengths are being revealed. Using their core assets, each of the following firms has put in place tactics and corresponding ways of making things that engender a far more desirable outcome for all stakeholders. These companies, therefore, help put an end to the "strategy of tragedy."

It is essential to point out that most of what the following firms currently produce has historically wreaked havoc on society and the environment. Cars, sneakers, coffee, hardware, hamburgers, and packaging are their final output. Additionally, many of these companies are notorious for labor problems, health care problems, environmental problems, and the like. Some firms have thus far been able to address only one key part of their business constructively, while they have left other parts relatively unaddressed. We highlight their changes because they are monumental, although we expect that some readers may be incensed to see flawed companies in this section.

This chapter is about turnarounds. It is about major changes of heart and mind, followed by momentous changes in policy and practice. Every company mentioned here has altered its ways—seriously and measurably, not just symbolically. No company has completely transformed itself yet and serious defects might still exist. Despite each company's past actions, questionable practices, and ongoing imperfections, each begins to turn the wheel of progress in a positively healthy direction. Each has recently reprioritized—and signals that reprioritization loud and clear—because each sees the shortcomings of its previous ways. Actually, each sees flaws in the entire system, or corporate machine, and therefore steps away from the herd. The step away is crucial because without the step away, again, the system remains stagnant. As McDonough reminds people in his press interviews and presentations, "The Stone Age did not end because humans ran out of stones. It ended because it was time for a rethink about how we live."[1]

THE INTENTIONAL BUSINESS

How does a company with a history of doing things ineffectively or unjustly, either from an environmental or a social point of view, suddenly become effective in terms of its ability to produce a positive overall impact on *all* stakeholders? This is a huge leap, an enormous feat that starts with the step of setting better goals and priorities. Setting intent means deciding exactly what outcome you're aiming for and which side you're on: Are you on the problem side or the solution side? If you are against corporate responsibility in principle, or if you refuse to be for it in practice, then you're likely on the problem side of the spectrum. However, if you truly understand the need to change, can face the truth, and are willing to break free from tradition, then you're likely on the solution side.

In conducting research for this book, several things sparked a sense of elation and joy within our group. One of them was finding a newly intentional business—a company that perhaps had been so brutalized by CR advocates and NGOs that many people had written it off as hopelessly misdirected or just plain bad. A company that, despite all this, had proactively and even dramatically decided to revise its course and move in a whole new direction. Often, these companies called themselves out to us through stunning new announcements. One of the clearest examples we found of a company that recently expressed intentionality followed by newfound purpose is Ford Motor Company.

In a 2005 speech describing his intentions for Ford's future and how he sees achieving them, company CEO Bill Ford Jr. confided this to his colleagues:

The questions for me are personal: how can I help some of the most innovative thinkers on earth feel free to surface their breakthrough ideas, to see things in a different way, and to push our company to new heights? I am asking these things of you and of myself at a time when our company faces daunting challenges, a time when our competition is as fierce as it is strong, a time when others would gladly grant us our place in history, but would raise questions about our role in the future.

People are fond of saying that when Ford stumbled it was because products were weak and that when we came roaring back it was because products got stronger. There's truth in that, but that's not the whole truth. We have succeeded when we found ways to let the innovative spirit of our people soar. And we have failed when we allowed that spirit to be harnessed. We have done that in the most innocent ways and with the best of intentions. But we've done it—and that must end now. From this point forward, innovation is going to be the compass by which this company sets its direction.[2]

Ford's speech is just one of numerous crystal-clear indications that massive change is afoot at the world's second largest automaker. As readers likely realize, Ford is struggling and has been for some time. Sales have slipped in recent years and company employees are rightfully worried about ongoing restructuring efforts, which by 2012 may include the elimination of some 30,000 jobs. In light of this, workers, engineers, and bean counters are especially skeptical about Bill Ford Jr.'s plan to marshal more resources for initiatives designed to make the company a better corporate citizen and in particular, a better environmental performer. Ford senses this, and in response, he sent another unmistakable sign that change is imminent.

In an audio message e-mailed to company employees in November 2005, Ford addressed hesitations with swift resolve. He asked those inside the company who would dare impede either environmental or operational progress to either embrace his vision or leave: "Anyone who thinks or attempts to convince you that it's business as usual at Ford is wrong and would best serve us all by pursuing their interests elsewhere . . . Our heritage of innovation must be reclaimed and renewed or the greatness of our company will become part of our past. It's that simple."[3]

In examining most of the company's recent communications, particularly those targeted at employees and shareholders, we noticed the exact same change-or-die theme. Innovation is Ford's new mission. The mandate to change from an inefficient polluter into an eco-effective performer is plainly reflected in Ford's national advertising, public relations, CR and annual reporting, Web sites, and perhaps most tellingly, in Bill Ford Jr.'s personal speeches and employee dispatches. Lately, he talks a lot about vision, an expression of intent. On the company's Web site, Ford is quoted as saying: "Our vision for the future is simple: We want to build great products, a strong business and a better world." While the first portion of his vision is what one would expect the CEO of a major corporation to say, the last part trips some activists up.

Various groups have a terribly hard time believing that as a company, Ford is serious about building a better world and prioritizing environmental performance, especially in light of the company's track record and current financial challenges. They remind people that Ford broke its promise to increase fuel efficiency by 25 percent by 2004 and that the company currently has the worst-performing fleet of vehicles on the road. In 2005, the Environmental Protection Agency (EPA) reported that the average fuel efficiency of Ford's current lineup is a lowly 19.1 miles per gallon. Similarly, the Union of Concerned Scientists reported that Ford's current fleet has the worst greenhouse gas pollution performance of all the Big Six auto manufacturers. "By producing a fleet of cars, trucks and SUVs that are the worst global warming polluters in the industry, Ford is driving climate chaos," insists watchdog group Jumpstart Ford. Jumpstart Ford is the most outspoken of all the company's detractors. "More than any other U.S. automaker, Ford bears responsibility for global warming," they say.[4]

For every move or announcement Ford makes, Jumpstart Ford casts a response. In 2004, after Ford launched the Escape, a vehicle it touted as America's first SUV hybrid, Jumpstart noted that although the Escape is a "fine product," the company produced only 20,000. "That's six-tenths of one percent of Ford's total vehicle lineup. A little more than a drop in the gas tank."[5] In September 2005, Ford announced that it would increase production of the Escape to 250,000 vehicles by 2010, as well as use gas-hybrid engines in more than half of all Ford, Lincoln, and Mercury vehicles. Again, Jumpstart said that wasn't good enough: "We need Ford to improve the fuel efficiency of its whole fleet by 2010, and build a fleet that has zero tailpipe emissions by 2020." Jumpstart did, however, take some credit for Ford's decision, saying that the commitment to hybrid technology "shows that we're having an impact."[6]

Our assessment of Ford indicates that the company jumpstarted itself. In recent years, a great many of Ford's more significant choices appear to stem not from external pressure, but from a clearer sense of internal direction. There is undoubtedly a wider scheme at work as the company increasingly measures its success against higher ideals. This becomes particularly apparent when one observes how the company has allocated a certain portion of its wealth. Whereas what Ford makes is one thing, how the company makes its products and other of its investment decisions is something else.

FORD'S NEW MODE

Ford's new mode commenced approximately six years ago, with the $2 billion makeover of the company's Dearborn, Michigan–based Rouge manufacturing facility. In its previous, 1930s heyday, Rouge employed 100,000 people and encompassed 15 million square feet of building space. The plant was the literal manifestation of founder Henry Ford's dreams: production on a mass scale leading to affordability, profitability, and company growth. Interchangeable parts moved through assembly line conveyor belts and became automobiles in just ninety-three minutes. Rouge was a symbol of the times, embodying the spirit of the Industrial Revolution and the corporate machine. But by the 1980s, many of the technologies utilized within the complex grew obsolete, and the physical environment became contaminated with carcinogens. In 1999, a boiler explosion killed six Ford workers and injured twenty-four. The unfortunate modern-day incident was a metaphor for the tension between the times, calling for a new approach.

Back in 1999, Bill Ford Jr. decided to set that approach by transforming Rouge into what he calls a "model of twenty-first-century sustainable manufacturing." Perhaps not surprisingly, Bill McDonough was the person who initially convinced Ford that the feat was equally possible and in the company's best interest. Apparently, the two really hit it off. "He's got a hell of a sales pitch," Ford recalled after their initial meeting. "He's very persuasive, and we were on the same wavelength immediately."[7]

Before the Rouge makeover could commence, Ford, with the help of McDonough, needed to convince shareholders to take an enormous leap of faith—a gamble, really. Ford shareholders were called upon to make a decision that they were not inclined to make: invest heavily in a revolutionary overhaul, the likes of which had never been seen and the advantages of which have never been proven, at least not on an industrial level. This was to be done during a financially challenging period for the company. "When I went in and said, 'I want to produce the world's largest green roof,' you can imagine the response," says McDonough. "We held very tightly to the idea that if we didn't produce shareholder value then we wouldn't be able to do it."

After a great deal of deliberation, Ford and McDonough got approval to forge ahead. Ford engineers became enthusiastic about the vision, new concepts began to flow, and Rouge was redesigned into a healthy and productive new environment. Today, nearly half a million square feet of the Rouge facility's remodeled rooftops are "alive," just as McDonough imagined—brimming with soil and plants called sedum that help trap rainwater, filter emissions, and protect the structure from thermal shock and UV degradation. Shallow green ditches planted with additional vegetation are scattered about the grounds and trap and naturally purify millions of gallons of storm water, saving the company an estimated $35 million in water treatment costs. Flowering vines on trellises, as well as other plants, produce additional oxygen, provide shade, and keep the buildings cool. An innovative air delivery system decreases energy use and creates a healthier and more pleasant internal atmosphere. Renewable energy sources including solar and fuel cells help to power the facility as skylights and glass walls flood the space with natural sunlight, enabling engineers to turn off lights during the day to save $50,000 annually in electricity bills. Waste management is intensely strict, and shipping containers and other materials are sent back to suppliers for continual reuse and recycling. And perhaps most notably, a naturally occurring chemical process called photoremediation uses a dozen or so plant varieties to absorb and safely neutralize the rancid ground contaminants that have been festering for decades.

These and other improvements make Rouge an ecological marvel and certainly an anomaly in the automotive and manufacturing industries. But again, Jumpstart along with Thegreenlife.org, Dontbefueled. org, and several others gave the effort an overall thumbs-down. They dubbed Ford's attempt to leverage the Dearborn-based Rouge facility to its public relations advantage as evidence of greenwashing. "From all the PR that they are spinning out of Dearborn, you'd think they were the most environmental company on the road," Jumpstart says. "The Dearborn Truck Plant may be considered an environmental dream for its water-preserving green roof, but the products coming out of it are an environmental nightmare."[8]

Jumpstart's point is well taken. The Dearborn plant does, in fact, produce some of Ford's more polluting, least efficient vehicles, like the F-150 pickup, which gets twelve city miles per gallon and received a 2005 EPA air pollution score of one out of ten. However, what Jumpstart ignores is that it would have been far cheaper for Ford to just pull up stakes, abandon Rouge, and build a new eco-friendly facility somewhere else. But the company did not do that. Why not? Could it have been because Ford believed that making the investment was the right thing to do for the future health of the company, surrounding communities, and the environment? "I think the issue here is a signal of intention," says McDonough. "Moving a big organization with a hundred years of history is not a quick process, but transforming the way we think about a building is something that can be done as a way of signaling a new way of thinking."

To McDonough's point, the thinking behind Rouge is something different. And the new thinking is no longer confined to the Rouge facility. By now, it has spread throughout the company. For instance, Ford's Windsor Engine Plant in Canada currently sends all shipping containers and pallets back to suppliers for continual recycling. Its Bridgend Engine Plant in Wales uses enough solar panels to light 108,000 square feet of space and save 4,400 U.S. tons of carbon dioxide annually. Its Ohio assembly plant uses an innovative fumes-to-fuel process that transforms paint fumes into electricity. In fact, since Rouge was rebuilt, all of Ford's plants around the world have become ISO 14001 certified. Also, Ford's suppliers are encouraged by the company to become ISO 14001 certified. If Rouge really were a token, a $2 billion publicity stunt, then why would the company roll out similar models and environmental management systems all around the world?

Though doubts regarding Ford's will and ability to transform into an environmental performer may still exist in the minds of some, one recent decision sets the record straight. Ford *is* changing for real, right now. As reported by the *Detroit News* and *Time* magazine, Ford is currently involved in a "secret research project" that will do for Ford's products what the Rouge facility redesign did for the company's manufacturing processes. The plan, officially named "The Piquette Project" after Ford's Piquette factory plant, where the Model T was born, is a recyclable, environmentally friendly car that is engineered using a novel approach for the auto industry. McDonough, along with a team of Ford engineers, will design the new car using two tools: McDonough's *Cradle to Cradle* design model, which ensures that the materials used to make the car produce maximum value but are also perpetually circulated in "closed loops" and thus cause no damage to ecosystems;[9] and a clean sheet of paper. Is this yet another signal of intent? McDonough says no. "That's a signal of earning your stripes. You have to understand that Rouge led us to the process that allowed us to transform the way we think about large buildings. That process has now been applied the way we think about the future of the car."

Ford may have a long road ahead of it, but in Rouge the company found a central purpose. The purpose, which the company now rather broadly defines as its "innovation mission," is crucial not because it makes a statement to the public about where Ford wants to go, but because it aligns people within the organization and creates momentum. McDonough indicates that this common purpose leads to great change, and that it plays out through Rouge and Piquette. "We're bringing hundreds of people together who all believe in the same thing to format and daydream—and to go execute. It's a great moment," he says. "That's not greenwash. That's experimentation and process change."

Bill Ford Jr. is serious about not just recovering, but about taking the lead market position through such innovation: "My goal is to fight Toyota and everybody else and come out on top,"[10] he told *Time* magazine in a January 2006 interview. The CEO is convinced of the medium- to long-term advantages of the company's environmental transition. Of this, he recently told SustainAbility chairman John Elkington: "[The environment] is a highly motivating topic for the people at Ford to engage in. It not only rights a wrong that this company has done in the past, but it's also helping to build a better future, not only for their own children, but for the next generation of Ford workers . . . We are setting off on a path that will transform us from an old-line industrial company into a model company for the twenty-first century."

Following 2006 news of the company's efforts to stem losses, Ford pressed on with his message to shareholders and regarding the importance of continued investment in environmental technologies. He insisted: "We cannot succeed in the long run if we're only focused on the short term."[11] And in Ford's first major corporate advertising campaign since 2001, Ford personally tells the public: "We're driving American innovation with advancements in hybrid vehicles, safety, and design." The head of a hundred-year-old, $171 billion American icon is telling the world with guts and grit that this corporate responsibility stuff needs time to settle in, but that it just might help make or break his company's future fate. That's nothing to sneer at.

THE RIPPLE EFFECT

Financial and operational challenges, like the ones Bill Ford Jr. currently faces, provide leaders with a difficult integrity check. In such circumstances, executives with visions to improve their company's impact on the world at large are challenged to stay the course and are tested by the conventional wisdom that says that one must trade between serving shareholder interests and wider societal interests. This has to be one of the most taxing trials that any purpose-driven leader could conceivably face in the course of his or her career. Moreover, the outcome of such a trial—whether or not Ford is able to prevail in growing his company in an environmentally *and* financially healthy direction—has enormous implications for the business community and for society at large. There is a great deal riding on Ford's shoulders.

Integrity checks come in other forms as well. External circumstances of all sorts can trigger defining moments or simply sharpen a leader's resolve. Apparently, this latter case in point came about for Lee Scott, chief executive of Wal-Mart, following Hurricane Katrina. Like most around the world, Scott is said to have found Katrina horrifying, both from a humanitarian and an environmental point of view. The storm did, however, reportedly help to put several things into perspective for him, including his corporation's former environmental posture, which in retrospect he sees as "more like a public relations campaign than substance,"[12] and more important, his company's highest possible potential.

Here's the thing about Wal-Mart: the company's approach to health care, equal employment, and pay disparity, and its influence on the outsourcing of American jobs are the source of constant controversy. But there is no dispute surrounding the company's response to community crises, at least not to Katrina. Immediately following the storm, as FEMA fumbled to grasp hold of the situation, Wal-Mart managers bulldozed their way into a flooded Waveland, Mississippi, store to salvage critical supplies like diapers and water. The company dispatched over 1,500 trucks loaded with donated food, clothing, and other products to affected communities and five additional trucks to the Houston Astrodome, along with forty-five associate volunteers. It immediately coordinated with the National Guard to offer truckloads of free ice, and emergency supplies in Waveland, and handed out free seven-day supplies of prescription drugs to dazed and desperate evacuees from a double-wide trailer. Wal-Mart also donated the use of twenty-five of its facilities as temporary shelters, 12,500 of its associates as volunteers, and $20 million in cash assistance to aid in relief efforts. In all, Wal-Mart used its enormous scale, streamlined logistical abilities, and vast resources to temper a gradually worsening catastrophe. According to sources inside Wal-Mart, today the U.S. government is asking: "How did you do what you did?" and the company is sharing that information.

"Our culture of communication gets us answers very quickly and makes what needs to happen, happen very quickly to support our associates, facilities, and communities," explains Jason Jackson, Wal-Mart's director of emergency management. Jackson says that based on its structure, Wal-Mart has a leg up on FEMA: "We have the advantage of less bureaucracy." Wal-Mart also has the advantage of a state of the art emergency operations center (EOC), which tracks weather, storms, fires, quakes, and other environmental situations that may impact any of the company's 5,000 locations or its millions of customers or suppliers. "We actually knew that Katrina was taking a turn for the worse and estimated its destructive intent the Friday before it hit. By Sunday, evacuations were well in progress," Jackson says.

In describing Wal-Mart's Katrina response, Jackson relays an orchestrated timeline of events. During the first days after the storm, the EOC kept in constant communication with associates and teams to assess the level of devastation and corresponding local needs. "Ground forces" composed of associates and managers were dispatched in hard-hit areas to ensure the welfare of other associates and to reconstitute facility operations. The EOC expanded its operations to include an eighty-operator call center to support and aid the company's thousands of displaced associates as rapidly as possible. The EOC also scaled up a security operations center, a health and safety operations annex, a strategy annex, and an "information systems war room" for what Jackson characterizes as "a massive home office response." Yet at the same time, Jackson downplays the full scale of Wal-Mart's reaction: "What we did really amounts to doing the same thing that we do every day: shipping product efficiently and quickly to take care of our customers. In some places, we knew our stores and clubs would be the only place open where people could get food, water, pharmaceuticals, and other supplies, and it was more about supporting those people in their time of need than it was about making the almighty dollar."

Times of severe crisis can either bring out the best or the worst in people, and according to Wal-Mart sources, this was a tragedy that made people shine. Ray Cox, store manager at Wal-Mart in Waveland, site of the company's hardest-hit store, says he saw direct evidence of interorganizational goodwill immediately after Katrina hit and still sees it today. "I've always been proud of my company, but I'm even more proud of the way they've responded to their associates and to the Mississippi gulf coast following Katrina. They stepped up when we needed them most." Cox explains that Wal-Mart corporate granted every request made by management during the period when the Waveland store was trying to regain its bearings and help its associates and local community members to survive with just the basics. "Wal-Mart has more than taken care of us, and therefore, we more than want to take care of our company. That feeling is not just coming from me in my leadership role—it's coming from every associate that's employed with us in this store." Apparently, Waveland customers, and particularly evacuees, feel similar emotions. "I can't tell you how many times a day I have customers come and shake my hand and say 'thank you, we needed what you did,' with tears in their eyes," Cox recalls. Wal-Mart corporate registered altruistic moments, as associates in various states throughout the country were reportedly calling in during their off hours, asking superiors: "What can I do to help?" All during the aftermath, individuals throughout the company seemed to experience a contagious sense of pride and mission.

From this vantage, Scott seemingly liked what he saw. Any way you sliced it—from the way people came together to the way the company's logistics and communications teams worked together—there was a perfect synchronicity in Wal-Mart's Katrina response. What if that synchronicity could be harnessed and used to help the company reach its higher goals? For that matter, what if Wal-Mart's higher goals became progressively more reliant on the concept of what it means to be a great corporate citizen in the twenty-first century?

A few months after the disaster, Scott addressed Wal-Mart associates, saying:

Katrina asked this critical question, and I want to ask it of you: What would it take for Wal-Mart to be that company, at our best, all the time? What if we used our size and resources to make this country and this earth an even better place for all of us: customers, associates, our children, and generations unborn? What would that mean? Could we do it? Is this consistent with our business model? What if the very things that many people criticize us for, our size and reach, became a trusted friend and ally to all, just as it did in Katrina? . . .

As one of the largest companies in the world, with an expanding global presence, environmental problems are our problems. The supply of natural products (fish, food, water) can only be sustained if the ecosystems that provide them are sustained and protected. There are not two worlds out there, a Wal-Mart world and some other world . . .

There is crowd of smart people who think that if a company addresses the environment, it will lose its shirt. I believe they are wrong. I believe, in fact, that being a good steward of the environment in our communities and being an efficient and profitable business are not mutually exclusive. In fact they are one and the same. And I can show you why . . . To be successful and continue to grow, we must operate in a world that is healthy and successful.[13]

Scott's words, which are somewhat incongruous with the token environmental messages released by the retail giant in years past, are but icing on the cake. The cake is Wal-Mart's $500 million annual commitment in environmental technologies at its more than 5,000 stores and distribution centers around the world. This financial commitment is backed by concrete goals, timetables, and metrics, which include a plan to increase Wal-Mart's massive truck fleet's fuel efficiency by 25 percent over the next three years and double it within ten years, saving an estimated $52 million annually in the near term and $310 million annually by 2015. Another target is to reduce company-wide greenhouse gas emissions by 20 percent in the next eight years and to redesign Wal-Mart stores in order to make them 25 to 30 percent more energy efficient over the next three years. "Doing this will bring cleaner air to our communities, help address an urgent environmental problem, and save us millions of dollars at the pump and on electricity bills," the company tells people on its corporate Web site, http://walmartstores.com/ environment.

In 2005, Wal-Mart made four other promises that signify its intent to continue to think big picture and develop business solutions that benefit both the environment and shareholders. First, Wal-Mart pledged to share all learning and technologies with the world, including customers, suppliers, and even competitors. It decided that, for instance, the viable green building store prototypes it engineers should be made available to as many companies as possible for replication because "the more people who can utilize this type of technology, the larger the market and the more we can save our customers"[14]—and also, the more Wal-Mart can save itself. While this decision contrasts with the company's dominating reputation, it makes business sense.

Next, rather than hammer suppliers for lower and lower margins at any cost to the earth, Wal-Mart pledged to show preference to suppliers in China and the U.S. that implement environmental management systems. Today, suppliers with their own green programs and that meet Wal-Mart's other criteria are more likely to win contracts than suppliers without such programs. In this case, Wal-Mart is making the burden of going green a greener proposition for suppliers, while also reducing the reputational risks associated with doing business with subpar suppliers who do not comply with the company's new, higher standards. What's really interesting is that this policy stands to a have serious influence on China's development pattern, as approximately one-sixth of China's exports are channeled through Wal-Mart.

Another of Wal-Mart's big green promises is to bring cleaner, environmentally friendly products into the marketplace. The company did not specify any major worldwide targets or broad forecasts in relation to such products, but recently, it did shift its North American buying decisions in certain key categories. For instance, in February 2006, Wal-Mart pledged to source all of its wild-caught fresh and frozen fish from fisheries that meet the independent environmental criteria set by the Marine Stewardship Council (MSC), a London-based group that promotes sustainable fishing practices. Experts say that Wal-Mart's support of the MSC will lead to better standards across the industry as well as dozens of fish products bearing the MSC's distinctive blue eco-label, thus making mainstream consumers aware of the importance of responsibly sourced fish. Similarly, Wal-Mart placed organic cotton yoga outfits in 290 of its stores in 2005, and according to the company, they sold out in less than ten weeks. Wal-Mart has enormous influence on its 68,000 suppliers and, therefore, what is sold in its stores and elsewhere. The minute the company decides it wants to sell organic at a reasonable cost, all it has to do is ask its network of suppliers, and eventually, it shall receive. Wal-Mart, as some environmental advocates point out, has the power to become the world's largest purchaser of organic products practically overnight.

Wal-Mart's fourth and final promise was to aggressively pursue regulatory standards that encourage utility companies to invest in low or no greenhouse gas sources of electricity, as well as reduce barriers to integrate these sources into the power grid. Because Wal-Mart's influence might help make renewable energy more accessible, in this case environmentalists might grow to appreciate the company's muscle and direct influence on regulators.

Naturally, not all environmental advocates view Wal-Mart's latest promises or its direct and indirect influence on stakeholders as potentially positive. As with Ford's recent commitments, activist groups of various sorts portray Wal-Mart's newest stance as a "publicity stunt," "empty actions," and "elaborate and calculated greenwash."[15] However, also as with Ford, there is clear evidence that Wal-Mart's current environmental initiatives are indeed the final product, not of marketing or publicity teams, but rather of years of work at the highest engineering, operations, and management levels of the company.

Over the past decade, Wal-Mart engaged the help of leading-edge experts in market-oriented environmental solutions, like environmental group Rocky Mountain Institute (RMI). Amory Lovins, chief executive of RMI and author of *Winning the Oil Endgame*, says that his organization began working with Wal-Mart in the nineties on a single project that later developed into a two-pronged effort: the total redesign of Wal-Mart's trucking fleet and the retrofit and redesign of Wal-Mart stores and distribution centers for maximum energy efficiency.

"We will not be a party to greenwash," insists Lovins. "We only work with firms with a sincere desire to change how they do business and that are culturally ripe for that sort of change. If we didn't think that Wal-Mart was sincere, then we wouldn't be working with them." Lovins says that Wal-Mart engaged RMI because it was clear that by using known technologies, Wal-Mart's trucks could become up to five times more efficient without experiencing any difference in safety or performance, and that by building green buildings, energy costs would decrease while store productivity skyrocketed. The triple bottom-line differences were key determinants in the assessment of each project that Wal-Mart undertook and currently undertakes—from the pursuance of regulatory standards to the selling of organic products.

Lovins explains that, in terms of operational changes, the advantages of Wal-Mart's newest moves were abundantly clear to the company. Green building designs, for instance, are less toxic, make more efficient use of water, and use alternative sources of energy. Therefore, they result in less overall environmental impact. But the benefits of these buildings do not end there. "They are also fiscal," explains Lovins. "And these fiscal advantages exist on several levels. One level is the saved energy costs you get with alternatives. You also get less volatility with energy prices because you reduce both your costs and your business risk in energy supply since you are not relying on energy sources that fluctuate. There are social advantages, too. You get happier people." Wal-Mart's internal research suggests that indeed, higher productivity, lower absenteeism, and happier workers do occur in green design stores that are drenched with sunlight and have more harmonious and visually appealing configurations. A highly controlled study conducted by an outside research firm hired by Wal-Mart found a 40 percent gain in sales pressure in the green stores. "On top of the financially valuable reductions in overhead costs, Wal-Mart also has reason to expect better associate recruitment, retention, motivation, and sales in well-designed, efficient green spaces," Lovins concludes.

Just as with Ford's latest investments, what Lovins describes is not an environmental campaign, but rather, an operational overhaul designed to make Wal-Mart perform better. This is a shift in the company's approach to managing its operations, or an upgrading. Like every company in this chapter, Wal-Mart is in the midst of a learning process and always will be. No doubt, Wal-Mart will trip along the way. It concedes this by telling consumers what to expect in terms of green products at "everyday low prices": "We believe you should not have to pay more for healthy and environmentally preferable products. We have a long way to go to make this happen, and because we are learning and listening in new ways, we expect to make mistakes."[16]

Though its path might not be entirely smooth, Lovins indicates why Wal-Mart will achieve its goals: "They have the power and scale to change the market overnight." Again, the moment Wal-Mart's organic produce or organic cotton clothing hits its thousands of stores worldwide or nationwide, they will have made an elite category instantly accessible to the masses. Lovins also notes Wal-Mart's unique brand of wisdom: "They're not a 'ready, aim, fire' company, they're a 'fire, aim, ready' company. That is, they just do things and then figure the strategy out over time, and they give their people the room to figure it out, make mistakes, and then learn quickly." Whatever the exact term for describing Wal-Mart's approach to making operationally led changes and environmental progress, the inaccurate term (although critics will hate to acknowledge this) is most assuredly "greenwashing."

Here we have the largest retail company on earth not just sending a message and not simply setting the pace, but through its most recent moves, directly influencing the corresponding policies of nations, suppliers, regulators, competitors, and eventually, the lifestyles of millions of consumers who might very soon be able to afford to buy organic products. Both Wal-Mart's synchronistic response to Katrina and its fiscally sensible approach to tackling climate change set off a ripple effect that could feasibly continue to produce results both inside and outside the company for years, perhaps decades to come. At the very least, both factors give Wal-Mart associates and management something meaningful to stand by and customers something worth talking about and shopping for. Both factors diminish the need for spin at a corporation so often condemned for it.

THE BIRTH OF PURPOSE

The ultimate goal of corporate responsibility is not simply to lessen a company's negative impact on the world, but rather to establish a purpose that's bigger than the end product. The committed pursuit of a higher purpose leads to a better end product or superior results. The endeavor is valuable because, as Ford and Wal-Mart show, it reinvigorates the whole organization by giving everyone something inspiring to aim for. It enhances a company's significance, strength, creativity, potential, and standards. The pursuit of a higher purpose also naturally lessens a company's negative impact and makes the world a better place. This combination of benefits makes the endeavor worthwhile.

As more companies willingly leave old models behind and set their sights on optimal outcomes, more uncover such a driving force. In the Ford and Wal-Mart examples, the force came from the top down. Bill Ford Jr.'s and Lee Scott's personal convictions and visions set forth specific agendas and projects, creating some internal disruption but ultimately setting the basis of a greatly improved course for the whole organization. The top-down model is common among companies with exceptionally charismatic leaders. However, this is not the only way in which higher purpose originates. Frequently, higher purpose emerges from the bottom up as smaller, fringe initiatives gradually take hold, form a critical mass, and eventually begin to direct and define the entire company.

In the process of our analysis, we observed that this second form of evolution—where purpose migrates from the roots of a company upward—seems to occur more often. If you look closely at the nature of the projects that over time germinate into wider, transformational schemes, you will notice all varieties. The initial seeds of corporate purpose might spring from the jurisdictions of philanthropy, marketing, human resources, environmental management, design, procurement, operations, or research and development. Such projects are typically guided by people who function in distinct departmental "silos." Said another way, the projects are usually designed independently, as department managers in large companies rarely collaborate with other department managers on a daily basis. However, every so often, results or circumstances allow managers to cross borders. When this occurs, people grow empowered, sparks fly, ideas grow, senior leaders get onboard, purpose begins to take shape, and the business begins to change in fundamental ways. This is precisely what's happening at multiple companies we observed, including a Canadian professional football team called the Montréal Alouettes, McDonald's, and Nike— three totally different organizations and cultures. And yet, in each, purpose trickles up from below.

FROM SILO TO SYNTHESIS

One of the more vivid illustrations we found of how purpose can emerge from the sidelines resides at the Canadian professional football team the Montréal Alouettes. The Als, as their fans call them, are a low-frills operation, and their management is low-key. Compared with their American NFL counterparts, players in the CFL league receive little in the way of personal fanfare or endorsements, and Als players make an average of only $65,000 per year. In the past, it was difficult for CFL teams like the Als to fill stadiums as Canadians didn't revere football the way they did hockey. As a result, the Als have experienced what team president Larry Smith and VP of operations Mark Weightman describe as many "twists and turns" over the years. In 1996, the year the team returned to Montréal after a ten-year hiatus, the situation seemed hopeless. "The crowds were small, media coverage was spotty and the city's sentiment was cool," recalls the team on its Web site.

As a means of fostering public support and a stronger organization, Smith and Weightman began experimenting with a bunch of supplementary programs. Some of those programs provided fan perks and lowered operating costs. Others were more community directed. For instance, the Als partnered with Pfizer and the Canadian National (CN) Railway to help battle escalating dropout rates in Quebec high schools. Now called CN Adopt an Alouette, the program brings Als players into schools to provide mentorship and guidance on issues like relationships and conflicts, time management, and career planning. Each player involved in the program receives training from specialists on issues of adolescent development and presentation, and many use their own stories of perseverance, hard work, and determination as a means of inspiring the students. Today, Als players make more than three hundred community appearances through the Adopt an Alouette program every year. In addition, a similar partnership with the Big Brothers Big Sisters Association allows neighborhood kids to get to know and spend time with Als players, while players also mingle with local fans through annual friendly neighborhood basketball and hockey games that raise money for charity.

While these and other events bring fans and players closer together, the Als also sponsor programs that get young people interested in the game. For instance, a bursary program awards C $23,000 annually to young students who excel at football in a recognized secondary, collegiate, or university-level, while the Alouettes Classic brings one hundred chosen student athletes who perform on and off the field together for an exciting annual game hosted at Alouette home base, McGill's Percival Molson Stadium in downtown Montréal. A junior football camp and other programs also embody the Als' commitment to supporting youth. "Our objectives are to consistently encourage young athletes to follow their dreams and to stay in school," says Smith. "We believe football is one of the best ways of teaching the discipline needed."

The benefits of the Als' commitment to its community can be seen, heard, and felt on multiple levels. To start with, the Als helped revitalize the sport of football in Quebec. In the ten years since the Als have been back in Montréal, Quebec's amateur football league has mushroomed from 150 to over 300 teams. "Though we aren't conceited enough to say we are the sole reason for the recent upsurge," says Smith, "we do play a significant role in helping the league develop young talent and in encouraging young Quebecers of all skill levels to play football." This newfound appreciation for football reaches the wider population, too, as Molson Stadium is now typically packed with cheering, loyal fans. "You can really feel the excitement," says Als fan and McGill research team member Jamie Wald about his experience at a recent game. "The Als are known for bringing so much back to the community and to the city, and the work they are doing is extremely important to people. They set a great example. I'm also personally impressed by individual players' and the executive team's commitment to serving their community. They buy into this because they understand the results they can achieve." Today, Als games are sold out and media coverage is consistent, not spotty. Players like quarterback Anthony Calvillo have become local heroes for good reason. In November 2005, Calvillo was nominated for one of the CFL's most prestigious honors, the Tom Pate Award, which recognizes players who best exemplify fair play on and off the field and contributes to his team and community.

The benefits of the Als' commitment to its community can also be quantified. Smith estimates that due to the social equity built by the team's ongoing community efforts, the Als can lose an entire year's worth of games without experiencing a decline in ticket sales. Absent this social equity, Smith says, the lost games would register as lost sales almost immediately. Thus, our research group determined that the Als have evolved past the intent- and purpose-setting phase in the progression, but the story of how they did so is special.

Over time, the little "giving back" initiatives created a winning direction for the reconstituted Canadian football team. They amount to what Smith and Weightman describe as "a purpose beyond the playing field." Smith explains: "This is a relationship business. To build relationships with fans, we realized that we needed to be about more than just football or entertainment. Now we are a team that strives to achieve more than visibility in the community, but rather *integration* into the community." Most American professional sports teams walk above the crowd and make public appearances here or there during peak seasons like Christmas, but the Als walk *with* the crowd and have found ways to ingrain themselves deeply, to the point where they are a crucial part of the regional character and a symbol of the local culture itself.

The Als are lucky, of course. They didn't have to wrestle with past negative CR performance. As a result, they discovered their higher purpose quite effortlessly. Als senior leaders had the authority, will, and room to experiment. It's not always that easy. More often, it takes companies a little longer to hone in on their purpose and to see results. Also, corporate chiefs are not always the ones setting the corporate responsibility pace or even, frankly, the corporate responsibility agendas. Managers are frequently the ones responsible for developing the compelling ideas and goals that allow a company to create the greatest possible impact. This is what happened at McDonald's.

Mats Lederhausen, managing director of McDonald's Ventures, has spent a lifetime with the company, as his father opened Sweden's first McDonald's in 1973. "I started my career very young, working for my dad when he was an owner operator. When I was eighteen, I became a shareholder," says Lederhausen. "After business school and a few years at Boston Consulting Group we restructured the company and I became a joint venture partner with McDonald's corporation. It was during that time that I connected with what I really was about and what I think business ought to be about." In 1992, Lederhausen's McDonald's Sweden group began working closely with the Natural Step, an organization that trains companies to understand the environmental challenge and what to do about it. McDonald's Sweden began recycling, separating waste, and phasing out plastics. It started buying organics and switched over to 100 percent renewable sources of electricity. "We built state-of-the-art restaurants that were as sustainable as they could possibly be using the technologies available to us at that time," explains Lederhausen. "We put some of our company cars on ethanol, and we put our truck drivers on a bonus system that encouraged them to get better gas mileage. We trained all of our people in the language of sustainability."

However enterprising, McDonald's Sweden is just a distant daughter to the McDonald's mother ship. She is one of 30,000 siblings worldwide. It is often cited that McDonald's corporate spends more money on advertising, targets more children, gives away more toys, and purchases more beef than any other company in the world. While nutritionists estimate that fast food is a top contributor to obesity, heart disease, and diabetes, environmentalists calculate that it takes McDonald's 600 gallons of water to produce one quarter-pounder, and 10 calories of energy for every calorie of food produced.[17]

Knowing all of this, Lederhausen thought the McDonald's mother ship could learn from the knowledge and benefits gained by McDonald's Sweden. "Our model was working well in Sweden, and meanwhile, I saw McDonald's in the U.S. going nowhere. The very spirit of what this company was about in the 1970s was lost. The stores looked like crap," he says. "Corporate wasn't paying attention to any of the big trends that were going on environmentally or socially, so I got increasingly vocal with them. I started sending memos, and I started letting them know what we were doing in Sweden and what they needed to start doing in the U.S."

One day in 1998, Lederhausen deemed his efforts futile. He resolved to resign from the company because he thought there was no way that he alone could convince McDonald's senior leadership to make the drastic changes necessary. "My idea was to go to Oxford University to write a book about corporate philosophy," says Lederhausen. But things took a turn. First, some of Lederhausen's closest colleagues, like renowned leadership expert Richard Barrett, convinced him that he needed to stay inside the corporate world—not outside looking in—to have the desired impact. Also, McDonald's leadership wouldn't accept his resignation. They ultimately agreed with his criticisms, liked his suggestions, and gave Lederhausen a promotion to global vice-president of strategy.

Since then, McDonald's has made unusual environmental progress with the help of Lederhausen and a team of committed others. Today, McDonald's is the largest user of recycled materials in its industry. According to the company's corporate responsibility reports, in 2003, approximately 47.2 percent of the paper packaging the company used was made from recycled content, while McDonald's has purchased more than $4.1 billion in recycled packaging in the past fifteen years. Between 2002 and 2003, McDonald's reduced its packaging weight from nearly 11 percent to approximately 16.4 percent per $1,000 in sales. In 2004, the company reduced packaging by another 3.2 percent per $1,000 in sales. In Denmark, McDonald's runs the world's first hydrofluorocarbon-free restaurant, while in Australia, France, Italy, and Brazil, McDonald's recycles its cooking oil into biodiesel fuel. McDonald's has also worked with environmental groups like Conservation International to develop global guidelines for protecting fishing stocks, animal welfare, and forest resources. In 2005, the company won approval as a sustainability performance group Ceres partner and pledged to make continual worldwide improvements in its social and environmental performance.

While these efforts are notable, changes in McDonald's product line are what interested us the most. As of 2005, some of those menu updates include premium salads served with Newman's Own dressings (of which the company has sold over 300 million), additional fruit and vegetable items, and a nutritionist-designed Happy Meal for adults. McDonald's also adjusted its kids' Happy Meals to provide low-fat milk, real fruit juice, and water rather than soda, and apple slices versus sugary snacks. Its Chicken McNuggets now are made with white meat only, not by way of the whole-chicken-plus-filler-in-blender process illustrated in the popular film *Super Size Me*. Additionally, as of 2006, McDonald's is serving Fair Trade and organic coffee in 658 restaurants in the U.S. and only organic milk in the UK. Around the world, McDonald's is in the process of phasing out the use of meat treated with antibiotics and growth hormones, thus putting enormous pressure on suppliers to comply with higher health standards.

Needless to say, McDonald's is neither a perfect nor an entirely transparent company. It has yet to quantify or report on certain metrics like worldwide water usage or greenhouse gas emissions, let alone its estimated impact on future generations. However, in proactively implementing more incremental, positive changes in the past ten years than any other fast food company in America, including Burger King, Wendy's, Domino's Pizza, KFC, and Taco Bell, McDonald's more than demonstrates an intent to transform. It sets the pace, consistently leading the pack on key issues like pollution, recycling, genetic engineering, food safety, and yes, even nutrition. "If you look at the turnaround in the portfolio of food, if you look at the turnaround in how the company runs its operations, if you look at how the company currently runs its people programs or food sourcing or environmental impact programs, then it's obvious that the work that McDonald's has done over the past five years has resulted in good, solid improvements," says Lederhausen. "I'd give the effort a B plus. The company could go further still, but the intent to change is there."

While McDonald's corporate has yet to home in on its particular purpose in the world, several of McDonald's ventures have, and movement within these firms positively affects the parent corporation, Lederhausen says. In his current role as managing director of McDonald's Ventures, Lederhausen oversees a portfolio of purpose-driven companies including Chipotle Mexican Grill, which serves "food with integrity" including organic vegetables and free-range meats, and also gives away all its daily leftover food to local charities. Lederhausen's portfolio also includes the European natural food restaurant chain Pret A Manger which supports numerous charities helping the homeless, as well as the Ohio-based restaurant Donatos Pizza, which through its food and outreach serves the purpose of "spreading goodwill through business." "In its own way, each company in our portfolio embeds corporate responsibility in the fabric of its business without ever mentioning the term 'corporate responsibility' in any of their communications. Each is set up to be a positive force for good," says Lederhausen.

Of all places, McDonald's corporate is an atmosphere where a person like Lederhausen can reach his personal potential and where evolution can unfold. This is surprising for several reasons. First, it makes one think twice before supposing that such responsibility-led transformation isn't possible in all corners of corporate America. Second, it makes one grateful that it is. It also makes one consider how important corporate culture is to change itself.

An internal atmosphere that sets up impossible circumstances where visionary people have no breathing room, where great ideas hit brick walls, and all odds are against truth limits the possibility for movement and success. At McDonald's—as at Ford, the Montréal Alouettes, and even Wal-Mart—there is a willingness to make positive progress. Therefore, positive progress is being made. This sounds obvious, but it is surprising just how many companies set themselves up for failure corporate responsibility-wise through cultural roadblocks and mental resistance. Change is a process that requires experimentation and a willingness to break free from negative patterns and thought forms— sometimes even from basic rules.

At Nike, luckily, rule breaking has always been the rule. The company is rooted in novel principles, and they are reflected throughout the corporate culture. "Legendary track coach and Nike cofounder Bill Bowerman believed, 'if you have a body, then you're an athlete,'" says Hannah Jones, vice-president of corporate responsibility. "Nike has adopted that basic tenet, along with a commitment to bring inspiration and innovation to every athlete in the world."

While as a brand Nike stands for innovation and inspiration, the company defines its larger role in the world as that of a "potent change agent," according to Jones. As a company, Nike embodies change or evolution—of personal best, of the athlete, of sport, of research, of design, of materials, of solutions, and of certain world problems. The company promotes positive change through its activities, while its higher "potent change agent" purpose is the product of an interorganizational grassroots process. Nike is still undergoing that process and, in fact, hasn't really formally acknowledged the process as grassroots the way it has its approach to marketing. Nevertheless, Nike's corporate responsibility executions are undeniably built on individual creativity and groundswell. Thus far, they have resulted in some pretty terrific outcomes.

Cultural conditions within Nike allow stakeholders—including employees on Nike's marketing, design, philanthropy, and operations teams, and even suppliers, retailers, and other partners—to contribute new, good ideas that might help the company to improve its impact on the world at large. The company is always looking for ways to advance. "Every season, we ask our designers: 'What is the one thing you are going to do differently?'"[18] said Darcy Winslow, global director for women's footwear, apparel, and accessories in a separate interview. The company collaborates with its partners from around the world and allows ideas to germinate. Essentially, it considers environmental impact a key part of the creative process. Nike then test-drives the good, new ideas as pilot programs. The pilot programs that generate triple bottom-line results are maintained, while the ones that don't work are phased out. Nike has always been known for this type of emergent strategy. Rather than isolate a specific cause or charter and then launch corporate responsibility programs under that charter right off the bat, Nike experiments. The company lets the market tell it which sorts of corporate responsibility initiatives are the most valuable.

In 1998, for instance, Winslow's group launched a pilot program to assess the environmental impact of the process the company used to manufacture footwear. The group determined that certain hazardous chemicals could be effectively replaced with safe materials that were either biodegradable or reusable. Thus, describes Winslow, sprang forth a concept shoe with "a fully compostable rubber sole that abrades nutrients for the soil during a long Sunday run and a nylon upper that can be returned to Nike through the new 'Reuse-A-Shoe' recycling program. Our goal [was] to take responsibility for our product through its entire life."[19]

That was eight years ago, and multiple components of the program proved to be very useful. Nike ran with those. Since 1998, thousands of pairs of used Nike shoes have been collected, disassembled, and reborn in the form of 170 donated sport surfaces for children's schools and recreational facilities across America through Nike's ongoing Reuse-A-Shoe program. In addition, Winslow's shoe design concept merged with similar ideas and pilot programs from other creative people, and those ideas have collectively influenced wider corporate environmental policies. To date, the new corporate environmental policies include the current phase-out of polyvinyl chloride (PVC) from all Nike products, the move to environmentally friendly water-based adhesives, improved management practices that divert 60 percent of waste from landfills, and the development of a unique rubber that is 96 percent less toxic than other rubbers commonly used in the marketplace.

Nike is starting to close the conceptual loop and apply its newly instated corporate environmental policies and innovations into the design process. "We've moved beyond the first chapter of addressing and measuring our social and environmental impacts as a company, and are writing the next one, which defines our corporate responsibility work as brand-enhancing with the potential to transform not only our business, but also our industry and beyond," says Jones. "We see this next phase as core to our success moving forward, with the potential to help us enter new markets, improve our supply chain performance, and leverage the power of our brand."

In Nike's next chapter, the company crosses the border between emergent and deliberate corporate responsibility strategy by seizing new opportunities that serve the company's triple bottom-line goals. For instance, in 2005, the company launched Nike Considered, a smaller line of products that uses less energy, materials, and chemicals to make and also produces less waste. "Nike Considered is not just a new pair of shoes. It [symbolizes] a creative new paradigm—and a new way for us to integrate corporate responsibility into how we work,"[20] says the company. Similarly, back in 2002, Nike introduced Nike Organics clothing made from 100 percent certified cotton in its U.S. women's line, and later followed with similar offerings in its U.S. men's, European women's, and European kids' categories.

Although these lines represent a relatively small portion of Nike's overall revenues and portfolio, they are becoming more of an emphasis for the company and certainly represent a move in the right direction. Ultimately, the more adept Nike grows at applying its policies and innovations to the design process, and the more success it has in honing in multiple company efforts around an ultimate goal, or "potent change agent" purpose, the further up the progression the company moves. "Our goal is to add on to these achievements by bringing sustainability into the very first conversations of design," says Hannah Jones. "It is to design innovative product with a decreased environmental footprint so there's no compromise between great athletic performance and great environmental performance. We know that sustainable design can add value."

ON THE CUSP

There are so many companies like Nike that are just on the cusp of passing the litmus test. In fact, during our analysis, we realized that while the High-Purpose Progression does represent a general developmental cycle or change process, it does not perfectly translate to a rating system and should not be viewed as such. While the firms profiled in the next chapter clearly passed the point of no return and thus undoubtedly qualify as High-Purpose Companies, we noticed a significant gray area that exists between the Set Intent . . . Then Purpose phase and the Transcend and Include phase. For this reason we spent hours deliberating over the appropriate placement of companies including Starbucks, Microsoft, Dell, Cisco Systems, FedEx, General Mills, Target, UPS, and a few others.

The group agreed that each of these firms had moved significantly beyond me-too rhetoric to invest in corporate responsibility initiatives that help them perform better both as businesses and as global citizens. The issue of contention for us was whether or not those initiatives had become *invaluable* to the company and by extension, its stakeholders.

In evaluating whether purpose had indeed become invaluable, we looked for the presence of at least one of two conditions:

- **Condition 1**: Higher purpose as the primary source of innovation.

- **Condition 2**: Higher purpose as the primary source of distinction.

Under the first condition, a company's higher purpose serves as the dominant developmental force, literally guiding technological and product development, as well as growth strategy. This, we believe, is the case at DuPont, Toyota, General Electric, John Deere, and SC Johnson, the first five studies explored in the next chapter, Transcend and Include.

Under the second condition, a company's higher purpose is what a company is most known and revered for in the marketplace and also one of the top reasons why it performs consistently. This is the case at JetBlue Airways and Wegmans Food Markets, the sixth and seventh studies explored in the next chapter.

In the process of our research, we discovered two important subconditions:

- **Subcondition A**: Deliberate versus emergent or haphazard corporate responsibility strategy.

- **Subcondition B**: "Permanently ingrained" purpose (In other words, the removal of the higher purpose would either cripple the existing business or else force it to turn into a totally different kind of business).

Whether companies fell into category one or two above, both subconditions applied to each company that incontestably passed our litmus test. From a research point of view, this is how we attempted to define the term "invaluable."

Despite our attempted rigor, however, we still found ourselves making some judgment calls. Our objective in the gray cases was to decipher: how valuable is invaluable? To be totally candid, this is a difficult question to answer with complete conclusiveness. For instance, how do we determine what value or lack of value certain "intangible" variables have to a company and its stakeholders? In many of the gray cases, the companies themselves did not know, for instance, to what degree employee morale or consumer loyalty had been influenced by specific community outreach efforts because they themselves had not conducted any research, so our best guess was only as good as the company's guess.

Nevertheless, we found it worthwhile to ponder inconclusive issues rather than simply dismiss them and move on or characterize them as evidence of program ineffectiveness the way corporate responsibility cynics often do. Just because the output of a variable isn't black, white, or on paper does not make it meaningless or negative. In qualitative research especially, there are always new questions worth asking and the answers are also worth exploring from different angles as they often lead to valuable insights. For instance, consider what might happen if a huge corporation like Starbucks were to suddenly stop investing in responsible coffee purchasing? Like most companies worth studying, Starbucks has its critics, but it represents big shoes to fill.

Even Starbucks questions itself. The company opens its 2004 corporate social responsibility report, entitled *Striking a Balance*, with the query: "Is Starbucks responsible?" In his upfront letter to shareholders, chairman Howard Schultz responds to the question by telling readers: "You will have to determine for yourself whether Starbucks is a responsible company." What he doesn't say is that the question is itself a little vague, and maybe even moot because the answer depends on whom you're asking. Perhaps it is more constructive to frame the question another way: How would society be worse off *without* Starbucks Corporation? What *value* does Starbucks provide to stakeholders that others can't or don't? We asked a few experts in the field of responsible coffee purchasing the latter two questions and found their answers fairly interesting.

Nicole Chettero of Fair Trade certification organization TransFair USA says that support from major member companies like Starbucks is crucial to millions around the world: "Fair Trade coffee has provided coffee farmers in some of the poorest communities in Latin America, Africa, and Asia with over $70 million more than they would have earned selling their harvests to local middlemen. Each dollar of Trans-Fair USA's budget has been translated into more than seven dollars in supplemental income for farmers and farm workers since 1999." Chettero concedes that although it is impossible to surmise *exactly* how Starbucks's sudden cease in support of Fair Trade might influence the decisions of other retailers, the organization does believe that momentum is growing within the retail community thanks to the support of Starbucks and other major corporate supporters like Dunkin' Donuts and Procter & Gamble. Chettero also explains that collectively, Fair Trade projects sponsored by these and other major corporate partners fund sustainable local development projects, including health systems, scholarships, women's leadership initiatives, and microfinance programs in over fifty countries around the developing world and benefit over 5 million farmers, farm workers, and their families. Thus, on a socioeconomic level, the potential negative results of even Starbucks's pullout could be substantial. However, as is to be expected, there are others in the field who view things rather differently.

"Unfortunately, our research shows that Starbucks is tooting its own horn with respect to how much it is actually doing to support the Fair Trade cause," says Craig Minowa, environmental scientist at the Organic Consumers Association. "When you walk into Starbucks stores, one of the first images you see is coffee farmers in foreign countries, and this creates a feeling that Starbucks is supportive of its suppliers, but when you look at the statistics, you see that less than 3.7 percent of the coffee Starbucks sells is Fair Trade, and that Fair Trade coffee is not available at all Starbucks locations." Minowa points to an initiative launched by a group of activist bloggers called "The Starbucks Challenge." The bloggers suggest that a substantial number of Starbucks customers have attempted to order a cup of French-pressed Fair Trade coffee at Starbucks stores with negative results. Customers participating in the challenge report their feedback on http://greenlagirl.com and a string of other sites. "Two months into the challenge, things STILL haven't improved much," says Siel, the site's host. "The [company] STILL hasn't answered our questions—How does Starbucks plan to fix the problem? When? Regardless of politics, most of us agree on one thing: If a company makes a promise, it should stick to it."[21] As we said, the answer to Starbucks's framed question depends on the vantage of the viewer.

Seen Starbucks way however, the technical standards of Fair Trade appear to be the minutia. As the company points out through communications of its own, coffee can be Fair Trade certified only when it comes from small-scale, family-owned coffee cooperatives that meet specific requirements imposed by Fair Trade labeling organizations like TransFair, while only two percent of the world's coffee supply is Fair Trade certified. This means that medium- and large-scale farms and plantations from which the company has been buying coffee since it was founded do not qualify, nor do smaller farms outside the system. Whereas 11.5 million of 312 million pounds of coffee that Starbucks purchased in 2005 was technically Fair Trade certified, Starbucks paid an average of $1.28 per pound for all of its unroasted coffee—a price 23 percent higher than the average commodity market price during that time frame. The average commodity price does reflect prices paid for mediocre coffee whereas Starbucks buys premium coffee, but one might consider "responsible coffee purchasing" to be a broader concept that extends beyond the Fair Trade label. Starbucks surely does, and it applies this broader concept to company-wide supply chain standards.

Through its C.A.F.E. (Cafe and Farmer Equity) practices, which are buying strategies that provide incentives to suppliers to contribute to the social and economic well-being of coffee farmers, Starbucks pledges to help preserve ways of life and protect the environment. In 2005, the company reports that it purchased 76.8 million pounds of coffee from approved C.A.F.E. suppliers in seven countries worldwide. By 2007, Starbucks pledges to source 225 million pounds through the system. Although numerous groups like OXFAM have questioned the validity of Starbucks self-imposed C.A.F.E. standards, most—though not all—in our research group agreed that C.A.F.E. represents a useful mechanism through which the company can adapt to changing stakeholder demands, thus gradually becoming more responsive and valuable. Additionally, various initiatives within Starbucks overall directly impact coffee quality. For instance, one initiative offers microcredit loans to coffee farmers, who can then invest in their farms and cultivate superior coffee beans. In this particular instance, Starbucks would be worse off without its responsible purchasing efforts because its coffee might suffer, and customers might taste this difference, too.

Is Starbucks responsible? Perhaps this question is still a subject of debate in certain circles. (What is a *wholly* responsible company, anyway—and who gets to be the judge?) To be sure, the issue of responsibility is an increasingly important attribute to Starbucks, and one that is playing itself out across ever more of the company's core operations and policies—from health care to customer relations and environmental and supply chain management. Starbucks's intent hasn't completely taken shape as a formal purpose that powers the company, we deemed, but every year, the general pursuit of purpose tips the scale a little more. And the company does try to measure what it calls "the Starbucks Effect," or the impact Starbucks has on the world at large. That impact is huge, as the company touches the lives of 25 million farmers in seventy countries. "We recognize the relationship between the success of our Company and the strength and vitality of all communities in which we operate. And it all begins with a cup of coffee,"[22] says Schultz.

Overall, it is one thing to know what corporate responsibility activities a company like Starbucks partakes in, but it is quite another to consider what might happen should those activities cease to exist. We found it useful to attempt to determine to what degree a company values its values, or derives value from its values, and in doing this, we found the what-if questions to be far more meaningful than the one-dimensional "what" questions alone. In fact, since we ran this exploratory process with a number of our gray companies, it helped lead us to one of the central findings in our study.

DEPTH VERSUS BREADTH

Companies that dabble in every conceivable corporate responsibility facet (community, philanthropy, diversity, environment, employees, human rights, etc.) tend to be *less effective* than companies that pursue deliberate strategies in a focused area—both in terms of making a substantive social and environmental impact, and in terms of generating a financial return on their corporate responsibility investment. That is our conclusion, and it runs somewhat contrary to the way that companies are often rated on Best Citizens lists.

Best Citizens lists typically quantitatively rate companies across the various performance dimensions listed above and then add up cumulative scores and rank companies accordingly. However, in this study, we evaluated corporate responsibility "effectiveness" in terms of the *quality* of triple bottom-line returns generated from corporate responsibility investments. In doing so, we noticed that the companies producing the best quality returns went deep where they knew they could make the biggest difference. Then, over time, the companies gradually broadened their reach into other areas, and continue to do so. The companies that "graduated" to the higher phases of our progression did not commence their corporate responsibility–related efforts by taking on everything at once. Instead, there was a focused strategy at the onset, or at least an area or several key areas of concentration. Whatever it was, that concentration was vitally important to the business, and thus, it became a company-wide initiative that was embraced by the senior management within each company.

As we have seen with the prior cases, at Ford, the key corporate initiative is environmental innovation. At Wal-Mart, the primary emphasis is also on environmental innovation, supplemented with community crisis response. At the Montréal Alouettes, it is all about community integration. At McDonald's, the primary emphasis is mostly on food sourcing along with environmental performance. At Nike, efforts are mainly directed toward improving design materials used. At Starbucks, the central focus is on responsible coffee purchasing, in addition to employee health care. This form of execution, where there is an alert emphasis on one or two areas of critical importance, we believe, is a basis for triple bottom-line effectiveness. Conversely, too much diversity or fragmentation at the onset tends to dilute results in the initial developmental stages—much the way too much stimulus can stunt growth.

Equally if not more important, broad-based corporate responsibility programs without a particular strategic emphasis typically draw from a company's financial and in-kind resources and then channel those resources to many areas that may not apply to the business, whereas depth corporate responsibility programs tend to bring the core strengths of a corporation to bear in solving social or environmental problems that have a high level of strategic relevance. Relevance to business goals helps to ensure that the corporate responsibility programs will provide shareholder value. And as previously mentioned, shareholder value ensures that the programs themselves can be sustained over time. Simply stated: *strategy is preferable to a lack of strategy*. Thus, ranking companies on the basis of their "overall responsibility" or "goodness" when they can make more of a difference and provide better *value* to society and shareholders by going deep occasionally, dare we suggest, risks missing the point.

Microsoft is a great example of why and how depth works better than breadth. While over the past eight years, Microsoft might not have topped Best Citizens lists due to antitrust or public opinion issues, the company currently homes in: "Some people inside and outside the company feel as if we've ought to have done more, for instance, environmentally, or talked more about what we have done environmentally or on other levels," explains Pamela Passman, vice president of corporate affairs. "But over the past couple of years, we have really tried to focus our efforts on problems where we know we can make the biggest contribution, whether that's socially or economically, because of our competency in that area and because of the nature of our business."

Microsoft is presently using its greatest strengths as an organization to attack two of the world's worst problems: poverty and online security. In these two areas, the company is reaching out in a way that no other business company quite could. Recently, Microsoft made the commitment to helping close the digital divide by bringing the benefits of technology—and technology skills—to one quarter billion underserved people by 2010. It currently partners with NGOs, schools, and government groups to develop technology-related solutions to social problems like computer illiteracy and unemployment. The company found a neat intersection between its business and philanthropic strategies, amounting to the wider purpose of "creating opportunities in the communities where we do business."[23] According to Passman, "Our citizenship efforts are all core to our business. They create an educated base of future consumers and also ensure that our technology will be accessible to all people and to other companies."

Microsoft's outreach programs also create a safer online environment. "As 'bad actors' become even more creative, we have a responsibility to keep ahead of that," Passman says, and also mentions that the creativity of Microsoft's 60,000 employees are the company's secret weapon. Over the past few years, employee innovations and ideas have led to solutions that help combat serious problems ranging from child pornography to the trafficking of women. For instance, a Toronto police officer e-mailed Bill Gates, frustrated that he didn't have the tools necessary to deal with online predators of children. Microsoft's Canadian subsidiary responded with a solution called the Children's Exploitation Tracking System (CETS). "Now we're working with the Indonesian, Australian, UK, and U.S. governments using this tool," explains Passman. "The tool is a big hit, and the original idea came from a group of employees who were trying to respond to the needs of local law enforcement officials. That's what it comes down to. That's how we can make a difference."

What's most interesting about Microsoft's depth approach is that it signifies a level of maturity, because the company is not approaching the realm of corporate responsibility as a popularity contest. Passman feels that in this way, Microsoft is coming into its own: "We're shifting from the adolescent that we were in the 1990s into an adult," she says. "In the 1990s we dealt with a lot of government and public opinion issues and problems. We know that. We also know that we're a company whose product is essential to people's daily lives. All of these factors have contributed to our current approach. We have to be much more focused and much more articulate about what motivates us, about what matters most to us as a company, and about why we are excited about the potential that our technology has for people." Although Microsoft may still be perceived as an "evil empire" by some, that perception is immaterial to the company's ability to produce a significant social and economic impact. Microsoft has both the tools and the ambition to deliver. Equally important, employees inside Microsoft have the will and wherewithal to help the company achieve its purposeful goals: "I get hundreds of e-mails every week from people who want to be a part of this." More than anything, Passman says, they keep the momentum building.

Dell Computer is another technology giant with a depth focus, as its current e-waste initiative is among its competitive group's most extensive. Dell was the first U.S. computer company to commit to a formal, global recycling program. Consumers buying a new Dell computer can opt to have their computers taken back at the end of their lifespans at no cost to them, and Dell will also take back current unwanted electronics for a flat fee per item. The company then recycles the collected PCs and monitors for reuse. In 2004, the company recovered more than 24 million pounds of used computer equipment from customers. In 2005, the company increased its used computer equipment recovery rate by 50 percent to 36 million pounds. Dell hopes to increase its product recovery rate by another 50 percent in 2006. In addition to worldwide recycling, Dell is in sync with the European Union's new toxic materials directives described in chapter 3. Under its Restricted Materials Program, Dell began voluntarily phasing out the use of cadmium, hexavalent chromium, mercury, flame retardants, and other chemicals in advance of regulatory requirements, keeping it well ahead of the curve.

Currently, Dell seems to be shifting its strategic emphasis from end-of-life solutions to what it describes as a more holistic, "life cycle approach."[24] Although Dell hasn't launched any green products yet, the company is ahead of competitors like Apple with respect to environmental issues, and its product development group is currently in the process of becoming ISO 14001 certified, meaning that it is undergoing rigorous environmental evaluations. Again, as with Nike, when Dell engineers environmentally benign, yet effective electronics (or other momentous innovations) from the start, and those innovations become invaluable to stakeholders, then it crosses the border.

True to its name, Target Corporation also keeps its eye on a focused area. While it might not be perfect with respect to managing all the labor issues it faces, the company does a remarkable job when it comes to philanthropy. Each week, Target manages to give back $2 million to education, the arts, and social services—three niches that perfectly fit with the brand's youthful, creative, and energetic persona. Whereas so many corporate attempts to win the hearts of Americans through charitable donations seem scatterbrained or awkward, Target's attempts are positively formulaic and truly constructive. For instance, in addition to giving 5 percent of pretax profits to prescreened charities, Target's ongoing Start Something initiative, developed in conjunction with the Tiger Woods Foundation, generates measurable improvements in students' self-esteem, goal-setting abilities, and attitudes toward learning. Target's art and educational grants enable students and families to gain access to things from reading workshops to symphony tickets, while the company's better-known Take Charge of Education program lets Target customers funnel 1 percent of their Target credit card store purchases to the school of their choice. Thus far, that particular program has raised $154 million for over 110,000 schools through 9 million participating Target cardholders. Reportedly, schools have used these unrestricted funds to purchase everything from library books and classroom tools to gymnasium equipment, musical instruments, and drama costumes.

In effect, Target steps in where there is a lack of funding or government support. Its philanthropy programs serve unmet needs and fill gaps in the system, which is one reason why they work so effectively. Another reason Target takes a special interest in kids is because, as the company says, "there is no better place to see a masterpiece than reflected in the eyes of a child; there is no greater return on investment than seeing a child excel; and because a happy home encourages a child to dream and achieve."[25] The company ties its vision of success to that of a future generation's. Idealistic as this may seem, the company's determination is widely acknowledged, as in 2005 alone, Target was named by *Forbes* a "Most Charitable Company" and by *Barron's* as a "Most Respected Company." It also received the National PTA's Commitment to America's Children Award, the Americans for the Arts Corporate Citizenship in the Arts Award, the American Red Cross Good Neighbor Award, and several other accolades.

THE POINT OF PURPOSE

Reviewing results like these, one can't help but notice how adept certain companies are at making a marked difference and how, in general, more companies are increasingly driven by purpose. In fact, we noticed a growing trend in corporate communications: the purpose statement. Unlike the traditional mission statement, which typically focuses on a unique business proposition (e.g., Google's mission "to organize the world's information and make it universally accessible and useful"[26]), or the now commonly used corporate vision statement, which typically captures a business goal (e.g., Mattel's vision, "to be the world's premier toy brands—today and tomorrow"[27])—the purpose statement offers something a little more motivating, even for shareholders.

Making accessible products and services, making money, meeting the needs of consumers today and tomorrow and operating with integrity are *rules* of the game of business. But what's the *point* of the game? The purpose statement tells people what in the world the business is here to do.

For example, Procter & Gamble tells its shareholders: "Our purpose is to improve the everyday lives of the world's consumers. We fulfill this purpose in many ways: through P & G brands, first and foremost, but also through our support of humanitarian, educational and social cause efforts."[28] Similarly, Unilever, the parent company of Ben & Jerry's, tells people that its corporate dedication is to "Add vitality to life." Like P & G, Unilever purports to fulfill its purpose through existing brands— as with Dove's current advertising campaign aimed at raising girls' self-esteem, and also through community outreach initiatives around the world.

Tex Gunning, president of Unilever Bestfoods Asia, is a true believer in the power of corporate purpose, and his group has managed to make something meaningful and substantive out of Unilever's higher calling. Every day Unilever Best Foods Asia reaches out to "bring vitality" to many poor and starving children throughout Asia with a combination of affordable products and philanthropic helping hands. That is both the group's social objective and also its growth model. According to the company, emerging markets like China and India account for 37 percent of Unilever's group sales, and underlying sales in such areas are rising at twice the rate of the overall company. In China alone and under the leadership of Gunning, Unilever's business grew 20 percent in 2004, and the uptrend is expected to continue. Undoubtedly, there is profit to be made in serving a higher purpose, particularly in emerging markets, but for Gunning, this isn't the pot of gold at the end of the rainbow. The larger reward, in addition to the positive societal impact, is the personal meaning that purpose brings to the people working in his group. "We as individuals should entirely integrate our personal lives and our search for meaning with our business lives," he says. "Businesses with a meaningful intent will bring meaning to the lives of their employees . . . then, we'll only need half the policies, half the training, half the values statements that are usually needed because people will be living out their deepest values everywhere in their lives."[29]

Reading insights like this made us think twice about our own analysis. Perhaps whether or not gray companies barely passed or are poised to pass the litmus test is immaterial in the wider scheme of things. The important issue is that purpose is having an incrementally positive affect on each of these companies, infusing them with meaning and direction, and diminishing the need for extraneous rules and regulations. Through the pursuit of purpose, each of these companies comes to terms with its past and also grows progressively self-directed. Each turns into more of a whole as individual thoughts, strategies, and efforts get organized, and everyone begins working toward the same central goal. That central goal becomes the dominant force for transformation. The next skill is to surrender to the purpose and allow the change process to completely unfold. For the optimal results to manifest, all major engines must be powered by purpose, and yet, at the same time, the company must allow itself the freedom and flexibility to experiment with the purpose in the various ways that suit it best.

Brainstorm: Identifying Your Company's Higher Purpose

1: Set Intent
  a. Which side (for or against corporate responsibility) is the company really on?
  b. What are the worst results that the company creates for stakeholders? (Externalities)
  c. Can the company commit to stop creating these? (If so, then when?)
  d. What ideal results does the company desire to create for stakeholders? (Highest goals)
  e. How do team members envision effectively generating these desirable results? (List all possible ways, regardless of current know-how)

2: Then Purpose
  f. What was the original founding philosophy of the company?
  g. Has the company grown apart from its original founding philosophy? (If yes, then how so?)
  h. What does the company stand for today?
  i. What principles does the company hold most dear?
  j. What stakeholders are influenced by the company's activities? (Prioritize)
  k. Besides make money, what is the company here to do?
  l. How would society be worse off without the company?
  m. What value does the company provide that others can't or don't? (Core strengths)
  n. How can the company best apply its core strengths to solve or approach items b or d above?
  o. Conversely, how can the company best apply its strengths to solve a critical social or environmental problem relevant to item j above?
  p. Distill the answers to all of the above down to a meaningful action statement that encapsulates the company's higher purpose and embodies its ultimate value proposition.

(See purpose statement examples in the following chapters.)

6:

Transcend and Include

Evolution is a process of transcendence, which incorporates what went before
and then adds incredibly novel components.
—KEN WILBER IN *A BRIEF HISTORY OF EVERYTHING*

Many companies, as they increase in size, fall into the trap of abandoning their roots and lowering overall quality. This chapter is about the opposite phenomena: that of good growth. Good growth occurs when companies experiment with making better things in better ways, leading to progressive improvements in stakeholder prosperity, nourishment, happiness, safety, and the like. Companies in this transcendent and inclusive phase seize enormous market opportunities by ingeniously leveraging their greatest strengths. As a result of good growth, such companies become measurably healthier as they gradually increase their reach, significance, and influence.

DuPont has been locked into the good growth cycle, also known as sustainable growth, for well over a decade. DuPont makes industry-grade chemicals, not crunchy granola bars. It is in the process of transcendence and inclusion but is not a company without blemish.

In 2004, air carcinogens released by DuPont rose a hefty 25 percent over the prior year, while hazardous waste rose 7 percent. In 2005, the company settled an ongoing matter with the U.S. Environmental Protection Agency (EPA) involving four counts of reporting violations filed under the Toxic Substances Control Act and relating to the chemical compound perfluorooctanoic acid (PFOA), which is used to make products marketed under the Teflon brand name. "We still have far to go. There are many ways in which we need to improve," concedes Dawn Rittenhouse, DuPont's director of sustainable development. Nevertheless, DuPont is a High-Purpose Company.

DuPont passes our litmus test because despite its shortcomings, its investments in good growth permeate most every aspect of its business and because those investments yield triple bottom-line returns so substantial, so clear and measurable, that they prompt the company to continually reinvest. If DuPont stopped investing in good growth, its overall quality as a company and medium- to long-term financial performance would greatly suffer. DuPont literally *cannot afford* to stop investing in good growth, while its degree of good growth relies on its ability to serve its higher purpose. Similarly, the more and better DuPont serves its higher purpose, the more the world benefits. Based on the company's innovations, contributions, and strategic plan, society would be significantly worse off without DuPont.

To be specific, DuPont owes its high-purpose status to its pioneering "zero injuries, illnesses, and incidents" approach to safety; its "zero waste and zero emissions" commitment to the environment; and its history of meeting or exceeding its own performance goals in the majority of these areas. Its high-purpose status is also due to its rigorous method of "continuously improving processes, practices and products" and to the *billions* of dollars in shareholder value it has thus far generated from socially and environmentally advantageous scientific developments.

These include bio-derived chemicals, biofuels, and high-performance polymers—as well as numerous products and services. DuPont Safety Resources help enable global businesses to operate injury free; Bullet-proof Kevlar has helped to save thousands of law enforcement officials' lives; and heat-resistant Nomex has helped to save countless firefighters' lives. On the environmental front, Avaunt, a low toxicity insecticide, allows poor farmers in drought-prone nations to protect their crops; Sorona, a fabric derived partially from corn sugar is both eco-friendly and durable; and Tyvek Home Wrap, a sealed roof system, saves sub-stantial energy costs and also reduces carbon dioxide emissions. It is with technologies and products such as these that Charles Holliday, DuPont's chairman and CEO, forges an integral piece of the company's future. He tells shareholders:

> We have the choice to view major societal concerns like climate change, fossil fuel energy use, the impacts of chemicals to hu-man health and the environment, and the introduction of new technologies such as nanotechnology as things that we must defend. Or we can see them as opportunities to create solutions that not only improve our bottom line but also create tremen-dous benefit for society. We have chosen to see these as opportu-nities and to use these to drive our business growth. . . . We are on a journey to transform DuPont into a more sustainable com-pany. We are doing it not only because it is the right thing to do, but also because it is our core strategy to grow the company.[1]

DuPont exists, Holliday explains, "to create sustainable solutions essential to a better, safer, healthier life for people everywhere."[2] The concepts "better, safer, healthier" signify DuPont's higher purpose—its desired meaning and effect on the world at large—and this higher purpose plays out in tangible ways almost anywhere you look, from the culture inside DuPont to the nature of shareholder communications to the discovery methods used to unleash the firm's latest scientific break-throughs.

MEASURES OF CORPORATE HEALTH

In September 1999, following Holliday's initial announcement to the world that he would dedicate vast company resources to sustainable growth, the *Economist* published an article entitled "DuPont's Punt," which read: "[Holliday's] environmental goals, which include shifting to non-depletable inputs, reduction of greenhouse gas emissions, while maintaining returns on investor's capital in the high teens, is subject to much criticism . . . [A DuPont rival] thinks of voluntary environmental investments as a cost, and says it is naïve to see it as a source of profits . . . Salomon Smith Barney, an Investment Bank, does not really see the point of the green initiatives." The article concluded with the statement, "If Mr. Holliday wants to convince the world that DuPont is becoming green, perhaps he should consider living downwind from its dirtiest smokestack."[3]

Today, Holliday and his shareholders must chuckle, or at least smirk, all the way to the bank. In addition to achieving a myriad of intangible benefits related to the pursuit of purpose, such as happier and more motivated workers and a far better public image (DuPont was recently selected as one of *Fortune* magazine's prized Blue Ribbon companies), the company also reached multiple major milestones since 1999. Each of these milestones is a result of DuPont's "better, safer, healthier" purpose; each is an indicator of the company's ever-increasing health, while each translates into improved financial value.

- **Measure 1: Healthier people**. DuPont is one of the safest companies in the world. It was the first industrial corporation to embrace a "zero injuries" culture in the early 1990s and has since then operated with the belief that all workplace accidents can be prevented.

"Although we know we can't achieve the zero goal overnight, it translates into a commitment to learn from every mishap and to work in each location to complete one day, one week, one month at a time without injury," says Rittenhouse. "The best measure of our degree of success is the rate of improvement." Since the 1990s Du-Pont's global injury rate has steadily dropped, so that in 2005 it was less than half of what it was in 2000. The company also counts near-term progress, as its overall injury rate declined from 1.358 to 1.190 between 2004 and 2005, representing a 12 percent improvement. But what's more interesting is how DuPont views injuries overall: "We're not just counting injuries in terms of major workplace incidents," says Rittenhouse. "We're also taking into account ergonomic issues and accidents that occur offsite, at home or on the road. We're promoting total safety and accident prevention." Du-Pont weaves safety into everything from employee and management performance evaluations to pay progression and career promotions. This, Rittenhouse explains, is essential, because it establishes a precedent that translates into improved performance and productivity, employee well-being and lowered risk.

- **Measure 2: Healthier processes**. Although the *Economist* questioned DuPont's 1999 vow to reduce greenhouse gas emissions by 65 percent below 1990 levels by 2010 while keeping energy use flat, the company exceeded both of these goals. By 2003, DuPont's emissions were already 72 percent below 1990 levels, and by 2006, the company also cut its energy use to 7 percent below 1990 levels and derived 17 percent of its revenues from nondepletable or green resources. "During the decade of the 1990s, we improved our environmental footprint by about 60 percent, and shareholder value increased by nearly 340 percent," DuPont chief financial officer Gary Pfeiffer told shareholders in a 2000 speech. "I will not try to convince you of the mathematical causality of those two facts. I would suggest for your consideration that they are more than coincidental."[4] Today, DuPont is engaged in emissions trading via the Chicago Climate Exchange, the UK Emissions Trading Scheme, and Canada's emerging trading system in order to help it reach its greenhouse gas targets in a cost-effective manner. In addition to preventing eleven metric tons of carbon dioxide from entering the atmosphere, DuPont's environmental efforts have thus far saved shareholders more than $2 billion in costs. Overall, the company's increasingly strategic approach to becoming cleaner and leaner enables shareholders to calculate the link between these two variables for themselves.

- **Measure 3: Healthier products**. "The cornfields of today could be the oil fields of tomorrow," says Holliday in a sound bite that characterizes DuPont's latest product development philosophy. Whereas in the 1990s, the question was how to make existing DuPont products more efficiently, today, bold thinking leads the way as the company engineers the right kinds of things from the onset. In the following section, some of DuPont's most significant new technologies and products are featured, along with the unique innovation process they were born from. For now, it's worth mentioning that in a November 2005 presentation delivered to shareholders entitled "Actions to Increase Shareholder Value," DuPont senior executives conveyed "clear [financial] momentum" brought on by new products like the previously mentioned Sorona, Avaunt, and Tyvek. The report indicated that overall, new products that improved "core value performance" and that are in line with the company's "better, safer, healthier" purpose accounted for 30 percent of the company's total sales. In a separate 2005 announcement, Holliday conveyed his optimism over future "better, safer, healthier" revenue streams by saying: "We are pursuing market opportunities for products to meet the climate challenge . . . We are broadly moving our operations away from reliance on fossil fuels and raw materials and increasingly toward renewables . . . We are leading a research process that will convert the entire corn plant into bio-derived chemicals, like Bio-PDO, and biofuels, like ethanol. The integrated biorefinery will create a new business model for sustainable production of chemicals, fuels and energy."[5] Though not every product that DuPont currently sells is better, safer, and healthier for the world, more are, and that is the decided direction in which the company's resources are moving.

- **Measure 4: Healthier projections**. It might seem peculiar to suggest that a measure of corporate health is the existence of the right kinds of measures. This idea was implied in a previous chapter, and DuPont demonstrates the notion on a few levels. First, there is the zero metric. When DuPont aims for zero waste, it effectively aims for 100 percent product. The closer DuPont gets to achieving zero waste, the more of the resources it buys to make products actually gets sold as products. Similarly, when DuPont aims for zero injuries and incidents or zero downtime, it says yes to 100 percent safety and 100 percent uptime. DuPont's own self-imposed projections encourage it to redefine excellence, not simply achieve good enough or best in class. As it stands, DuPont might not have reached its zero goals yet, let alone its longer-term vision of becoming fully restorative to society, but the company is aiming for interim milestones between now and 2010. These milestones are tangible, deliverable, and in line with the company's higher purpose. According to Holliday himself, these milestones include: saving the life or reducing serious injury to 1 million people; being recognized as among the top three enablers of human connectivity worldwide; being recognized as among the top two enablers of healthy, safe, affordable food; and deriving 25 percent of company revenues from nondepletable resources. "We view these goals as major opportunities for DuPont to create more value for our shareholders," says Holliday. "They also challenge the people of DuPont to create a more sustainable company that will provide tremendous and measurable societal value."[6] Again, design is the first signal of human intention, and at present, DuPont's scientists are at work engineering the company's future reality around "better, safer, healthier" goals.

CONSCIENTIOUS INNOVATION

In 1903, DuPont's scientists worked mostly with black powder. Their charter was to research cellulose chemistry in order to improve the power and efficiency of explosives. By the mid-1900, DuPont's objectives had changed. The company sought to become a world leader in the chemical and materials industry. "We transitioned into using technology to enter new markets," explains Rittenhouse. Using cellulose chemistry and new technologies, DuPont's scientists developed basic cellophane. "That development basically launched the packaging industry," she says. During this same time period, DuPont's researchers also invented nylon, the world's first synthetic fiber; neoprene, the world's first synthetic rubber; and also Teflon and spandex, two ingredients found somewhere in nearly every American home.

Today, DuPont's scientists are working toward a new objective, but as Rittenhouse notes, this objective was born from a gradual process: "When the vision to move in a 'better, safer, healthier' direction was made, it wasn't like someone from downtown corporate headquarters suddenly handed down the decision. That was the direction in which we had been moving for twenty-five years or so, and it was a matter of committing to that direction and seeing if we could drive the momentum even faster." Rittenhouse says that today, the official 'better, safer, healthier' purpose gives DuPont's scientists, and everyone else in the company for that matter, a structure and a clear end goal. "When our official charter of making 'better, safer, healthier' solutions came about seven ago, our scientists had already been experimenting with biotechnology for some time. But with the new commitment, we started thinking about how we could combine the benefits of biotechnology with the benefits of chemistry, for example, in order to create new products that make real differences in everyday life."

A key part of the company's ongoing research and development process is the task of understanding exactly *how* to make the biggest differences in everyday life around the world. To fulfill its purpose and retain a competitive edge, DuPont's research team, housed in the company's famous Experimental Station, make it their job to unearth unmet societal and environmental needs around the world. "We have a process that involves seeking out new business opportunities," explains Rittenhouse. "Our goal is to go out and determine; 'What do our customers need?' 'What does society need?' and then, knowing where the company's core competencies lie, we combine these factors in order to draw the next generation of research and development. We also have people out in the marketplace trying to make our current products better, safer, and healthier. For example, in the last few years, we've identified emerging energy efficiency needs in Europe driven by the Kyoto Protocol, and we've modified DuPont Tyvek, our sealed roofing system, to better accommodate those needs."

Rittenhouse describes market adaptation. DuPont is responding to the changing conditions and needs of the global marketplace. Its products do not lag behind market needs, and also, they are not too far in front of them either. DuPont's current portfolio is incredibly innovative and forward thinking, yet in sync with the world around it. Unlike so many other companies driven by technology, DuPont does not develop its technologies in isolation, then invent applications for those technologies, and then fabricate needs for those applications and push the packaged technology applications into the marketplace through aggressive marketing. Rather, the company first looks to the market for major unmet needs or potential applications, and then, using its existing technologies and assets, it forms new technologies and applications that meet the demand. In its search for unmet needs, DuPont dives for the deeply rooted and substantive issues—such as malnutrition, poverty, drought, climate change, energy inefficiency, and safety—all problems that cannot be solved immediately and that are substantial enough to nourish business performance over time. Thus, both the social value and the commercial viability are built into many of DuPont's "better, safer, healthier" solutions from the start, and the ratio of new product success improves, because a larger proportion of DuPont's new products respond to a vital demand curve.

In short, many of DuPont's products are simply more necessary and therefore of more value to society and shareholders.

PURPOSEFUL BEST-SELLERS

Not too far into the future, DuPont says, its latest high-performance polymers and biomaterials could lead to foods that help prevent diseases and brittle bones, smart materials that can adjust performance on their own, microorganisms that produce biodegradable products, and innovative fabrics that can be used for personal (safety) protection.[7] For the time being, however, many of DuPont's "better, safer, healthier" advancements are already making a measurable difference in people's lives, generating revenue, accelerating company growth, and furthering worthy causes.

Safety is one area that DuPont is widely known for, and DuPont's Safety and Protection division is the company's fastest growing business unit, with $5 billion in annual sales. DuPont sells a range of safety products, including bullet-resistant Kevlar, fire- and heat-resistant Nomex as well as contamination-proof medical packing and other innovations. Through DuPont Safety Resources, the company also sells training and knowledge about how to better promote workplace well-being and establish injury- and incident-free work environments. "In our view that's totally relevant to our purpose because we're helping to reduce deaths and serious injuries around the world," says Rittenhouse. Similarly, DuPont's Security and Solutions unit, a related business, offers lifesaving innovations like its bullet- and bomb-resistant security glass treated with Butacite glazing technology. It also provides safety infrastructure consulting services to clients including the U.S. Department of Homeland Security. In DuPont's *2004 Sustainable Growth Progress Report*, the company highlights these business units and views security and safety as among the world's top societal concerns.

The impact of chemicals on human health is another of DuPont's chief concerns, and this issue is addressed by the company's $6.6 billion Performance Materials division. That unit recently developed Bio-PDO, an innovative polymer made from corn that uses less energy to manufacture and also produces less waste. "This polymer was born when we discovered how to marry biological and chemical processes," explains Rittenhouse. "Originally, we started by asking: 'How do we combine our technologies to provide a better value and more innovative product?' But later we realized that the end result was not just about a slightly better value or a cleaner manufacturing process. We developed Sorona, a totally unique new material. This discovery led us to ask ourselves: 'If we can make a new material from biology instead of chemistry, then what else can we do?' " Bio-PDO and Sorona represented more to DuPont than an eco-friendly cachet. Rather, the innovations marked a new era and signified huge potential. "We determined that using the Bio-PDO polymer, we could also make a carpet that is naturally environmentally friendly, naturally stain resistant, that takes less energy to make, that produces less waste, and that doesn't require any chemical treatment. That alone, we think, consumers are going to be very interested in," says Rittenhouse. "The advantages of developments like these have so many layers of benefits, so many components to them, which is why we're so excited about the new technologies."

Other DuPont groups are equally thrilled by their latest discoveries, which hold similar promise by addressing global issues like poverty and ecology. DuPont's Crop Protection unit, which competes with Monsanto and is part of DuPont's Agriculture division, a $6.2 billion business, is guided by the motto "A growing partnership with nature." That group recently developed Avaunt, a low-toxicity insecticide specifically designed to meet the needs of some of the world's poorest farmers. "For the West African farmer, *Helicoverpa armigera* caterpillars head the list of problem insects," explains the company. The insects can destroy crops and devastate farmer's incomes. Avaunt is designed to counter the problem and be affordable by being applied in low doses and used with less water. It comes in small packaging that, according to DuPont, "can be destroyed without harming people or the environment—crucial attributes in this market." Statistics collected by DuPont indicate that farmers' cotton yields increased 15 to 20 percent after using Avaunt. "[This is] an extraordinary benefit in poor countries where cotton fiber exports represents the principal source of foreign currency."[8]

Other DuPont divisions, including DuPont Electronics and DuPont Fuel Cells, tap into serious issues, including energy inefficiency, fossil fuel use, and climate change. Various of the products and technologies spun out of these groups offer real social and environmental benefits as well as great market opportunities for DuPont.

"We can't say that all of our product portfolio is 'better, safer, healthier,' or that every new product we design is designated to be environmentally sustainable," says Rittenhouse, who explains that DuPont is constantly challenged to meet the needs of customers and wider society. "The needs of these two groups don't always cross over," she acknowledges. "What we can say is that 'better, safer, healthier' are our aspirations, and that we are always looking at where society is going and what demands exist not just today but in the future. Our success absolutely depends on our ability to use our technologies to meet changing world needs. This is a journey and we are not 'there' yet."

THE CYCLE OF SELF-IMPROVEMENT

The companies that pass our litmus test share an attribute: a reliance on innovative and responsive products and services. As was previously mentioned, so many companies tend to react to the corporate responsibility trend by simply slapping "green" labels on existing brands and products. However, like DuPont, the companies in this chapter and the next go steps further. They reverse engineer new technologies, products, and services around deep-seated social and environmental needs and problems. Therefore, given their occasionally imperfect track records, High-Purpose Companies aren't really best described as the world's most responsible corporate citizens. Rather, it is more accurate to portray them as the world's most *responsive* corporate citizens.

High-Purpose Companies answer to changing human needs; to shifts in the economy, society, and the environment; and to emerging trends. They prepare themselves for inevitable turns and are the first to market with progressive solutions that are vital and necessary, not frivolous or easily replicated. High-Purpose Companies make themselves *invaluable* to society—and to all stakeholders. It is not that they seek to serve society at the expense of shareholder interests, as the anticorporate responsibility curmudgeons would have you believe. On the contrary, it is that they understand that in order to continue to serve shareholder interests, they must better meet the growing demands of society. That is precisely *why* they do so well.

There is also the matter of *how* they do so well. At this Transcend and Include phase, High-Purpose Companies move into a continual cycle of self-improvement, where the rewards associated with serving a higher purpose spike significantly. This is chiefly because, as explained above, they are *selling* products and services that stem from purpose. Whereas the chief business benefit experienced by most companies invested in corporate responsibility, particularly those investing the bulk of their dollars in environmental management systems and the like, is cost savings, High-Purpose Companies advance beyond this. By selling responsive products and services, they generate triple bottom-line returns that are far greater than what could be achieved through any other permutation of corporate responsibility activities. What companies make and market has an enormous impact on the way people live, the impact that companies have on the earth, and the return they generate for shareholders. Ultimately, if companies can generate great *profit* and *growth* plus cost savings by being environmentally and socially responsive, then the whole system will be far better off. The triple bottom-line results presently produced by High-Purpose Companies indicate that this is indeed true.

For years, various corporate responsibility experts have suggested that the best CR programs work when companies align their philanthropic goals with their business goals. However, to suggest that a company like DuPont—which has used its purpose to spur new business models and sequential new technologies in addition to evolutionary products and services—has merely aligned its philanthropic and business goals is a vast understatement. In entering into the cycle of self-improvement, DuPont's "philanthropic" goals have largely merged with its business goals—to the point where they no longer qualify *as* philanthropic goals. Rather, they are now business goals with a purposeful edge. Also, DuPont is now engaged in something other than what would normally qualify as corporate responsibility. The entire business innovates in a new way.

Based on the mechanisms DuPont has built for itself, the better the company meets its "better, safer, healthier" purpose, the better it meets shareholder expectations. The better it meets shareholder expectations, the more it invests in "better, safer, healthier" solutions.

Those who would be skeptical of the argument that companies *should* seek to profit from their responsible endeavors might do themselves a favor and attempt to think broadly, beyond what we narrowly

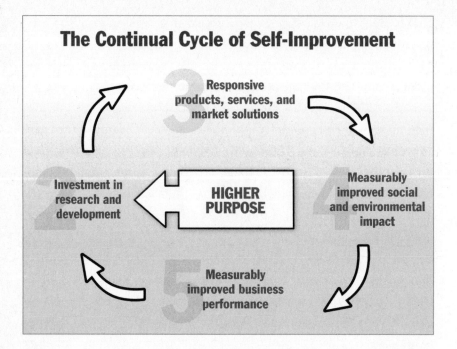

The Continual Cycle of Self-Improvement

frame as "corporate responsibility." High-Purpose Companies see past this limited notion, as they are in touch with wider needs, contexts, and conditions. They invest in corporate responsibility not only because it makes them money, but because the world needs them to. There is a great demand for what they do. Correspondingly, there is enormous value in what they provide.

Therefore, High-Purpose Companies do not abandon the system of capitalism. They do not reject basic business principles, nor do they do disservice to their shareholders. They join no bandwagon either. Contrary to what the *Economist*'s Clive Crook said in his January 22, 2005, article, "The Good Company," these most progressive and responsive firms absolutely, positively do not opt to "worry less about profits and become socially responsible instead."

Rather, High-Purpose Companies transcend and include. They simply integrate incredibly novel components into their existing system or infrastructure. They innovate and keep a few steps ahead of market forces. In fact, owing to their success, they partially direct market forces. They simultaneously play by the rules and advance the ball, as any business worth its higher share price does. This should not be a controversial issue, or a notion that causes the old capitalist guard to get up in arms and launch confrontational debates.

The corporate responsibility debate is, in fact, passé. As the evidence presented here and elsewhere blatantly suggests, we as a society would do well to move past the "good company" versus "bad company" labels because those labels aren't particularly useful or constructive. They don't help us to learn anything new or achieve anything worthwhile. Similarly, the business case for corporate responsibility is equally obvious, because corporate responsibility is not a narrow philanthropic practice area. Rather, it is a broad concept that applies to a level of preparedness for what presently exists within and around the business pipeline and, more important, for what is coming down the business pipeline. Corporate responsibility means taking responsibility for a company's past, present, and future behavior. It means being responsive to conditions that affect a business, rather than remaining impervious to them. Who in their right mind would suggest that businesspeople ought to ignore the impact their companies have on the world; the trends, needs, and market conditions that affect their stakeholders; or the avoidable risks that could harm shareholder interests? These are the three key areas that encompass the *real* corporate responsibility. As was mentioned in the prologue, it is not about charity. It is about change. And coping with change requires not just a conscience, but also a level of competence.

The marketplace has indeed transitioned. A major shift is under way. We are exactly where the "environmental economists," such as Bill McDonough, Bill McKibben, Amory Lovins, Michael Braungart, and Paul Hawken, predicted we would be decades ago. We are at the end of an old economic cycle, moving into a new one. We are currently entering a new economic S curve, which both McDonough and Hawken coin "the next industrial revolution," and which author Daniel Pink describes as "the conceptual age." Regardless of how the new era is branded, it is signaled by an enhanced creatvity coupled with an awareness of how all things relate, a relentless exploration of new ideas and solutions to old problems, and, as Hawken and McDonough emphasize in their depictions, it is guided by the laws of nature that were avoided or ignored during the last economic cycle. (The new cycle we are entering into was briefly described in chapter 3.)

High-Purpose Companies represent the breed of business that is particularly savvy about settling into the new S. They have made the leap to synchronize with budding conditions. High-Purpose Companies embrace the change. They are the *early adopters*, the alphas of the modern business world.

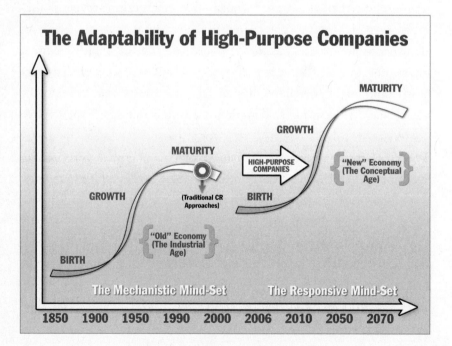

The Adaptability of High-Purpose Companies

CREATIVE LEAPS

Toyota is way ahead. The company saw and managed to respond to the new S miles ago—before Ford and well before Nissan, DaimlerChrysler, and General Motors. This is remarkable for a company that, as *Fortune* magazine's Alex Taylor recently pointed out in his article "The Birth of the Prius," has long been characterized as a " 'fast follower,' a risk-averse company in which process—the famous Toyota lean production system—trumped product."[9] As Taylor makes clear, Toyota is at once a conservative, slow-to-change, and yet incredibly innovative firm. In contrast, over the past fifty years, the American automotive industry could be characterized as conservative, resistant to change, and slow to innovate. That disparity explains a lot about Toyota's current lead in the market. And now Toyota is picking up momentum. In the process of developing the iconic Prius, Toyota broke its own traditions and developed some invaluable new ones.

Toyota found its purpose in the world, which is to "make sustainable mobility a reality." Just like DuPont, the company's purpose is relevant to shareholders, in line with its greatest strengths, and vitally necessary to the world. Of this the company says: "Toyota is acutely aware that the significant social and economic benefits of the automobile cannot be sustained forever simply by producing more vehicles. Continued vehicle production at current levels will congest our cities and foul our air."[10]

To offset further damage, Toyota commits its engineers to making constant quality improvements. It takes a dramatically different approach to quality than has, say, competitor DaimlerChrysler in years past. Toyota considers all the implications of its decisions and defines quality in multiple dimensions: quality of goals, quality of ideas, quality of team input, quality of design, quality of technologies, quality in manufacturing, quality of environmental impact, quality of social impact, quality in meeting consumer expectations, and so forth. The company measures these things, and more importantly, Toyota practices *kaizen*, setting tough benchmarks and striving for continual improvement in each of these areas. The output of this multidimensional focus on quality translates to exceptional processes, products, and market performance. As Taylor observes in his article, "Toyota is becoming a double threat: the world's finest manufacturer and a truly great innovator."[11]

The Prius, Toyota's most ingenious creative leap and one that it considers to be its "most notable environmental success,"[12] was born when the company allowed itself to think big picture and allow its best people, processes, and technologies to come together to uncover just the right solution. It was apparently a scary, painful process as there were huge obstacles to overcome. There were major differences of opinion between Toyota's engineering and sales teams as to whether hybrid was the right solution to the problems of fuel inefficiency and fouled air. There was the concern that the final output would be too expensive to produce and sell. Once the decision to go hybrid was made, Toyota's president, Hiroshi Okuda, decided to move up the go-to-market deadline by a year, giving the design team only twenty-four months to perfect the finished product. Eighty mechanical system design permutations were evaluated before the company settled on the right one.

Toyota launched the Prius two months ahead of schedule in Japan in October 1997, and Japanese consumers loved it. Forecasts were adjusted, and Toyota's production of the Prius for the Japanese market doubled to two thousand vehicles per month. In July 2000, the first-generation Prius hit the United States, but the American press was less than receptive. Two *Car and Driver* writers gave the vehicle this sluggish review: "The gas pedal is just an electronic link advising the computer how fast you would like to go—someday. It acquires super-sensitivity at mid-throw, resulting in annoying power surges in what should otherwise be steady-state cruising. Mash it at inappropriate times, say in neutral, and the engine simply ignores you."[13] But consumers didn't care. They liked the car's other assets—its environmentally conscious association, greater fuel efficiency, lower emissions, and new technology. Cameron Diaz and Leonardo DiCaprio each bought one.

Then came the second-generation Prius in 2003, a car now synonymous with the term *hybrid*, although Honda had its versions on the market before Toyota. The redesigned Prius cast Toyota in an excessively favorable light with movie stars, technophiles, environmentalists, and average folks alike. By 2004, Toyota had sold 120,000 Prius vehicles. People fell in love with the car's attributes, as *Wired* magazine reports: "Prius owners can make TiVo users and Mac addicts seem blasé. A typical newsgroup posting from one of hundreds of customers who frequent fan sites like PriusChat.com: "This is the greatest car ever invented!"[14]

The love affair with Prius is mutual, as Toyota is currently in phase two of its strategy to move the car and its mother technology, Hybrid Synergy Drive (HSD), into every North American driveway. In this second phase, the company's strategic priority has shifted from creating mass appeal to enabling mass accessibility. Currently, Toyota offers five hybrid vehicles, the bestselling Prius, the Highlander Hybrid, the Lexus RX 400h luxury hybrid, and the newly introduced Lexus GS 450h hybrid luxury sedan and Camry Hybrid. Since 1997, Toyota has sold over 500,000 of these vehicles. By the early 2010s, Toyota says that it hopes to radically increase that number to a million hybrids sold each year. In order to achieve this sales goal, Toyota plans to "halve the cost of hybrid powertrains as early as possible," thus making HSD, or "sustainable mobility," affordable to a much wider percentage of the population.[15]

Toyota is leveraging the assets of its newest products and technologies to the fullest extent—making their benefits widely known to customers, environmentalists, and society at large. Recent statistics released by the company reveal that as of December 2005, Toyota's HSD technology has saved Americans more than 100 million gallons of gasoline. In addition to lowering fuel consumption, Toyota also reported that its

Prius, Toyota, and Lexus brand hybrid vehicles have also prevented nearly 900,000 metric tons of carbon dioxide from being emitted into the atmosphere; saved 4 million barrels of crude oil from being consumed; and checked more than 3 million pounds of smog-forming gases from being created.

Carlos Ghosn, CEO of Toyota rival Nissan, recently told *Fortune* magazine: "Some of our competitors say they are doing things for the benefit of humanity. Well, we are in a business, and we have a mission of creating value."[16] We sincerely hope that Nissan will do just that. And in the process of creating value for Nissan shareholders, we hope that Nissan will perceive the multipronged value that Toyota creates and the implications that such value generates for the rest of the automotive market.

Toyota isn't plugging itself as an environmentally conscientious player for the sake of appealing to the likes of Cameron Diaz and Leonardo DiCaprio. "We're at the edge of making the internal combustion engine similar to regular film for the camera,"[17] says Ernest Bastien, vice president of Toyota's vehicle operations group, making an obvious reference to the influence of digital photography. Five years ago, it might have seemed inconceivable that the company best poised to overshoot GM's global vehicle output is on a mission to "make sustainable mobility a reality" and render the combustion engine obsolete. But that's exactly what the company intends to do. Toyota's success is making believers out of doubters and causing disruption within its class. Reportedly, Volkswagen, Audi, Porsche, DaimlerChrysler, and perhaps most notably, GM, have followed Toyota's proven success with hybrid programs of their own. Five years from now, history will tell how Toyota's creative leap helped to move not just a single company to the head of its class, but an entire industry into the modern age.

General Electric is another leading-edge company that follows a similar opportunistic formula and causes competitors to stir through purposeful and disruptive advancements. Like Toyota, GE sets its eyes on the future and sees green in all forms. In transforming his $152 billion conglomerate into an eco-effective leader, GE chairman and CEO Jeffrey Immelt has a clear objective in mind. In a May 2005 speech given at the George Washington University School of Business, he made that motive widely known:

> We commit to increase our sales and profits based on this initiative. Let's be clear about this. GE's obligation is first and foremost to our shareholders. The GE stock is the most widely held security in the world. We have some five million shareholders, about 40 percent of whom are individuals. And we're investing in an environmentally cleaner technology because we believe it will increase our revenue, our value, and our profits.
>
> We're launching ecomagination not because it's trendy or moral, but because it will accelerate our growth and make us more competitive. Today our revenue of ecomagination products is about $10 billion. This number will double to $20 billion by 2010, generating organic growth of 15 percent. Our revenue growth will take place across the company in Energy, Transportation, Water, Consumer Products, and Materials. It will also help our global growth. Europe has been a leader in renewable energy. They've set clear goals: 12 percent renewable energy by the year 2010. China offers immense business opportunities. Of the twenty most polluted cities in the world, fifteen are in China. The Chinese government has set aside $85 billion for environmental spending. This will require substantial commitments in new power-generating technology and desalination, so GE investors will be rewarded by our leadership in ecomagination.[18]

Immelt's message must have caused GE's competitors to stir, because in it, he wasn't talking about joining a global bandwagon. He was talking about dominating global markets. Immelt was laying down an aggressive growth strategy. And anyone who is competing with GE knows that when that company sets an agenda, it delivers and others follow. Immelt's speech received a great deal of publicity. But like Wal-Mart's latest environmental pledge, it turns out that Immelt's speech along with GE's much celebrated ecomagination campaign are just gestures. They are frosting on the cake. It's what is behind them that is significant and in GE's case, something to behold.

On top of having established trade relationships with powerful foreign nations that represent potentially huge contracts for the company, GE has a diverse array of proprietary environmental technologies and products in the marketplace, right now. With GE's full capacities in place, and with the company working toward seizing the environmental opportunities that Immelt reveals, results would surely appear—almost instantaneously. And to date, they have.

Consider clean power, one of GE's fastest growing business divisions. GE Energy's Wind Power unit increased its revenues by 300 percent between the day it opened its doors for business in 2002 and year-end 2005, when its annual sales reached $2 billion. The company touts its highly efficient wind turbine technology, and as a result of that technology, expects revenues to increase by another $2 billion in 2006, making it a dominant player in the fastest-growing segment of the global energy industry and generating enough offshore clean power for millions of people around the world.

GE also capitalizes on water scarcity, a severe problem that affects over a third of the world's population. GE entered the water purification industry only a few years ago, and has already sold $2 billion worth of filtration systems, chemicals, and services. According to the company, by tapping into new sources of water, GE's Water Scarcity solutions remove saline from brackish and seawater—producing fresh, usable water for drinking, irrigation, and industrial uses, which lessens stress on limited sources of fresh water, as well as dependence on environmental

factors, like irregular rainfall. One of GE's ongoing desalination projects in Africa, for instance, will reportedly supply 25 percent of Algeria's
capital city's population with desperately needed drinking water. Going
forward, GE expects the global market for desalination projects to
grow from $4.3 billion in 2005 to $14.1 billion in 2014 and then doubling or even tripling by 2025.[19]

Rather than make its creative leap via one or two central technological developments the way Toyota did, GE makes the best use of its
means and forges ahead via multiple, parallel innovations. Currently,
these parallel innovations manifest in the form of consumer products
like compact fluorescent light bulbs that are 75 percent more energy
efficient and last ten times longer than the average bulb; SmartDis-
pense dishwashers that are 25 percent more efficient than the average
model and could save more than 700,000 tons of dishwashing deter-
gent from being washed down the drain each year; and Profile Har-
mony washers that could conserve enough water to save Americans $1
billion in water bills every year and support total U.S. water consumption for an entire year. On the transportation front, GE's innovations
manifest in the form of the new fuel-efficient GEnx jet engine, which
produces emissions 98 percent below 2008 regulatory standards and,
if airlines replaced twenty of their older twin-aisle aircraft with the
GEnx, could save $5 million in fuel costs annually; GE's Evolution
locomotive, a train that burns 3 percent less fuel, puts out 40 percent
less pollution, and costs 10 percent less to operate than its immediate
predecessor; and, due out in 2007, a 4,400 horsepower, 207-ton hybrid
train that reduces fuel consumption by another 15 percent and emissions by as much as 50 percent compared to the locomotives used today. On the industrial front, GE scientists recently developed Noryl
resin, a recyclable and nontoxic form of wire coating, as well as Lexan
SLX, a new pigment process that eliminates the need for costly emis-
sions-producing automotive paints. GE scientists and engineers are
reportedly at work designing everything from eco-friendly lightweight

plastics to replace the steel in cars to electricity plants that emit nothing but water vapor.

Is GE a perfect company? By no means. One sharp thorn in the side of both Immelt and environmentalists is the legacy the company leaves behind with its ongoing $460 million plan to dredge PCBs from the Hudson River. The start date for the cleanup keeps getting postponed, and the current kickoff isn't slated until 2007. Lots of environmentalists suggest that this tardiness completely contradicts the company's reputed commitment to eco-effectiveness. They also point out that GE has a history of blocking environmental regulations that conflict with the company's interests. For instance, in 2000, GE reportedly asked the U.S. Supreme Court to throw out EPA standards for smog and soot, while in 2003, it lobbied against various other pollution controls.

Has GE faced the truth about the environmental skeletons in its closet? Remember, this is the company that, under previous leadership, reportedly claimed "living in a PCB-laden area is not dangerous."[20] Clearly, the answer would seem to be no. But under the current administration, the tone is different, and the environmental policy is improved. "GE is a 126-year-old company, with facilities across the globe. Many of those facilities began operating at a time when scientific understanding and regulatory requirements were far different from today," the company explains on its global citizenship Website, http://www.ge.com/en/citizenship. "Changing standards and knowledge require that these 'legacy' issues must be addressed. We are currently involved in 87 sites on the Superfund National Priorities List. At many of these sites, GE's involvement is very small. We have sole responsibility at just eight. We have reached agreements with federal and/or state regulators at almost every site about the right way to proceed." Incidentally, GE's "legacy issues" also include additional cleanups at the Housatonic River in Massachusetts and in Rome, Georgia, and amount to hundreds of millions in liability and cleanup costs incurred for GE. The company has proceeded to work with government agencies to address issues and to begin cleanup efforts in all three cases. Although some might see this as a step forward, many consider it too little too late and Immelt himself seems to feel the weight of the company's past on his shoulders. In response to journalistic inquiries about how he can justify GE's new environmental stance in light of the company's polluting legacy, Immelt generally says things like, "I'm not gonna be burdened [going forward] by stuff we did years ago."[21]

According to *Fortune* magazine's 2006 reader poll on the Most Admired Companies in America, GE is prized for its uncanny ability to live in the moment and improve its future rather than reinvent its past. The results of that survey ranked GE at number one—making it the sixth time the company has claimed the top spot in the past ten years. "Why does the world love this company so much?" the magazine asks. "Through the good years and the bad, GE consistently does things the rest only wish they could."[22]

With respect to the company's current forge ahead, we were surprised to see such disparate journalistic headlines such as: "It Was Just My Ecomagination," "GE's Greenwashing," "GE Joins Green Bandwagon," and "Green Electric?"[23] Is it just our imagination, or is there a general lack of understanding and care in drawing distinctions between the diametrically opposed concepts of greenwashing and good growth or bandwagons and behavioral changes? In another pessimistic setup of GE's ecomagination campaign, as presented by the *New York Times* in a December 2005 article entitled: "It's Getting Crowded on the Environmental Bandwagon," one journalist noted, regarding environmental do-goodism, that: "Customers can't buy it. Shareholders can't invest in it. But a growing list of big-name companies (including GE) appear to be spending ever-bigger chunks of their advertising budgets to promote it."[24] To this reporter's opening line, we can only suppose that Immelt himself might respond by saying, "Yes they can. Yes they do. And that's because we're promoting something worthwhile."

There may come a day when journalists and bloggers feel confident enough to avoid reverting to the standard rhetorical clichés and cynicism often used. Not that foolish optimism is the choice option, but certainly the practice of following the money trail—of evaluating where and how a company invests in the beliefs and solutions it purports to uphold, as well as how stakeholders ultimately benefit from those investments—gives one a more accurate read of a company's true colors than a crass judgment call does.

Overall, *what's behind* the ecomagination campaign indicates GE's present and future colors and for that matter, the high-purpose charter. Ecomagination is all about using responsive technologies and innovations to solve serious world problems and, therefore, achieve superior business results. GE's near-term and potential long-term triple bottom-line results are outstanding by any account. The company makes itself invaluable to stakeholders by unlocking its full potential in order to alleviate serious problems like our diminishing domestic oil and natural gas reserves, our continued reliance on foreign sources of energy, the increasing scarcity of natural resources like water, and the unmistakable signs of global climate change. GE, just like DuPont and Toyota, solves such problems as no other company could and thus leaps far, far ahead.

SUBTLE CREATIVE LEAPS

Not all corporate transformations are dramatic, and not all creative leaps are accompanied by glittering campaigns. Many High-Purpose Companies operate under the radar screen, so to speak. John Deere and SC Johnson are two companies that advanced their way up the progression discreetly over the years, although the triple bottom-line benefits produced by both companies are equally as substantial for their respective stakeholders.

As a straight-shooting, no-frills agricultural products company, John Deere isn't much for glossy marketing slogans, and it has yet to pencil an official purpose statement. Despite this, Deere lists commitment as a fundamental value and says, "Along with our other core values of quality, integrity and innovation, commitment—to our customers, our employees and our communities continues to be a cornerstone of our business."[25] In particular, Deere emphasizes supporting the livelihood of farmers and the land on which they depend. That's a tall order, considering that farmers have to keep productive and profitable while the land they cultivate constantly needs to be nurtured, replenished, and protected. Serving both productivity and protection goals meant that Deere had to invent new modes of eco-effectiveness, so it began rolling out notable new technologies in the 1990s.

Deere's initial purpose-driven developments centered primarily on improving machine performance. For instance, one 1999 innovation was a new two-stroke engine that reduced carbon dioxide emissions by 70 percent while improving fuel economy by 30 percent with only a minor cost increase. A subsequent innovation improved operator visibility of Deere's field tractors by 300 percent, as well as increased their overall safety. Later in 2003, Deere began working with partner company Hydrogenics to develop forklifts powered by fuel cells, and then went on to win a Materialica Design Award for its renewable, soy-based material called HarvestForm, which reduces the use of petroleum in the building of agricultural machine parts.

By 2005, Deere's corporate performance counted a range of purposeful products and technologies, from its 2500E Hybrid Tri-Plex lawn mower to its cleaner-running CNG engines to farm equipment both powered by biodiesel and made from corn- and soy-based components. Currently, Deere markets the Timberjack 1490 slash bundler, which bundles tree cutting residue to use as biomass fuel; virtual reality training labs that help operators harvest trees more safely and with less disruption to the environment; forestry products and services that help customers responsibly manage timber resources; and GreenStar AutoTrac global positioning system technologies that help make farming safer and more environmentally friendly. Purpose invades the growing majority of Deere's existing portfolio and product development strategy.

Going forward, Deere is looking into how it can play a bigger role in crucial environmental projects that extend beyond traditional agriculture. The company recently announced plans to invest $8 million in wind energy projects, and expects to invest up to $60 million in the initiative by the end of 2006. Through its investment, Deere created a business unit to provide project development, debt financing, and other services to those farmers interested in harvesting the power of the wind. "John Deere is especially well positioned to support our farm customers in this growing industry," said Robert W. Lane, Deere & Company chairman and chief executive officer. "For generations, the world's most productive farmers have used John Deere equipment to provide food to the world and now, through wind energy, the same farmers can help meet the growing demand for electricity."[26] Deere is the leading manufacturer of agricultural and forestry equipment in the world. Also, it seems, the most forward thinking.

The same thing can be said for S. C. Johnson & Son. One might wonder how a 120-year-old company that markets such creations as Shout, Windex, Mr. Muscle, Raid, and OFF! *could* become purpose driven. The answer is, that company simply followed the guidelines by both engineering new solutions and redesigning old ones around stringent, purposeful goals.

SC Johnson officially entered the sustainability game in 1935, when the company's third-generation family leader, H. F. Johnson Jr., led a flight expedition to Brazil in search of the carnauba palm tree, a sustainable source of wax for the company's products. The ante was upped in 1955 when SC Johnson introduced the world's first environmentally responsible, water-based aerosols. In 1975, SC Johnson was the first company to voluntarily remove chlorofluorocarbons (CFCs) from all its aerosol products—three years before the U.S. mandate—and to this day the company maintains an environmental edge.

"Our vision is to be a world leader in delivering innovative solutions to meet human needs through sustainability principles," the company tells people. Through most of what it does—from social investments and corporate donations to workplace excellence, environmental leadership, improved operational processes, and certainly, through its products—the company intends to promote "global well-being."[27]

SC Johnson clearly comprehends the term *sustainable business*. The language the company uses conveys this. It's not the usual corporate responsibility rhetoric, but rather a demonstration of how systemic connections work:

> *Prosperity and responsibility can coexist. It's our success that enables us to add value and serve the greater good.*
>
> *We create economic value by offering innovative solutions and products to meet unmet needs and establishing new business to create jobs across the globe.*
>
> *We strive for environmental health by increasing our use of environmentally preferred raw materials and seeking cleaner sources of energy to power our operations.*
>
> *We advance social progress by investing in cultural, educational and public health projects that enhance quality of life.*[28]

Our analysis of both SC Johnson's corporate responsibility strategy and its related returns on investment indicate that the company indeed operates on a higher plane. Over the past fifteen years, SC Johnson has taken a deliberate, phased strategic approach. Between 1990 and 1998, the company focused on eco-efficiency, or, reducing the impact it had on the environment. During this time period, the company buttoned up its operations and eliminated over 460 million pounds of waste from products and processes worldwide, resulting in annual cost savings of more than $125 million. It was during this timeframe that the company was honored with the World Environment Center Gold Medal for International Corporate Achievement in Sustainable Development and also became one of the first consumer packaged goods companies to publicly report about its sustainable development programs and policies. After 2000, the company's strategic emphasis turned, and SC Johnson sought to become eco-effective. That is, it began actively sourcing superior materials that are less environmentally damaging in order to make end products that are more in line with the company's global well-being purpose.

In 2001, SC Johnson launched Greenlist, a first-of-its-kind environmental classification system that enables the company to better monitor what it describes as its "total purchase footprint," or the impact of the raw materials used in the company's products on the environment and human health. Greenlist, the company explains, is not about meeting regulatory requirements, but rather about SC Johnson improving its products beyond those requirements and meeting the company's own high standards.

Under the Greenlist system, raw materials are rated as either "good," "better," or "best" by level of toxicity, ultimate biodegradability, nature of source or supplier, and other significant concerns. "Greenlist is actually a process we use to measure, track and advance our products," says Scott Johnson, vice president, Global Environmental and Safety Actions. "We use Greenlist as part of the new product development process. It's also part of the reformulation process, as our products get reformulated at least once every five years. By doing so, in many cases, we are taking an already environmentally responsible product and making it better. We've now applied the Greenlist process to nearly all of the categories that we purchase—currently seventeen product categories." Going forward, Johnson says, the challenge for the company is to determine how to make all of its products totally environmentally sound without sacrificing efficacy and whenever possible, actually improving the product's effectiveness.

Each of SC Johnson's brands, from Glade to Windex, Pledge, Shout, Ziploc, Saran, and even Edge and Raid, use the Greenlist process during formulation. The idea is to move more of the product line to better- and eventually best-rated ingredients over time. The company has essentially boiled down a complex environmental issue to simple terms so that it can be more easily executed by everyone involved in product development within the organization. "Not everyone has to be trained in this," explains Johnson. "We've systemized it so that anyone working here can call an ingredient up on our formula system and get a simple number: 1 for good, 2 for better, or 3 for best. Our corporate goal is to get our overall average score higher, so it's easier for our scientists to start working with a 2- or 3-rated material from the start. You don't need to be an environmental toxicologist to understand Greenlist. You just need to know what 1, 2, and 3 are." Johnson explains that when the company first implemented Greenlist, between 2000 and 2001, the average baseline score for all of SC Johnson's raw materials was 1.12. By 2005, the company had achieved a score of 1.41, which was the goal for the 2007–2008 fiscal year.

The impact that the Greenlist system has had on the company's overall operations is great: "This is affecting all of our products via every raw material that's in them," says Johnson. "The process itself has helped us to set higher goals and led us to move towards the 'best' end and to reduce our total environmental footprint. As we reformulate and put superior products in the market, we're constantly looking at ways of reducing the total purchase footprint of the company."

Like all High-Purpose Companies, SC Johnson writes its environmental strategy into its corporate strategy, and no one group within SC Johnson specifically owns the environmental charter. "We have a full environmental plan, and it is only one of seven other objectives that we run our company by," says Johnson. "Everyone shares the responsibility of helping to meet the company's environmental goals." Environmental stewardship is visibly interwoven into SC Johnson's global well-being purpose. Even the individual Greenlist initiative is not really an individual initiative at all, but rather just a part of the way SC Johnson is. It is difficult to distinguish one part of SC Johnson's environmental approach from the other, or one specific initiative from the other, and even if there are two parts or two initiatives, then they are so integrally connected to each other, so dependent on each other, that the act of drawing the distinction is itself senseless.

SC Johnson's high-purpose system functions like a living organism. Every piece serves a clear purpose within the larger context. "Because of the way Greenlist operates as a process, it's instantly global, it's instantly understandable, it's instantly widely applicable," says Johnson. "Now that we've added in nearly every category of material that we purchase and have rated those materials, it covers much of what we do."

Now locked in a period of good growth, in November 2005, SC Johnson announced a voluntary partnership with the EPA in the agency's Design for the Environment Program (DfE), under which the two organizations work together to develop improved, innovative products that benefit human health and the environment. "This program applies the same approach to product development that the Greenlist process did in trying to drive us toward the sourcing of environmentally responsible raw materials in order to make those products," explains Johnson. "The two programs have the same goals: the continuous improvement of formulations, increased safety for humans, and the planet. The goals are very well-aligned."

The partnership launched with two official partnership products, including Scrubbing Bubbles Trigger Bathroom Cleaner and Shower Shine Daily Shower Cleaner by Scrubbing Bubbles, both of which are not only sourced with raw materials classified under the Greenlist process, but are also engineered to offer consumers products with a more positive health and environmental profile than those typically found in many conventional cleaning products. Six additional products are now under review. "The EPA has some aggressive targets in that they would like to remove all toxicity and nonbiodegradability from household cleaning products, and we are working with them in order to accomplish this," says Johnson. "We have the same goals as the EPA on these matters. There is a nice alignment here as well." Essentially, the two organizations learn from each other. Using Greenlist, the EPA can better evaluate SC Johnson's products and learn about how to work with big business more constructively, while by using the EPA's extensive tools, SC Johnson learns how to raise the bar for its products much higher than it would by working on its own.

In the press release announcing the DfE partnership, SC Johnson's chairman and CEO, Fisk Johnson, reiterated that the program was just one part of the company's overall business philosophy: "Design for the Environment supports SC Johnson's commitment to put the environment and human health at the center of product development and formulation. Companies can and should continue to look closely at making investments that are about doing what's right for the business and the environment."[29]

THE MONEY TRAIL

SC Johnson's present emphasis on good growth calls attention to another clear and distinguishing factor that sets High-Purpose Companies apart, and particularly High-Purpose Companies that, like SC Johnson, belong to our innovator class—and that is: savvy corporate responsibility wealth allocation.

Our innovator class High-Purpose Companies approach corporate responsibility as the opposite of a cosmetic exercise. In general, the majority of corporate responsibility dollars spent by our innovator class

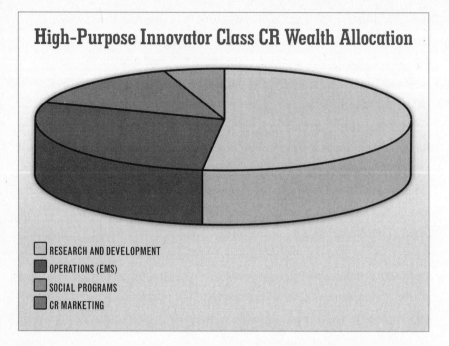

High-Purpose Innovator Class CR Wealth Allocation

- RESEARCH AND DEVELOPMENT
- OPERATIONS (EMS)
- SOCIAL PROGRAMS
- CR MARKETING

High-Purpose Companies, including DuPont, Toyota, GE, John Deere, and SC Johnson, went into the research and development of responsive technologies, solutions, and products first; operational improvements that reduced the company's environmental and social impact second (such as environmental and supply chain management systems); social programs third; and corporate responsibility–related marketing last.

For example, for 2006, GE allocated $1.5 billion to researching and developing new environmental technologies. According to sources inside GE, although the company does not allocate a specific budget for meeting its greenhouse gas, waste reduction, or energy efficiency goals, it does integrate environmental management systems (EMS) into its overall operational approach or "way of doing business" and also has committed over $799 million to hazardous waste cleanup efforts since 1999. At the time we were making our calculations, GE had yet to release 2006 forecasts for social giving or ecomagination advertising expenditures. However, GE gave $150 million in cash, products, and service to support local and global services organizations in communities around the world, and spent $90 million launching the ecomagination campaign in 2005, so we went ahead and plugged those numbers into our table. Thus, even discounting the company's hazardous waste cleanup efforts, we surmised that marketing, which could be considered cosmetic, represents a relatively small portion of the overall corporate responsibility investment pie at GE.

At SC Johnson, things broke down in a similar fashion, although the precise execution was different since the company has no landmark corporate responsibility initiative. Financially speaking, the company's corporate responsibility investments are not separately allocated or easily calculable at all. Rather, they are completely ingrained in the company's operational structure. Petrell Ozbay, senior manager of global public affairs explains: "It's not like there's a little group of scientists looking at how to make a select few products more environmentally responsible. By now, we're talking about all of our products across the board. The whole line has been reinvigorated and redesigned for better environmental performance. Also, everyone in the company is involved. For instance, we've got the production associates in our global manufacturing plants suggesting that we cool down the products with water that's two degrees cooler in order to save on energy and cut greenhouse gases. So our goals are embedded throughout our operations. Everyone knows about them, and everything we design and do is built from the standards up."

SC Johnson goes about things differently, but it allocates its wealth in a similar way as GE. Only in SC Johnson's case, it is the company's *total* wealth, not just a portion of its wealth that is at hand. The company's overall emphasis is largely on improving the quality of all the products it makes and also, the way it makes all of its products. "This is definitely the way it breaks down," confirms Ozbay in addressing SC Johnson's emphasis on environmentally led research and development plus operational improvements over publicity-related efforts.

Although the dollars spent and methods used by each innovator class High-Purpose Company varied, the rough percentage of spending in each category was consistent. Each company shared the same basic investment priorities, giving us a reasonably good sense of where things stand and where they are moving. The signs point to increased momentum for good growth. Essentially, none of our innovator High-Purpose Companies view or approach corporate responsibility simply as corporate responsibility, which is why they are investing in such a bullish manner—and also, why they are generating such stellar returns.

THE INTEGRATORS

As the corporate zest for shared pursuit escalates, different permutations take form. While the innovators are one class of High-Purpose Company, in the process of our research, we discovered another class: the integrators. Integrator High-Purpose Companies internalize their purpose. They absorb it and allow it to define their culture. They express their purpose from the inside out. Whereas at innovator High-Purpose Companies like DuPont, GE, and SC Johnson, the ultimate emphasis is on product, at integrator High-Purpose Companies, the focus is largely on people.

Integrator companies use their higher purpose to establish vastly motivating policies and functional internal atmospheres. Those policies and atmospheres have an extremely beneficial affect on employees, enabling them to produce exceptionally positive customer experiences. As a result of the consistent demonstration of purpose, both customers and employees repeatedly reward and acknowledge the company through supportive words and actions. Integrator High-Purpose Companies are widely revered for their dedication to both people and service. Their higher purpose enables them to succeed and also sets them apart in the marketplace.

JetBlue Airways' entry into the marketplace, along with its higher purpose of "bringing humanity back to air travel," could not have been better timed. When JetBlue exploded onto the scene, the major airlines were struggling to cope with their bulky infrastructures in addition to rising fuel costs and inefficient and aging aircraft. JetBlue, now widely hailed as the airline industry's miracle child, achieved sudden financial success during a time of economic struggle and industry cutbacks— principally because it took positions that opposed the ordinary. The fact that JetBlue was established with a humanity purpose implied that the rest of the airline industry was inhumane, which it essentially was.

Before JetBlue, the airline industry was notoriously unfriendly or indifferent to customers, hostile to unions and workers, numbers driven rather than experience oriented, old-school in terms of management strategy, and monopolistic in terms of competitive strategy. With respect to the touchy-feely stuff, forget about it. That was the last concern of senior managers running certain major airlines struggling to survive. As a result, their planes were dingy, decrepit, and polluting; the seats were uncomfortable; overhead and legroom was cramped; the bathrooms were filthy; the food was abysmal; flight attendants were often detatched because the airline had just cut their pensions; travelers were befuddled by the maze of increasingly complex pricing schemes, restrictions, and fees; and flights were changed or canceled without notice, with the cancellations often blamed on "mechanical issues" (sometimes code for employee walkouts). These problems and a host of others existed for years. They still exist. The airline industry was, and still is to some degree, quite soulless. Inhumanity became the travel industry norm, and weary travelers accepted the inhumanity because they had no other choice. This climate gave JetBlue the launching pad it needed.

After JetBlue, things changed, or started to. The airline industry grew a little more innovative, technologically savvy, environmentally progressive, and customer-oriented. JetBlue is arguably doing to the airline industry what Toyota is doing to the automotive industry: causing category disruption. For instance, shortly after JetBlue's launch, Delta tried to respond with Song (but closed the carrier down in 2006). Continental emphasized the relative youth of its fleet, and United and American vied to improve their customer service and employee relations. This market reaction was debatably driven in large part by Jet-Blue's humanity purpose. JetBlue is perhaps one of the greatest start-up stories ever, and probably one that deserves its own book or at least its own chapter. It is a crystal clear indication of how purpose can help enable both industry-wide change and brand affinity.

JetBlue was founded in 1999 and was profitable soon thereafter. The airline now has 7,500 employees and serves 36 cities in the United States, the Dominican Republic, Puerto Rico, Bermuda, and the Bahamas with a fleet of 89 new, fuel-efficient Airbus A320 aircraft, which are among the cleanest, most environmentally friendly commercial aircraft in the air. From the start, the concept at JetBlue was "high-tech, high-touch," and in terms of the latter goal, the company consistently goes out of its way to help people feel connected. For each policy Jet-Blue instates or promotion that JetBlue runs, there is a reason behind it and that reason often originates from the people the company serves. JetBlue surveys six hundred customers every day about their frustrations, needs, desires, and expectations. It figures out what people want and then delivers. JetBlue determined that, for instance, people wanted to buy a simple one-way fare without a Saturday-night-stay restriction, so it offered that. It inferred that people became easily bored on flights, so it offers thirty-six channels of live TV at every seat. It discovered that people typically found the coffee served on planes to be undrinkable, so it started serving more preferred Dunkin' Donuts blends. It realized that more of its travelers were environmentally conscientious, so it implemented an extensive sorting and recycling program. It grasped that people resented being treated like herds of cattle, so it cared for them like human beings.

JetBlue purportedly continues to apply what it learns from in-person and e-mail encounters. On its Web site, JetBlue.com, the company encourages users to speak up and lodge both compliments and complaints. "Customer feedback, the good and the bad, is critical to accomplishing our goal of getting better as we get bigger," the company says in its 2004 annual report. "We know we're not perfect, but we will always aspire to learn from every situation and improve."[30] According to JetBlue's internal survey results, the company is doing pretty darn well, as 94 percent of respondents recently ranked their JetBlue experience as "much better" or "somewhat better" than other airlines, while 99 percent said they "definitely would" or "probably would" recommend the airline to others. Frequent travelers clearly find JetBlue's high-touch personality irresistible, which is why they have rewarded the airline by voting it *Condé Nast Traveler*'s Best Domestic Airline four years in a row. In 2006, JetBlue was voted Best Airline Value by *Entrepreneur* magazine and given the Passenger Service Award by *Air Transport World* magazine, while in 2005, JetBlue was also voted *Condé Nast Traveler*'s Best Low-Cost Carrier; *Global Traveler*'s Best Airline for Economy Class; the *Wall Street Journal*'s Best Airline Quality; and was presented the Great Gay Marketing Award by *Out and About* travel magazine. The company responds to its consistent accolades through a clever marketing campaign that simply reads: "We love you too."

JetBlue is every bit as calculated when it comes to taking care of its own. Just as innovator High-Purpose Companies reverse engineer products around social needs and world problems, JetBlue constructs its management policies to fit the fundamental requirements and deepest wishes of its employees. Compared to mainstream airline industry standards, this is revolutionary. JetBlue conducts routine surveys to determine how employees feel about the company, its policies, and what could stand to be improved. According to the company, in 2004 for instance, surveyed workers said that JetBlue's medical Preferred Provider Organization network did not offer enough health care providers in certain regions. In response, JetBlue apparently added another PPO plan to fill the gap, even though it says that 98 percent of employees' needs were covered under the former plan. Similarly, JetBlue's 401(k) plan meets employee preferences as people have the flexibility to choose among twenty-one different funds, and all employees are made to feel part of the JetBlue team by sharing in 15 percent of the company's pretax profits every year.

JetBlue also followed employee suggestions by allowing its people to work from home. The company really ran with this one. At the moment, JetBlue's virtual office policy is so engrained into the corporate culture that its reservations center representatives are often depicted as housewives in bunny slippers. "That quote has definitely been around," says JetBlue spokesman Bryan Balwin. "But it's basically true. We have about 1,500 crew members who work for our reservations center and about 1,200 of those individuals work from home." The benefits of the program, Balwin explains, make the plan worthwhile. "We need to have people available to answer calls twenty-four hours a day because of the business we are in. This program offers flexibility for the crew members, where they can spend time with their families and still do their jobs. A lot of them are stay-at-home moms, and they need to be at home when their kids are at home. So this creates flexibility both for the representatives and for the airline, too. For instance, when call volume goes up due to inclement weather, instead of us having to wait for representatives to drive to the call center, crew members are immediately accessible to us and available to meet the demand." This saves JetBlue money, Balwin says. There's minimal overhead, no downtime, the company gets what it needs, and employees are as happy as crew members in bunny slippers. JetBlue reportedly has a waiting list of over 1,000 people eager to join the virtual call center team.

The ground and in-sky teams seem equally as satisfied with their jobs, according to statistics collected by the company as well as our own impromptu analysis. JetBlue received over 120,000 job applications in 2004, while it had new spots for only 2,700 people, and turnover at JetBlue is reportedly minimal. According to the company, pilot turnover is zero, whereas turnover among flight attendants, supervisors, and others is below 10 percent.

Checking in for the flight from Oakland to JFK, we asked the friendly fellow at the JetBlue ticket counter, "How do you like working for JetBlue?" He did not hesitate: "This is a supremely well-run airline. I just love telling people what airline I work for, especially people who work in the travel industry because they have the same reaction. Everyone thinks of JetBlue that way." Onboard, we asked several JetBlue attendants the same question. They gushed: "I absolutely love working for JetBlue. It's a great company." Another concurred: "They really listen and care about what people think. This is the best company that I have ever worked for." In describing their employer, people used the word "love" a lot. It's a humanity that shows.

Wegmans Food Markets is another integrator High-Purpose Company with a distinct humanitarian edge. For the ninth consecutive year, Wegmans was rated as one of *Fortune* magazine's Best Large Companies to Work For, capturing the number two spot in 2006 and the top spot in 2005. Apparently, employees love Wegmans because Wegmans loves them. That's the company's formula for success. "It's not about the food, it's about the people," says Mary Ellen Burris, senior vice president of consumer affairs. "At the heart of who we are is respect and care for each other and about the communities where we have stores. I know that probably sounds corny, but it's true," she says. "People come in and they gawk at the store. Competitors try and copy our physical environment, but they just can't replicate the culture that we've been able to develop over all of these years. We have hired people who really want to work here and who know our customers by name in many cases. There is an emotional bond. You just can't mimic that."

Wegmans is a unique example because, like JetBlue, its philosophy collides with those of most major grocery store chains, where low wages, long hours, high turnover, and labor unrest are more often the rules rather than the exceptions. Wegmans doesn't play that way. It offers both full- and part-time employees high-end salaries, comprehensive health care benefits, vacation and holiday pay, and scholarships. But perhaps among employees' favorite perks are Wegmans-sponsored knowledge gathering trips—like the one Mike Riley, wine buyer, recently took to Argentina, where he met wine maker Mariano de Paula, in order to sample what he describes as the country's "passionate" blends of Malbec, or the one that Terri Zodarecky, cheese manager, recently took to Europe in order to watch how cheese is made according to hundred-year-old traditions and to sample local varieties of Livarot, Pont l'Évêque, Saint-André, and Roquefort. These experiences translate into sophisticated selections, knowledgeable staff, and what Wegmans describes as "telepathic" customer service. According to the company, customers are very appreciative. In 2004, Wegmans received 3,500 letters from satisfied customers, who wrote to say how much they like shopping at Wegmans because they can find what they want or appreciate the way they are treated by Wegmans educated staff.

"We believe in investing in our people and giving them the knowledge and tools they need to create great customer experiences," says Burris. "We have found that when we invest in our people, they give back more than what we've invested in them." Since people development is a central emphasis at Wegmans, the company routinely makes changes to cope with any inefficiencies that it detects. Several years ago, for instance, Wegmans realized that as its stores had grown, store supervisors had become distanced from other employees. There were too many people reporting to them, and personal connections were getting lost. In response, the company moved things around so that now a

Wegmans supervisor never has more than thirty people to manage. "The result is that today our supervisors get to know their people better and they can more easily identify the concerns that may be affecting work performance. This has really helped to improve things," says Burris, who also indicates that it's about going the extra mile every day to fulfill even the smallest employee requests. "You have to take good care of your people. As a business, we can't take good care of our customers unless we take care of our own people."

The Wegmans brand motto, "Eat well. Live well," is also its purpose and the company clearly gives its people something to feel grateful for and even inspired about. The company's Web site, Wegmans.com, makes a point of this by posting commentary from some of its more satisfied stakeholders: "Wegmans believes in teamwork which makes the job good for now and for the future. Employees work together with good conscience and heart. Every employee is a member of the Wegmans family," cheers one enthusiastic employee. "I am proud to work for Wegmans because I think top management is focused on providing employees with the tools they need to achieve career and personal goals," gushes another. "There are endless opportunities in training available for everyone who has a passion for food and people. Everyone takes great pride in each person's success," promises a smiling café manager who epitomizes the company's people commitment. Such dedication attracts 127,588 new job applications every year, while keeping voluntary employee turnover at less than 8 percent. It also generates $3.4 billion in sales with growth of about 9 percent a year. Undeniably, wellness as a purpose translates into wellness on the balance sheet.

THE FIFTH ELEMENT

On closer examination of our high-purpose group, several distinguishing qualities become manifestly apparent: good growth; a reliance on responsive products, services, and policies; synchronization with the new market cycle; and savvy corporate responsibility wealth allocation. But there is another, fifth element that sets both innovator and integrator High-Purpose Companies apart. Within the companies themselves, inside most every person, there is an impetus.

People working for High-Purpose Companies tend to feel a deeper sense of satisfaction. Their jobs mean more to them because the company stands for and delivers something meaningful. The sense of stakeholder satisfaction produced by High-Purpose Companies, and particularly Integrator class companies like JetBlue and Wegmans, often transmutes into a form of love and devotion. The devotion can be measured quantitatively in terms of lower turnover rates and higher productivity, whereas the love can be detected qualitatively in the phrases that people use to describe the company. Both emotions, in fact, can be seen in people's faces as they light up in response and can be heard in the passion and conviction in people's voices. Love and devotion register as the actual words "love," "devotion," or "commitment" and "loyalty"—and they are also conveyed as the expression that what the company is doing is of extreme significance.

This might not seem like much, but in an era marked with scandal and in a climate where trust is at a deficit, the expression of devotion and love toward a corporation is highly unusual. When you multiply the significance of employee love and devotion for a corporation by the significance of consumer love and devotion for a corporation, then the potential for what a company can achieve and gain through its purpose is limitless. This love and devotion represents the key that can transform the good companies in the world into the greatest, most functional, and most successful companies in the world. These are the core concepts that we will explore as we move into the final phase in our progression: Anchor.

TRANSFORMING INTENT INTO REALITY

Company	Higher Purpose	Health Indicators
DuPont	"Create sustainable solutions essential to a better, safer, healthier life for people everywhere."	**PEOPLE:** Zero injuries culture lowered incidents by over 50% since 2000. **PROCESSES:** Zero emissions, zero waste policy saved 11 metric tons of CO_2 from entering the atmosphere and saved $2 billion in costs. **PRODUCTS:** Safety & Security Solutions, Tyvek, Bio-PDO, Sonora, Avaunt. **PROJECTIONS:** By 2010, save 1 million lives; derive 25% of revenues from nondepletable resources.
Toyota	"Make sustainable mobility a reality."	**PEOPLE:** Personal creativity and innovation-oriented culture leads to higher quality (*kaizen*). **PROCESSES:** Lean, green manufacturing reduces waste by 86%, with 8 facilities designated as "zero landfill" producing operations. **PRODUCTS:** Prius, Lexus RX 400h, Hybrid Synergy Drive technology moving across lineup. **PROJECTIONS:** Sell 1 million hybrids annually by the early 2010s; render the combustion engine obsolete.
GE	"Provide imaginative answers to the mounting challenges to our ecosystem."	**PEOPLE:** Workplace injury prevention program lowered incidents by 76% since 1996. **PROCESSES:** Environmental management system (EMS) reduced toxic emissions by 80% since 1990s. **PRODUCTS:** GEnx jet engine, Profile Harmony washer, Evolution locomotive, Water Scarcity and Wind Power solutions. **PROJECTIONS:** Sell $20 billion worth of ecomagination products by 2010; double eco-research spending to $1.5 billion annually.

TRANSFORMING INTENT INTO REALITY

Company	Higher Purpose	Health Indicators
John Deere	"Support the livelihood of farmers and the land on which they depend."	**PEOPLE:** "Zero injuries" goal resulted in reduction of incidents by over 11% between 2004 and 2005. **PROCESSES:** EMS reduced waste by 11% since 2003. **PRODUCTS:** HarvestForm, Timberjack 1490 slash bundler, GreenStar AutoTrac global positioning system. **PROJECTIONS:** Expects sales of AutoTrac to triple and will invest $60 million in wind energy projects by the end of 2006.
SC Johnson	"Promote global well-being."	**PEOPLE:** Safety program reduced injuries and incidents by 69.5% since the early 1990s. **PROCESSES:** EMS eliminated over 460 million pounds of waste; Greenlist process removed more than 13.7 million pounds of volatile organic compounds from SCJ products. **PRODUCTS:** Scrubbing Bubbles Bathroom Cleaner, Windex, Pledge, Shout, Ziploc, Saran. **PROJECTIONS:** Eventual goal of ongoing EPA partnership is to remove all toxicity and nonbiodegradability from household cleaning products.
JetBlue	"Bring humanity back to air travel."	**PEOPLE:** Responsive management policies improve productivity, plus reduce pilot turnover to zero and employee turnover to under 10%. **PROCESSES:** "High-tech" Airbus A320 aircraft offers superior fuel efficiency. **PRODUCTS:** "High-touch" customer experience consistently voted best in class. **PROJECTIONS:** Plans to add 200 eco-efficient Embraer E190AR aircraft, powered by GE's jet engines, to current fleet.

Company	Higher Purpose	Health Indicators
Wegmans	"Help people to eat well, live well."	**PEOPLE**: Employee perks and teamwork philosophy win Wegmans spot on *Fortune*'s Best Companies to Work For list for 9 consecutive years and keeps employee turnover at below 8%. **PROCESSES**: Waste reduction, recycling efforts, and food protection standards result in industry awards. **PRODUCTS**: "Telepathic" customer service results in repeated awards, loyalty, and 3,500 fan letters annually. **PROJECTIONS**: Be the very best company to work for by 2007.

7:

Anchor

Loyalty to petrified opinions never yet broke a chain or freed a human soul in this world—and never will.

—*MARK TWAIN*

"Fifty years ago as a child, I watched, on my small black-and-white TV, a somewhat fuzzy yet unsettling view of the definition of patriotism through the eyes of the Army-McCarthy hearings. A climate of fear and oppression was being fostered that did much to chill dissent. Fast-forward to today, my TV screen is much larger, the picture is clearer, but the view of patriotism perpetuated by our government is still just as narrow. At that moment many years ago, when Joseph Welch of Hale and Dorr confronted Senator McCarthy with that memorable phrase 'Have you no decency?' he became my hero. . . . Thus began my educational journey," said Robert Glassman, cochairman of Wainwright Bank & Trust, in a 2004 speech. In his speech, Glassman was accepting an award for corporate leadership and recalling his bank's civil rights origins. The speech continued: "I arrived at Harvard Business School in the fall of 1967. In the 1960s, HBS may have been the West Point of capitalism, but it was still a world of white male privilege . . . With financial assistance from the GI Bill, an inexpensive suit, and an antiwar button pinned to it, I could not have felt more out of place."[1]

The 1960s had left a formidable impression on Glassman, the HBS experience, in particular: "I always felt a little in over my head," he later told us. "I always felt as if Harvard had somehow made a mistake and let me in through the back door. I was a clear minority there." Glassman was for the peace movement, but he had just come off the Vietnam battlefield, where he had fought shoulder to shoulder with people of all races. And yet, there he was, swimming upstream in a sea of conformity, feeling conflicted about the viewpoints discussed in class and especially inspired by the convictions of Dr. Martin Luther King Jr. and Coretta Scott King—and with seemingly no refuge. Not from Harvard, not from his fellow classmates, and not from society. "At that moment, all I could really do was observe the situation, the inequity in the world and maybe attend a few antiwar rallies," he says. "Who knew that twenty years later I would participate in an institution that has come to be known for its commitment to social justice issues?"

Glassman insists that back then, he didn't know. He had no predestined vision of becoming a social entrepreneur. He indicates that to suggest that Wainwright Bank & Trust, a Boston-based publicly traded commercial institution with $725 million in assets, was born from the innate sense of morality that influenced his early life gives him far too much credit. But we respectfully differ with his viewpoint. Glassman deserves the credit, just as he deserves his Harvard degree.

Since Wainwright Bank opened its doors for business in 1987, it has fostered what Glassman and others describe as a "passionate love affair" with its employees, customers, shareholders, and local community.

The bank has committed over $400 million in loans for development projects that include HIV/AIDS services, immigration services, homeless shelters, food banks, affordable housing, and green building. The bank vehemently supports gay rights, diversity, and nondiscrimination as well as the anti-Iraq war movement. "These are edgy issues for a commercial bank to stand for," Glassman acknowledges. And yet, on the loans it issues to organizations working within these "edgy" sectors—and every sector, for that matter—Wainwright achieves a zero default rate. None of Wainwright's customers defaults on the loans.

Wainwright is recognized by SustainableBusiness.com as one of the world's Top 20 Sustainable Stocks and by the Social Investment Forum as one of America's Top 10 Green Banking Firms. In 1995, Wainwright was the subject of a Harvard Business School case study for its outreach to the gay community and for the lasting surge in customer loyalty that resulted from that outreach. Wainwright sticks to its gay rights guns, and more recently, it was the only publicly traded company in Massachusetts to formally protest the block on gay marriage and the extension of benefits to same sex couples. Wainwright similarly stands its ground with respect to the Iraq war, and frequently, during groundbreaking ceremonies where Wainwright has financed real estate development deals, Glassman and his colleagues use an online demonstrative tool that calculates how much money the local community could have saved had taxpayer dollars not been diverted. "In an effort to create economic transparency, we try to link the cost of the war relative to the tax base in that community to what otherwise might have been affordable housing units," says Glassman. "When people see an actual dollar figure, many find it pretty compelling."

Wainwright Bank happens to be the largest shareholder in Trillium Asset Management, having purchased a 35 percent interest in the firm in 1997. Trillium is itself the oldest and largest socially responsible investment management firm in the United States, and one widely known for devising shareholder resolutions that press corporations to adopt socially and environmentally just policies and clean up their messes. For instance, Trillium sponsored two separate resolutions on behalf of Chevron shareholders in response to the previously mentioned Ecuador environmental lawsuits. It sponsored a variety of other resolutions on behalf of shareholders of corporations such as Chrysler, Johnson & Johnson, and American Home Products—calling the public's attention to troubling issues, forcing corporate accountability, and by association, making Wainwright all the more influential in Fortune 5000 circles.

Upon first glance, Wainwright might appear as the quintessential example of a left-wing or fringe business for whom corporate responsibility makes sense under a particular set of circumstances. However, this bank deserves a closer look because irrespective of the particular social issues it embraces, its impact is undeniable and its business formula is widely applicable.

Most every company in the world has its brand of philosophy. But Wainwright's philosophy is more than just a philosophy. This bank gives its stakeholders something worth fighting for. It provides people with a crusade. "End injustice" is Wainwright's crusade. Wainwright also delivers a purpose, which is to "provide equality and financial empowerment."

Wainwright creates an equitable work environment and further promotes the political and social concepts of equality and justice through various forms of activism, such as its formal protests on behalf of gay couples and people living with AIDS. Through Wainwright's financial services, the bank enables its customers to achieve economic opportunity. Wainwright uses its purpose to structure responsive lending products—such as community development loans that encourage growth in the social sector and that are flexible enough to meet the needs of individual borrowers, as well as its Green Loans, which encourage the installation of energy conservation systems. The bank also uses its purpose to develop supplemental services, such as its Web site CommunityRoom.net, which offers nonprofit clients a means of connecting with one another and spreading the social justice message. Additionally, Wainwright uses its purpose to set internal management policies, like its same-sex domestic partner benefits to employees and its decision to maintain one of the most diverse boards and workforces in corporate America. In its community, Wainwright is widely known and prized for its purpose. The local press portrays it as "a bank that gives people strength," "a bank that keeps its promises," and "totally fearless when it comes to [its] beliefs."[2] For these reasons, Wainwright is both an innovator and an integrator, as are all the businesses featured in this chapter. It is the ultimate High-Purpose Company.

BANKING ON DEVOTION

Wainwright delivers the right message in the right way to the right people at the right time. That is how it has achieved an unbreakable bond with its stakeholders and record financial results. Loans issued at Wainwright grew 14 percent between 2004 and 2005 and 22 percent between 2003 and 2004. "When Wainwright was founded, it was one of fourteen thousand banks in an undifferentiated industry with fungible services and commodity prices," says Glassman. "Now we've ended up as one of the region's best-known banks with a constituency that knows exactly who we are and absolutely loves what we do differently."

Wainwright Bank does not attempt to court everyone. Glassman and his colleagues realize that it does not matter if all the public loves the company. What matters is that the ideal people love the company. It is irrelevant to Wainwright, for example, that some in Boston and elsewhere find the bank's support of gay rights or antiwar issues to be offensive because Wainwright does not care to attract business or support from those constituencies. Wainwright knows that it will never please everyone, so it does not waste its energy with fruitless efforts, for instance, shamelessly pandering itself as everybody's favorite bank or as the industry's best citizen.

Wainwright appreciates that to take a stand, to embrace a crusade meaningful enough to stir people to the point where they do love and devote themselves to the company exclusively, it must naturally alienate others. "On some issues, we have stood alone," says Glassman. Taking a stand means turning certain people off, a sure risk, but in this scenario, one worth taking.

From the start, Wainwright used a depth approach to corporate responsibility—and to purpose-driven business and growth strategy overall. "It was never about merchandising or cause marketing," says Glassman. "We had a genuine commitment to certain social issues from the time we were founded, and we suspected that because of this commitment, there would be a population of people within the greater Boston area that would want to go out of their way to do business with us." At Wainwright, business growth and success was less about the generic notions of good values or doing the right thing. It was more about taking opportune and substantive positions and backing the positions up in ways that were totally genuine, tangible, and productive. Wainwright has a specific target audience in mind. It has goals and metrics on paper. Some of the bank's goals are social and others are financial in nature, and Wainwright meets them all. "We always measure our success in terms of two bottom lines—the social justice platform and the business platform," says Glassman, who insists that one platform sustains the other.

Wainwright stands for the kinds of social justice issues, like gender, racial, and class inequality, that few other major corporations are supporting and that certain people *need* to feel passionately about. The company's support of these issues has been unwavering. For instance, Wainwright issued its first loan of $11 million in financing for AIDS housing back in 1993 and then went on to fund Boston's Gay Pride

Parade later that year. By 1998, the bank had issued several hundred million in loans to worthy causes, had testified before Congress in favor of antidiscrimination acts, and had also endorsed both Ceres (Coalition for Environmentally Responsible Economies) and NOW (by signing the Women-Friendly Workplace Pledge). Thus, Wainwright earned unswerving devotion not through one or two campaigns, Glassman explains, but through a lifetime of authenticity. Because of the way Wainwright executes its whole business experience—from the mailroom to the boardroom, bank branches, cybercafés, city hall, and local neighborhoods—stakeholders who connect with these issues can't help but be drawn in. Like Glassman said, everybody who matters most to Wainwright greatly appreciates the value that Wainwright provides. Not only does the bank use its greatest strengths to do what no other bank can, it does what no other bank would dare to do. Wainwright's products, services and social positions are all equally unusual, compelling, and consistent with each other. People admire that. As a result, employees, shareholders, customers, civic leaders, the press, the web of accountability, and much of the local community are equally devoted.

In Wainwright's case, effective outreach is evidenced by the company's relatively small marketing budget. Wainwright doesn't have to spend too much effort reaching prospects because prospects reach Wainwright. "Our clients find us," says Glassman. "I'd love to say that we've got a brilliant marketing strategy, but what it really comes down to is word of mouth. There are ten thousand nonprofits within our area and thousands more progressive customers and employees who are sensitive to these issues. The progressive community talks to each other and we've become sort of a fixture to them." Glassman says that Wainwright is flooded with applications and letters from potential candidates who want to work for the company. "We have no trouble finding the best people," he says.

The Wainwright culture innately produces the results of love and devotion. "We have set up an atmosphere where our people, and particularly the folks who are a part of the gay community, don't have to conform to some corporate notion of what a banker should be," says Glassman. "They can share whatever about their life they wish to share with their workmates, and they can be comfortable with who they are just the way anybody else is." Put another way, Wainwright bank employees do not have to look, talk, or act like Wall Street bank employees. Instead, they can relax, be themselves, and concentrate on doing great quality work. Wainwright's core concept is so simple. Through its policies and, by extension, its people, the bank is *being* that which it claims to stand for. "If we can't project an internal commitment to social justice, then we're not going to be perceived as credible externally," says Glassman. "The sense of openness and decency toward our employees generates benefits for the customer and also generates a sense among our wider constituency that we are the real deal. We are exactly what we appear to be."

CORRELATIONS OF SIGNIFICANCE

Anchored High-Purpose Companies reflect their purpose inside and outside. They don't have to fabricate elaborate means of conveying a responsible image for themselves because that image is intrinsic. It is who they are and what they are. As Glassman said, they are exactly as they appear to be and remain true to themselves, which is why the right people love them. This authentic, "being" trait helps to answer the question: how does a company foster unswerving stakeholder love and devotion?

Stakeholder love and devotion need not be invented. They are already there. All that needs to happen is for companies to unleash them. That sounds a like a self-help book speaking, doesn't it? It's true, though. The Wainwright story exhibits certain significant correlations that are both rudimentary and enlightening. If a company truly stands for something that people care about deeply and passionately, then people will tend to care about the company deeply and passionately. The significance and authenticity of a company's higher purpose is directly proportional to the level of love received. Similarly, if a company devotes itself to the well-being of its people, then in turn, its people will likely devote themselves to the company's well-being. The level of devotion given is often proportional to the level of devotion received. These relationships and positive correlations have been demonstrated throughout most of the cases reviewed in this book, though they are most clearly evident in this chapter.

The simple truth is that if companies want to attract love and devotion from their stakeholders, then they should become the desired result. They should transform themselves into the embodiment of love and devotion, rather than construct ideal perceptions through other means first. If they truly desire to change the world for the better, then in transforming themselves, they will also change the world. This is authenticity in its purest form. In this way, Anchored High-Purpose Companies are authentic.

As previously mentioned, so many firms say that their purpose or philosophy is reflected in "everything we do" and then behave in incongruous ways. However, in our analysis, we determined that in addition to Wainwright, several other companies such as IKEA, Patagonia, Eileen Fisher, Tom's of Maine, Aveda, and TerraPass, have visibly mastered the skill of anchoring. To anchor is to let go of all outside standards and judgments and use the company's higher purpose as the sole source of identity, stability, and energy. Anchored High-Purpose Companies do not often worry about regulatory standards because they far exceed them, just as they do not pander to public interest groups, public opinion, or the press because they remain true to their core. Anchored companies have no need for extraneous rules, policies, or rigid corporate hierarchies—despite their size—because in such companies, ethics are autonomous, while purpose is completely engrained throughout the culture.

In a simple world, this would be the last stop on the progression: the final phase in the transformative process. However, as will be made clearer further on, the transformative process is without end. Also, in our small sample of seventy-five firms, we found no examples of companies that made it up this high without the original intention to get there. Each of our anchored companies was founded with a higher purpose in mind, and each evolved in expression of that purpose. One could read this result in one of two ways: either the anchor phase is an exclusive echelon reserved for a certain kind of firm, or the other firms in our study have yet to decide and manage to anchor themselves. We tend to think that the second explanation is the right one.

Whereas it is challenging for companies that dedicate themselves to a higher purpose midcourse, such as DuPont or GE, to advance up to this stage, it is not impossible. More than anything else, what is required is the heartfelt desire to do so. Many large Fortune 500 institutions will simply not develop that kind of desire. They will take their higher purpose just so far. They will make a great difference in the world and to their shareholders and that will be enough, but they will not seek to transform their internal culture to the degree where human creativity and well-being are maximized, and therefore, even better performance is enabled. This is essentially the skill required at the anchor stage. Other companies, however, will venture further.

The firms that venture further will enable their purpose to override rigid structures and to generate the contagious stakeholder evangelism just described in the Wainwright case. More Fortune 500 High-Purpose Companies will likely anchor in the coming years, and we suspect that a host of firms not included in our study, such as Genentech and Herman Miller, might already have. The vision and tactics embraced by Anchored High-Purpose Companies, however effective, are by no means exclusive to green firms alone. As with the Wainwright example, each of the following High-Purpose Companies provides lessons that are widely applicable. Also, as it becomes more difficult to both differentiate and innovate in a crowded marketplace, companies will need to find ways to build reliable stakeholder loyalty as well as meet pressing new social, environmental, and economic demands—and this is surely one route.

Just as any business that wants to can see the bigger picture, face the truth, and set intent and then purpose, any business that wants to can also create the idyllic internal systems that foster the optimal external conditions. Beyond transcending and including, each Anchored High-Purpose Company in our study—from IKEA to Patagonia, Eileen Fisher, and TerraPass—effectively creates its own reality. Essentially, each invents its own little utopia or living laboratory, which sets off a powerful chain reaction. In doing this, each pushes the boundaries, even grappling with the larger esoteric questions, including not only: What is the modern role of business? But also: What *is* a business?

None of our anchored companies goes about doing things the "normal" way. They are each profitable capitalists, but beyond that, little about them is routine. Every one breaks the rules. None speaks the regular business language or uses the standard measures of success. Each firm evaluates business problems differently and identifies radical solutions. In fact, some in the mainstream business world view these companies, their solutions, and particularly, their purpose-driven leaders, as rather odd. In the past, certain of these leaders and companies have been frowned upon or even rebelled against. Other times, the company's dedication to purpose has been portrayed as a frivolous eccentricity, or even cast as some sinister plot for mind control.

Anchored High-Purpose Companies make some people uncomfortable because they are different. They tend to bring into perspective serious problems that no one else wants to talk about. What goes on inside of them is specifically designed to deal with these problems—to work on behalf of the betterment of the planet and the improvement of the way people live. Depending on the vantage of the viewer, one could interpret such companies as sidetracked, novel, or incredibly significant.

ATYPICAL BEHAVIOR

Since the dawn of his career, IKEA founder Ingvar Kamprad has been portrayed as somewhat of an oddball. He is one of the world's richest men but reportedly takes the subway to work, and when he does drive, it's in a rickety old Volvo. Kamprad is now officially retired from IKEA, but he still serves as senior adviser. "He is also a critical store customer, a watchdog for the IKEA concept and quality, a visionary and a constant source of inspiration,"[3] says the company. Kamprad apparently never cared much to emulate the business elite, although he is constantly billed as Sweden's answer to Sam Walton. Superficially, it would seem the pair had a lot in common. Both founded hugely successful ventures that sell vast volumes of goods at low prices. But in IKEA's case, success is largely due to other important traits, such as stylish design and function—along with the inimitable vision that keeps everything together. Kamprad has always had a strong point of view.

Some of the European press has been rather harsh about Kamprad's opinions, which he laid out for all to read in his hyperbolic 1976 tract, entitled *The Testament of a Furniture Dealer.* This essay delves into Kamprad's personal beliefs about business, society, and the ideal role of IKEA in the world. It is required reading for all new IKEA coworkers (Kamprad is philosophically opposed to the term *employee*). In his tract, Kamprad describes the original concept behind IKEA as something "sacred" and writes such things as: "We decided once and for all to side with the many," "Waste of resources is a mortal sin at IKEA," "Happiness is not to reach one's goal but to be on the way," "Only while sleeping one makes no mistakes," and "What we want, we can and will do. Together. A glorious future!"

Certain journalists interpret Kamprad's ideals as zealous propaganda, but Kamprad has always insisted that what his moral message comes down to are some rather basic tenets: that anything is possible, everyone is equal, hard work is necessary, and it is fine to make errors. Apparently, Kamprad originally founded IKEA as part of an egalitarian crusade. The concept of the company is such that it demands self-sufficiency from coworkers and even from customers who have to assemble furniture themselves. Thus, Kamprad indicates, IKEA exists to serve the dual higher purpose of both "creating a better everyday life for the many people" and also of "helping people to improve themselves."[4] But there are those who are unsettled by this underlying meaning: "[One gets] the creepy sense that IKEA is something more than just an extremely successful capitalist enterprise—that to work for it is to work for some kind of cult,"[5] said the *Guardian* in a 2004 article. Taken out of context, the *Guardian*'s review nearly suggests that a business that serves an interest other than the amassing of monetary wealth is necessarily some kind of cult.

In any event, before examining how Kamprad went about bringing to life his original "cult" vision or higher purpose (depending on how you see it), it is fascinating to first consider just how effective the efforts have been. Let's say for the sake of argument that IKEA's dearest stakeholders have indeed drunk the proverbial corporate Kool-Aid. First, observe how there are masses of them—far more converts than critics—who seem to be desperately thirsty for more of what the company is serving. Next, consider why this is so.

In 2006, over 310 million people visited IKEA worldwide. Additionally, 160 million copies of the IKEA catalog were printed and distributed, which, the company tells people, is appreciably more than the Bible. It has been calculated that on some Sundays in the UK, almost twice as many people visit IKEA as attend church and that 10 percent of Europeans currently alive were conceived in one of IKEA's beds. In the United States, when IKEA's Atlanta and Stoughton, Massachusetts, stores opened in 2005, thousands of people camped out by the store's entrances, and reportedly, diehard campers had been stationed there for weeks. In the Far East, when IKEA's second Shanghai store opened in 2003, the store welcomed 80,000 visitors on the first day of business. And in both 2004 and 2005, when two separate IKEA stores opened in London and Jeddah, they created such a frenzy among customers that at least twenty-five people were trampled after everyone tried to rush into the store at once. In the Jeddah incident, several people lost their lives.

In the case of Jeddah, Saudi Arabian cultural and political circumstances likely played a part in the customer frenzy, but still, one has to wonder about the growing global brand phenomenon. Stakeholder love and devotion is one thing, but what causes the fanaticism?

At present, there literally are thousands of IKEA "fanatic" sites, forums, and blogs hosted by users across the United States, eastern and western Europe, Asia, and even the Middle East who are hopelessly devoted to the company. One independently hosted site, Ohikea.com, run by Ohio-based Web designer Jen Segrest, exists because "man cannot live on Target alone." In addition to posting the latest news about IKEA, the site encourages people to "Wear your passion" with IKEA fan merchandise such as T-shirts, bumper stickers, and hats. Another blog, appropriately named Positive Fanatics, hosted by Illinois-based artist and photographer Armand Frasco, goes so far as to spotlight the original egalitarian vision of Kamprad and host philosophical discussions with IKEA fans, who bond over a mutual appreciation of the company's aesthetic and values.

We asked Frasco to describe exactly what motivates him to devote so much of his time to promoting IKEA, to which he responded with this mysterious portrayal:

There is just something about the experience. IKEA is radical. I am personally intrigued by the philosophy of the founders and the management style. I like that. That's why I started my blog. But when you enter an IKEA store, it's just different. I have asked a lot of people about this and they agree. You can't quite put your finger on it . . . There's a certain energy there. I guess, to sum it up in one word, it's cool.

Most IKEA coworkers appear equally as drawn in. Vault.com reflects feedback from hundreds inside the company who indicate that IKEA's values do translate to utmost personal loyalty. A store manager in Los Angeles describes why in a workplace survey:

> At IKEA *we are all coworkers. Socialistic? I don't think so. Unpretentious? Definitely. And, believe it or not, one can go from handling carts to being a store manager. Hours can be flexible, life balance is encouraged, women can move up, and diversity is promoted sincerely . . . Store managers can wear uniforms if they choose and skip the high clothing bills! . . . We encourage straightforward communication across all levels and, I believe, most people love working here! In fact, . . . we're hiring "Why-sayers"—people who ask "why" and dare to challenge old ways of working! We don't use a lot of titles, so you can be what you want to be and call yourself whatever.*[6]

No doubt, regular folks like IKEA for its good design and low prices. But the most enthusiastic stakeholders are attracted to the deeper elements. Frasco's sense of "energy" picks up on something considerable. The real secret of IKEA's phenomenal success exists beneath the brand's exterior. IKEA subliminally provides something that people feel thirsty, even desperately thirsty for. The company arouses people partly because it fills an emotional and spiritual void. More specifically, IKEA helps people to fill the void for themselves.

In today's society, a great many people feel empty and cut off. Apparently, Kamprad thinks that's because many of us have grown distracted by the wrong things. We've forgotten the value of hard work and lost touch with what is really important. Our everyday chores, namely shopping and working, which should provide us with enrichment, have become mindless activities. In many ways, life has lost its flavor. Kamprad envisioned IKEA as an antidote to these problems.

For instance, IKEA products—their clean lines, brightness, function-ality, simplicity, and environmental integrity—bring quality to the masses. They deliver on the IKEA purpose of "creating a better every-day life for the many people" by breaking down barriers that separate the classes. Now everyone can afford to beautify their surroundings, not just the very rich. Similarly, the IKEA retail experience—with its awe-inspiring blue-and-yellow 300,000-square-foot buildings, expertly staffed child play centers, lifelike displays, circular maze of rooms, Scandinavian aesthetic, and Swedish meatballs—foster amusement, exploration, and self-sufficiency. IKEA makes an adventure out of shopping. People are enthralled and culturally enriched by the experi-ence, *and* they have to load their own cars and unpack and assemble the products in their own homes. In his 1990 business case, "Ingvar Kamprad and IKEA," Professor Christopher A. Bartlett of Harvard Business School categorized these things as "gentle coercions," or ways of getting shoppers to stay longer and buy more. Indeed, all of these things have a way of engaging people to the point where they discover new items that they didn't previously realize they needed. The shop-ping experience at IKEA is part theater and part treasure hunt. But there is more to the IKEA phenomenon.

Inside IKEA, the higher purpose of "helping people to improve themselves" is equally abundant as the corporate culture is a deliber-ate antidote to the traditional mechanistic mind-set. The egalitarian crusade is brimming with life. Regularly staged Antibureaucracy Weeks put seniormost executives to work on the sales floor and be-hind cash registers, while new IKEA coworkers are given social and environmental training as they, too, will have to help meet the compa-ny's progressively tougher demands in these areas. The company has cultivated ways to make people become more self-reliant, more sup-portive of others, and also more prone to take initiative, regardless of their rank. For instance, coworkers are financially rewarded for devis-ing better ways of doing things as IKEA is always looking for ways of improving itself. "We like change," says the company on its recruiting Web site. "People in the IKEA Group are often more stimulated by finding ways of achieving their goals than by the goal itself. They take inspiration from discovery and are constantly 'on the way' to the next challenge." Conversely, leaders are financially rewarded for promoting a sense of well-being. "A leader at the IKEA Group can accomplish more by creating a good working environment than any other means," says the company.

The basic principles of IKEA's egalitarian crusade infer that everyone working at the company—from the seniormost leaders to cashiers—is equally valuable and that anything is possible. Additionally, the company conveys a level of fearlessness and resistance to the status quo, as well as to the mental barriers that could hold it back from achieving its highest goals. "We know exactly what we want, and our desire to get it should be irrepressible," the company tells people. Just as in any other case, IKEA's egalitarian crusade and purpose made real through the company's internal management atmosphere translate to a meaningful customer experience.

When one walks into an IKEA store and looks around; when one reads the signs that say, "Välkommen!"; when one engages with a hearty coworker, the ethos is reflected. This is an integral part of what makes IKEA work. One cannot separate the lifestyle brand that is IKEA from the lifestyle that is the corporate culture. These two things are one and the same. That's why people believe the retail experience. They buy into the whole IKEA concept because they have reason to. This added dimension of reality is Frasco's perceived energy. IKEA provides people with not just a story, but with an enveloping, unfolding, true story. IKEA is not just a company with great merchandising, it is a company with great merchandising that reflects an inspiring vision and purpose. Throughout the experience, that vision and purpose is reflected a hundred different ways. The combination of vision and purpose conveyed at IKEA are so inspiring, in fact, that they cause some stakeholders to become evangelists—and in extreme cases, fanatics. Therefore, at IKEA, it is not a superficial layer alone that draws people in, but rather the internal atmosphere that creates the external conditions that draw people in and keep them hooked. Kamprad himself has even said on several occasions: "Maintaining a strong IKEA culture is one of the most crucial factors behind the continued success of the IKEA concept."[7]

Another central concept born internally from IKEA's purpose and conveyed externally throughout the IKEA experience is economy. But when IKEA says "economy," it doesn't just mean it literally, in terms of lower retail prices, as most surmise. IKEA means economy in the wider sense of doing more with less. For instance, IKEA gets stakeholders, particularly coworkers, to reevaluate their life priorities and become less materialistic. Just as egalitarianism is embraced, status symbols are shunned throughout the corporate culture, and as the California store manager featured on Vault.com indicated, many people working within the company find this to be liberating. This sense of economic liberation, of not being a slave to fashion, is also conveyed in the IKEA brand experience, and customers appreciate it.

IKEA also hates the idea of wasted resources. Economy at IKEA additionally means taking every possible measure to ensure that no unnecessary natural resources, human resources, packaging, space, time, and especially money are spent at any point during the business cycle. "Doing more with less is" a mantra at the firm. IKEA is known for being frugal, and whether that means that all who work for the company— from the president on down—fly coach when they travel or that the company avoids working with complicated furniture concepts, expensive pigments, or undesirable suppliers, that mantra is carried out. IKEA guarantees customers "low cost, but not at any cost." Its product development model keeps prices low by relying mostly on renewable and recyclable materials and by minimizing the use of materials. For instance, IKEA's chair legs are hollow instead of solid, and particleboard cores are used in many furniture pieces in lieu of hardwood. IKEA has strict forestry requirements and does not use wood from virgin forests. Thus, various of IKEA's wood pieces are made from an inexpensive blend of wood chips, while some storage systems were born from things such as recycled milk cartons. IKEA is always looking for ways to refashion existing materials, thus turning trash into treasure. At the end of their life, most IKEA items can be disassembled, and all IKEA stores take back products and recycle or resell parts. IKEA also flat-packs its items in transport, thus squeezing more product into less packaging space and cutting down considerably on carbon dioxide emissions, waste, and costs.

Along these lines, IKEA often talks about taking "many small steps forward," rather than making large leaps at once. Recently, company president Anders Dahlvig was asked to characterize for shareholders IKEA's total social and environmental impact. Of this he said: "We're moving in the right direction, but we must remain humble."[8] It was yet another indication of the company's genuine trait.

THE PARANOID SURVIVE

It's interesting: we found that many of the firms in our study that loudly proclaimed themselves good citizens did some of the least progressive and productive things, while the ones that took the most novel approaches and generated the best returns more often than not *downplayed* their achievements. It is possible that this is a fluke or condition unique to our sample of seventy-five firms. More likely, however, it plays back to the adage that Intel founder Andrew Grove encapsulated in his book *Only the Paranoid Survive*, which is that self-satisfaction and complacency invite competitive disadvantage, whereas healthy self-criticism allows for continual advancement.

Perfection is never fully achieved, and market conditions are always changing. In his book, Grove notes that owing to this, the best companies are always engaged in critical self-assessment. They constantly regroup, rethink, and revise their strategic approaches because the competitive climate demands this. Also, deep down, even when their companies are succeeding by the traditional measures, the very best corporate leaders always feel a little restless, as if they ought to be doing more. Leadership experts characterize this trait as "constructive discontentment."

These two traits of critical self-assessment and constructive discontentment are exhibited in Anchored High-Purpose Companies. While each of the firms in this chapter is excessively idealistic, none is self-righteous. Not one has become contented, and none talks down to stakeholders. IKEA's Kamprad surely has fundamental and unswerving beliefs, and his company is engineered to improve the world, although he insists: "No one has made more mistakes than I have." Through his personal statements, Kamprad repeatedly conveys that the ability to compensate for one's own shortcomings helps to form the foundations for his company's culture.[9] Similarly, Wainwright's Robert Glassman communicated his feeling of unworthiness to us immediately, almost as soon as our interview with him commenced. He felt as if he didn't deserve the credit for the success of his bank. It was as if he realized that there was still so much work to be done and that to gloat would be akin to undermining the legitimacy of his mission.

In line with the trait, Michael Crooke, president and CEO of outdoor gear retailer Patagonia begins his speeches by telling people what a huge polluter his company is: "The bigger we get, the more we pollute," he always says. People in the environmental community typically regard Patagonia as one of the greenest, most responsible companies around, so Crooke's admission catches audiences off guard. After all, Patagonia was the first company in its category to use 100 percent organic cotton. It currently makes its PCR (post consumer recycled) Synchilla fleece clothing out of used soda bottles, consequently diverting tens of millions of pounds of plastic from ending up in landfills every year; relies on renewable sources of energy like wind for power;

builds its buildings using the latest in green design innovations; donates 1 percent of its sales to the preservation of the environment; promotes balance and family togetherness through an elaborate on-site child care facility (which includes toddler, preschool, and kindergarten programs); pays employees for their charity work; and gives them $2,000 bonuses for buying hybrid cars.

Patagonia also uses its marketing muscle to call attention to important issues, like the need to reduce threats to wild salmon, conserve water, save agricultural resources, and protect virgin forests. It devotes space on its Web site, in its catalog, and in its stores to voice its opinion and get people thinking and talking about what's most important. "Someone needs to be the loud voice out there, banging the gong. We want to be that," says Eve Bould, director of communications. "We help to amplify the voices of grassroots activists, so we really can't be whitewashing our messages or taking the traditional corporate stance on things when we're trying to give a voice to the people who are out there in the field doing the hard environmental work."

Certain community members throughout the nation would rather that grassroots activist voices remain muffled, and many have grown incensed by Patagonia's determination to be a loudspeaker for certain causes. In response to one of the company's local advertisements that promoted the message of virgin forest protection groups, for instance, one Oregon local yokel sent this letter:

Patagonia—
Greetings from Grants Pass, Oregon. Saw your ad in The Daily
Center. *I have a suggestion: Why don't you bastards keep your nose out of our business. And our lives!!! Come around here and we will take care of pukes like you! YOU LIE AND YOU WILL BE STOPPED. STAY OUT AND STAY HOME. MIND YOUR OWN BUSINESS.*[10]

According to Patagonia, for its support of forest protection, the company received thousands of similar letters and a box of one customer's Patagonia gear. One retailer in California stopped carrying Patagonia merchandise after heavy pressure from a lumber company, while another in Maine did the same thing after Patagonia supported the creation of a national park in the New England state. But just like Wainwright and IKEA, Patagonia does not stand down. It refuses to entertain those who would take offense to its environmental crusade. "We're not out to make everyone like Patagonia," says Bould. "Our founder, Yvon Chouinard, often says that he's perfectly happy if half the people hate us, as long as our core customers love us and know what we are all about." Indeed, let the people who could care less about the implications of human activity on the environment stock and shop other brands.

Patagonia remains true to its core beliefs and that is one side of its strength. Another side is the company's adjacent modesty. "We recognize that we're far from perfect," says Bould. "We never want to give the impression that we are patting ourselves on the back or congratulating ourselves for all of our environmental achievements." Bould's sentiment is consistently reflected throughout the company's communications. In Patagonia's corporate responsibility brochure, entitled *Louder Than Words*, for instance, the company makes this point by telling stakeholders: "We are a long way from calling ourselves an 'environmentally friendly' business." Together with Crooke's pollution demonstrations, Patagonia's public acknowledgement of deficiency proves a point: the more one knows about environmental problems and the role of business in contributing to those problems, the more one realizes how much needs to be fixed. That's why the companies that are the real leaders in the field would never dream of brashly casting themselves as leaders in the field.

When Patagonia selected its core statement of purpose, it was scrupulous. "[We] exist as a business to inspire and implement solutions to the environmental crisis," the company says. As one of the better corporate purpose statements out there, Patagonia's is short, spare, and lacks wiggle room.[11] However, it also presents its challenges. "One of Yvon's main philosophies is to always try to perform better but also to recognize reality and not sugarcoat the fact that we are in an environmental crisis. The reason we are in business is to address that crisis," explains Bould. "At the same time, we cannot deny the fact that because we are in business, we are contributing to environmental problems. So this creates a conundrum." The best part of the conundrum is that Patagonia really does take on the world's environmental crisis to the extent where the process of doing so causes constant growing pains for the organization. Patagonia's relentless pursuit of purpose is unsettling because it can make the company's prized breakthroughs suddenly appear faulty.

Patagonia creates organizational excellence by fostering constructive discontentment. It considers not one of its current environmental achievements to be good enough to be left alone. Take organic cotton and PCR fleece, two of Patagonia's chief materials and, many would say, top environmental contributions. Bould points out that cotton uses an inordinate amount of water to grow and that, after being grown year after year, permanently depletes the soil. "Everything takes its toll," she explains. Organic cotton also has to be dyed for production, thus adding to the material's environmental toll. In the same vein, PCR fleece is made from nonbiodegradable plastic, which in order to be made into fabric in the first place has to be melted down in a process that creates greenhouse gases. "We're frustrated with PCR fleece," says Bould. "Although we do recognize that the innovation was a good step forward, ultimately PCR garments end up in landfills. We're just delaying the waste process." Thus, from an environmental point of view, neither of these materials is ideal, but Patagonia is making progress. "Our goal for the future is closed loop, meaning that no waste is produced. If you can't compost it, then you should be able to recycle it," she explains.

Starting in fall 2006, Patagonia will be offering recycled clothing made from scrap fiber and recycled plastics marketed under its Capilene line. "These new innovations are a great step forward for us," says Bould. "They still aren't 100 percent closed loop, but are definitely a step in the right direction." The new recycled lines embody Patagonia's developmental approach, which is all about making incremental improvements and learning from the past. The company applies the incremental method to all of its projects, from product design to construction and remodeling.

Patagonia's 1984 Mission-style corporate headquarters in Ventura, California, is a good example of this incremental learning curve. Just like PCR fleece, the building itself was originally conceived as an environmental innovation but later viewed somewhat differently. The building is located near a prime surf break and appears as the antithesis of a sterile corporate environment, "with no acoustic drop-tile ceilings, aluminum window frames or pre-fab work cubicles," says Patagonia in its description of the original space. "Instead there is aesthetic simplicity—trim and molding of vertical grain fir and much artwork of wild nature—that embodies our environmental ethos. Or so we thought." It turns out that in the company's initial go, Patagonia got ahead of itself and was a little naïve. While the 1984 headquarters building reflected an environmental aesthetic, that was all. The company had chosen esthetic over priority and had used virgin materials throughout. "It's made from old growth forests that we are now fighting to protect,"[12] says the company.

By now, Patagonia has transformed the site, using recycled, reclaimed, and nontoxic materials. It has also approached new development projects using state-of-the-art green building innovations. Patagonia's 171,000-square-foot Reno Service Center structure was built mostly from recycled materials, while its all-steel framework has a minimum of 98.5 percent recycled content, and 90 percent of the wood used internally is "reclaimed" from forest fires, old barns, bridges, or buildings. "We even sweated the details using 100 percent recycled plastic bathroom partitions, low-flow shower heads and toilets, and lighting 'zones' that use motion sensors to shut off unneeded lights,"[13] the company says. According to Patagonia, these innovations plus others add up to annual energy savings of up to 35 percent.

Different areas of Patagonia's business have undergone similar reassessment. One such area is marketing communications. Apparently, Patagonia has been so engrossed in implementing its higher purpose over recent years that it has failed to effectively translate the significance of its activities to consumers. "We struggle with this because we don't want to engage in 'green marketing,' and we don't want to overstate our progress in green building or environmental fabrics," says Bould. "But then again, it's interesting to compare our brand's reputation to that of other brands. Some of our customers believe that our competitors, like REI, are more environmentally friendly than we are based on the advertising campaigns they run." In this instance, consumer ignorance is a risk. To inspire solutions to the environmental crisis, Patagonia realized that it needed to go public with its own.[14] "In the past, we have been quiet," says Bould. "To fulfill our purpose, get consumers activated, and even get other companies to invest in organic cotton and green building for instance, we believe that we have an obligation to make our voice heard more going forward."

Essentially, nothing at Patagonia is set in stone. Although the company now intends to ignite passion for its cause, it is unwilling to claim that it is the industry's "best environmental performer" partly because, owing to its pursuit of purpose, its environmental goals are always changing. The most important thing is that Patagonia gets to the systemic level by looking at the multilayered effects of its decisions. It relentlessly explores what "better performance" is and then innovates in pace with its discoveries.

IN THE FLOW

"The significant problems we face cannot be solved at the same level of thinking we were at when we created them." Although this illustrious Albert Einstein passage is often misquoted, most people get the picture. Patagonia's thinking was at a certain level when it invented PCR fleece, engineered its 1984 headquarters building, and stayed quiet about its higher purpose. Certainly, these things weren't originally viewed as problems. On the contrary, they were once viewed as solutions to problems. Only now, in retrospect, does the company see them as areas for improvement. That's because the company's thinking has advanced. Patagonia is in the flow. Through its internal process and culture, it invites progress and creativity in. It remains an open receptor for inspiration that helps it to reach higher planes of thinking or consciousness. Patagonia is deliberately becoming a more intelligent entity. If this flow is maintained, it will only help Patagonia to perform better over time.

Eileen Fisher, a retailer of upscale women's clothing, mastered the same skill. "We've figured it out by being in it," says Susan Schor, chief culture officer. "There is so much in our company that is done organically. We use this phrase 'In the river' a lot because we're always in the midst of changing. We're always creating what's coming next." As Schor indicates, the term *organic* applies to much of what Eileen Fisher does, ranging from the organic cotton used to make its clothes to the internal process that Schor describes. Just like Patagonia, Eileen Fisher constantly self-evaluates in an effort to determine what it can do better. Unlike many traditional corporations, Eileen Fisher does not approach the change process abruptly, or even deliberately, with stops and starts. "It just flows," says Schor. "We spend a lot of time visioning and revisioning. We allow ourselves the space and time to figure out what's right and learn as we go."

Some might consider where Eileen Fisher has managed to go during the course of its twenty-year existence to be quite remarkable, particularly if you contrast the company's path with those of other designers, who tend to come in and out of fashion rather quickly. Eileen Fisher boasts a healthy, steady $173 million business. Its assortments at major retailers like Nordstrom, Saks Fifth Avenue, and Neiman Marcus remain consistent from season to season, while the company marches to the beat of its own drum. Its unique "organic" philosophy translates into design. Customers remain loyal to Eileen Fisher because it is a brand that values simplicity over trend, comfort over edge, and versatility over multiplicity. Most high-end designers are always baiting women into throwing away the previous season's goods and buying more and more stuff for different occasions, but Eileen Fisher does not do that: "I want to wear—and make—clothing that works with all the dimensions of my life," says company founder Eileen Fisher. "I want to do yoga, go to work and go out for an evening in the same clothes—change a single piece instead of changing my entire outfit."[15]

Eileen Fisher is one of the only high-end fashion brands with a higher purpose, which is to "inspire simplicity, creativity and delight through connection and great design." While its clothing designs promote simplicity, the company's outreach, management practices, and internal culture promote utmost creativity and delight. Through grants and carefully designed social initiatives, Eileen Fisher fights for issues including women's health and well-being as well as women's independence and empowerment. In 2005, for instance, it issued $10,000 Vision Grants to women entrepreneurs. The company is also known to offer yoga, Pilates, qigong, and massage in its corporate offices and independent retail store locations. "We strive to develop a culture that encourages people to stop, stretch, and breathe," Schor says. Eileen Fisher additionally carries out its commitment to promoting social and environmental consciousness to the supply chain and manufacturing levels, and is one of a handful of SA8000-certified companies in its category. "Consciousness is all about awareness," the company says.

Rather than do less harm, Eileen Fisher intends to be productive: "We seek to improve conditions for our fellow factory worker, natural environment and women in our community."[16]

While these attributes surely set Eileen Fisher apart from other fashion brands, what establishes the company as an Anchored High-Purpose Company is its approach to leadership and organizational change. Above all else, Schor says, leaders in the company have four central priorities: ensuring the growth and well-being of the people they oversee, fostering collaboration and teamwork, maintaining a joyful atmosphere, and promoting the company's commitment to social consciousness. "These are our core practice areas," explains Schor. "We put a great deal of emphasis on these, particularly on the element of individual growth and well-being because that's what makes us stronger." Put into action, many of these practice areas manifest in rather counterintuitive ways. For instance, during the employee review process, the company's priority is to determine how it performed through the eyes of its people, as opposed to how people performed through the eyes of management. "The employee owns most of the review, and the emphasis is placed on thinking about what's next," says Schor. "It's about helping the person to recognize what they did really well, and then helping to replicate more positive experiences for that person going forward. We are always looking for ways of allowing people to pursue their passions."

Schor says that often, the outcome of the review sessions is such that work gets shifted from person to person so that the nature of work is always kept in line with people's interests. More significantly, however, the process says a lot about the company's management philosophy. "Our career development approach is more about shifting the shape of someone's job than it is about defining a specific career path," Schor explains. "We think about growing and expanding roles rather than sticking to rigid hierarchies or giving lateral promotions." Eileen Fisher's culture nurtures people's strengths and remains open and receptive to change at all times. The company creates internal conditions that lead to optimal external results. "The people working here feel taken care of and have opportunities to discover their passions. They feel valued for their best selves," Schor says. "The results of all this bring us their best."

Recently, the Eileen Fisher management team underwent what most in the corporate world would consider a dramatic restructuring. In late 2005, the company totally eliminated all signs of hierarchy. Rather than be directed by a chief executive, chief financial officer, and chief operational officer, Eileen Fisher is now led by a collective of fourteen people, who work together and make major company decisions via team dialogue and consensus. As to why the decision was made, Schor explains: "It felt right in an intuitive sense based on the way we were developing. We trusted our instincts and rolled up our sleeves. We decided to really integrate, be collaborative, and make our decisions from the whole."

Schor says that the company's new leadership team essentially taught itself everything that was necessary to achieve such change, "while being in process," of course. The learning curve for changes like these are constant, she explains, especially since there are no outside examples to draw from. "It's not just a matter of the leaders learning about leading collaboratively. It is also a matter of helping the whole company to understand that it is now not just one or two people at the top, but really a group of people that represent everyone in the company." This is a significant mental shift and one that to date, Schor says, the company has had a great deal of success instilling. At this point, the company's various divisions have also embraced the new structure, or lack thereof. "The whole organization is now applying the concept of collaborative leadership," says Schor. "So rather than the VP of sales or retail heading the show, that person is really facilitating his or her team of leaders to collectively lead that large business area." The results? Schor points to enhanced creativity and delight through connection—the company's primary reasons for being. When it comes to finding enterprising new ways of fulfilling its purpose, Eileen Fisher honors no conventional boundaries.

THE SIXTH SENSE

The truly innovative do not follow tradition, remodel old models, mimic competitors' moves, or look to focus groups or polls for answers about what to do next. Neither do the truly innovative ignore the laws of nature or the lessons of history. They do, however, use their sixth sense. Truly innovative companies draw on a skill that is underutilized in the mainstream business world: *intuition*. The most significant business breakthroughs illustrated in this chapter were not set by external standards, but rather were based on an internal sense of what was right. As Susan Schor explains, the leaders "just knew." They used a blank sheet of paper—the creativity in their minds combined with the power of collaboration—to invent something totally original. They leaped into the void, believed their visions were possible, trusted their teammates, and were unafraid of the unknown. This is Anchoring.

When a leader's sixth sense is strong, it feels like second nature to manifest the kind of internal atmosphere that makes people working in the company as happy, healthy, and productive as possible. If you spend time browsing the Web sites and CSR reports of the companies reviewed in this chapter, you will learn more about how most of them have instituted extensive management practices, employee benefits and wellness programs, child care facilities, and even extracurricular employee internship and off-site learning programs that reach beyond that which was described in this book. Every one of these companies has formed unbreakable bonds with consumers by creating an authentic, meaningful experience, and each has established an intricate internal environment, where individual expression is promoted and there are no artificial barriers, traditional hierarchies, or strict employee codes of conduct to be found. We do not believe that this movement toward intimacy is a coincidence, nor do we view the lack of structure as an eccentricity. It is clear that within certain companies—large and small, public and private—there is the desire and ability to cherish human relationships and to promote human creativity. And the same organizations that promote human creativity have achieved utmost ingenuity through their market solutions. Here is yet another correlation of significance: give people the room and desire to be innovative and they will be.

The process of Anchoring creates a sort of vacuum where High-Purpose Companies create their own inner world, and nearly get lost in it. For instance, upon telling Eileen Fisher's Schor how rare her company's management practices were, she commented: "We don't really view ourselves as different from the rest of corporate America. I guess since we're in it, it is hard to notice." Such companies become engrossed in their own process of perpetual change. By way of their own intentions and goals, Anchored High-Purpose Companies are prompted to continually search out their weaknesses, to refine them and to extend themselves further and further down their chosen path toward the fulfillment of purpose. Thus, the very process of Anchoring makes mediocrity unacceptable. Anchoring leads to greatness.

Anchored High-Purpose Companies care about little other than improving themselves and, in turn, the world. That is their top priority. Taking care of their people, establishing an inspired corporate culture, staying true to their core beliefs, discovering what better performance is, reaching better performance goals, and finding enterprising new ways of fulfilling their higher purpose is the mandate of such firms. These companies do not worry so much about the stuff that happens outside of this circle. As a result, Anchored High-Purpose Companies are totally inner-directed. They are purely proactive and, we argue, among the healthiest companies in the world. They are the corporate equivalent of what renowned psychologist Dr. Abraham Maslow identified as a

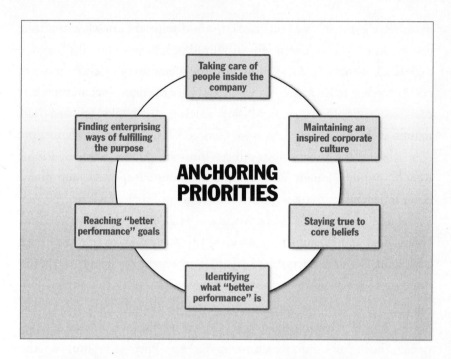

self-actualized individual in the sense that they become everything they are capable of becoming. In describing this state, which he viewed as the pinnacle in the hierarchy of human needs, Maslow said:

> *Human life will never be understood unless its highest aspirations are taken into account. Growth, self-actualization, the striving toward health, the quest for identity and autonomy, the yearning for excellence (and other ways of phrasing the striving "upward") must by now be accepted beyond question as a widespread and perhaps universal human tendency.*[17]

It is possible that this psychological need for self-actualization is what drives so many corporate leaders to seek out a corporate purpose in the first place. Perhaps self-actualization is a partial point human existence. Maybe we are all, as Maslow believed, hardwired to want to feel as if we have done our part to better the world. What is certain is that at this time more than ever, the survival of our world depends on self-actualized people. Maslow considered self-actualized people as among the psychologically healthiest in society and also the greatest contributors to society. According to his analysis, one factor begot the next—yet another key correlation of significance. In Maslow's articles and books, he often used figures such as Thomas Jefferson, George Washington, Abraham Lincoln (during his later years), Albert Einstein, Aldous Huxley, Pierre Renoir, William James, Walt Whitman, Eleanor Roosevelt, and many other independent thinkers as prime examples of such persons.

Like self-actualized people, Anchored High-Purpose Companies are exceptional and yet imperfect entities, still struggling to improve. Like their human counterparts, these organizations strive for health and at the same time, are painfully self-aware. They view and evaluate their own imperfections much more clearly and carefully than do most other businesses. This lucidity is an advantage, as it creates the inclination to evolve. In fact, the higher companies move up the High-Purpose Progression, the harder they work to improve and to climb higher still. The Anchor phase is not a finish line because companies do not stop developing. As Maslow indicates, this phase is more of a perpetual state of mind reinforced by spontaneous, self-affirming actions. The challenge to improve and serve the purpose is without end. *This is the point of the game.*

A higher purpose is best viewed as something that a company can spend its entire lifetime living up to. As with perfection, it is possible that the purpose is never fully realized. However, the journey is worthwhile because it can lead the company to some of its worthiest achievements. The cases and achievements throughout this book and the impact those achievements produce for individual stakeholders, society, business, the economy, the environment, and future generations all demonstrate this. When activated, a higher purpose leads to the most productive kind of progress imaginable. High-Purpose Companies are bound to have an enormous impact on the way the markets move and people live in years ahead.

THE NEXT GENERATION

The current crop of MBAs and recent business school graduates are another indication of the unconventional leadership mentality and vision coming to fruition. Businesspeople should look to this generation, many of whom can be found gathering at networking organizations like Net Impact, as teachers. These future leaders have a fresh perspective and are trained to be analytical. They question the rules and are not jaded or weighed down by too much experience. Their minds are free. Their will to change things is glaring. And in many cases, their business ideas are revolutionary.

"It's starting," says Tom Arnold, a 2005 University of Pennsylvania Wharton School graduate and chief environmental officer of startup company TerraPass. "You can see it reflected in chosen vocations, business plans, and investor confidence for new ventures." Arnold is talking about the student-led shift toward purpose and the consequential impact that the shift will have on tomorrow's companies. "This next generation of business leaders is looking at what their parents did and at what executives have been doing, especially over the past five or ten years, and we're cringing. We're saying: 'That is not the life that I want.' 'That is not the world I want to live in.' "

Arnold knows for certain that the world he wants to live in is not the one that previous generations built because, for one thing, he's seen global warming—up close and personal. While at Wharton, Arnold attended a leadership venture to Antarctica with twenty-two of his classmates. While there, each student caught a glimpse of the consequences that so many others can't quite conceptualize. "Literally everyone we met on the island was studying climate change," says Arnold. "Each researcher indicated that things that were really, drastically different in the past ten years since they had been keeping records." While data shows that parts of Antarctica endure a warming of anywhere from two to five degrees Celsius per year, Arnold's classmates experienced a coincidental, rapid climate change while they were on the island. The temperature rose dramatically over a twenty-four-hour period, and the frozen ground turned to slush, causing students to become drenched. "The whole island started to melt. It was insane. The volume of water these ice sheets release is just massive," says Arnold. The students visualized the power of melting ice and rising temperatures on a mass scale. They envisioned the real threat: not merely the difference of one or two degrees in temperature, but the resulting potential for cataclysmic floods and megastorms. Rising temperatures can mean a deluge of water in some areas, but it can also mean drought in others. The combination of drought and flooding can lead to famine, migration, and species extinction, along with increased risk of international insecurity. According to Arnold, the group had a crash course in Global Warming 101: "We all left wanting to do something to stop the cycle."

Arnold found his way at TerraPass, a capitalist venture specifically designed to reduce the impact of carbon dioxide pollution, a leading cause of global warming. "TerraPass is a really big experiment," says Arnold. "We're the first pure-play, for-profit environmental startup." TerraPass allows consumers to offset the emissions produced by their cars. Under the TerraPass program, consumers buy a pass with a fee proportional to their vehicle's carbon dioxide emissions—ranging from $30 annually for a hybrid to $80 for an SUV. TerraPass then invests the money in three types of leading-edge projects, including clean energy, such as wind and biodiesel; biomass, such as dairy farm methane; and industrial efficiency through the company's participation in the Chicago Climate Exchange.

TerraPass opened for business in November 2004, and by March 2006 it had signed up 3,300 customers and, by way of its clean energy funding projects, had also reduced over 50 million pounds of carbon dioxide pollution from entering the atmosphere. TerraPass has grown exclusively through viral marketing and word of mouth. Of the 3,300 customers the company counts, 450 were engaged enough to contribute blog posts on the company's Web site about key issues like energy conservation and the peak oil problem. "The whole experience we provide is key," Arnold says. TerraPass provides consumers with a forum and convinces them to participate in the carbon market, which is something that hasn't been done before. Though the company sells consumers nothing tangible other than a bumper sticker, it does present a value proposition that most environmental philanthropies do not. "When people buy a TerraPass for their cars, they get 12,000 pounds of CO_2," Arnold explains. "They're not paying for a lunch in DC. We're offering people a concrete unitization of environmental and social good. That's what enables our business model to work."

The fact that conscientious consumers are equally, if not more, willing to contribute to TerraPass as they are to, say, the Sierra Club opens the doors for a whole new generation of entrepreneurs. In Arnold's view, it also represents new level of opportunity for investment in consumer play in environmental markets, which much like the recycling market, could experience rapid development in coming years. "This could easily be a multibillion dollar industry," Arnold says. The right investors, like New Jersey-based GreenShift, apparently agree. "When we've talked about this idea to the philanthropic community, they've been intrigued but not ready, whereas the venture community is writing us checks," he says. Venture capitalists apparently better understand the TerraPass concept and appreciate the potential for expansion and growth. "They got the model immediately and liked the return that the business offered." It also helps that TerraPass speaks the native tongue. While the company is run by the cool, educated, somewhat nerdy and opinionated people that represent the mentality of its own target audience, it was engineered by people more representative of the venture mind-set than that of the philanthropist.

TerraPass was shaped in a classroom as part of an MBA problem-solving course offered by Wharton professor Karl Ulrich. "The first day of class, Karl walked in with a check for $5,000 and this idea of a student challenge for creating what he called a retail carbon offset business," says Arnold. "Something inside of me just clicked. I thought, this is such a strange combination of entrepreneurialism and making a meaningful contribution to the world." During the course of the semester, students would use different analytical means of determining the viability of the business. One of these means was a systemic analysis of global warming and how to go about presenting the issue to consumers in a way that was most compelling. "There appeared to be no leverage on the problem," explains Arnold. "Consumers needed a way to perceive it. We determined that in the past, the problem was marketing." Apparently, environmentalists hadn't sold global warming to consumers in a way that was meaningful enough. Students surmised that owing to this, linking TerraPass with consumers' cars was the right way to go since people could readily associate the connection between driving, tailpipe exhaust and atmospheric carbon buildup. "You can see auto emissions, and you drive your car everyday, so there is this mind-heart connection," says Arnold. TerraPass had an initial guilt hook with which it would draw consumers in, although students determined that to keep consumers engaged, it should focus on the opportunistic aspects of environmental activism rather than harp on the negative. This seems to be a winning formula for the company, whose goals are to reach 1 million members and reduce 10 billion pounds of carbon dioxide pollution in coming years.

"I think it's refreshing that a business like this came out of Wharton," says Arnold. Wharton doesn't make a big deal out of the study of social entrepreneurship, corporate responsibility, or philanthropy. It's a world-class academic institution that focuses on the practical teachings of management, finance, and strategy. "With the exception of Karl, if you look at the Wharton curriculum, it's not like the administration has purposed this as an area of concentration. I personally get great satisfaction from the fact that there were investment bankers in the class who took a keen interest in the project and who were great members of the team." Arnold says he wouldn't have it any other way. He views the lack of environmentalist and philanthropist team members as a good thing, and furthermore, sees the fashionable state of do-good curriculums in other business schools as something that could potentially derail the ability of future leaders to strategically address serious world problems.

"I'm not an advocate of getting a social entrepreneurship MBA," says Arnold. "First of all, what does that mean? Second, what do students sacrifice when they choose to think about just purely the issues of social enterprise? Third, the standard MBA curriculum really does prepare you for a lot of this stuff. It prepares you for decision making. It prepares you for leadership." To be sure, if sound corporate decision making and leadership in the twenty-first century *requires* that pervasive world problems and new market conditions be addressed, and that societal and environmental balance be restored, then why the separation? Why marginalize a broad concept that applies equally to every business sect?

"At the end of the day, these are just business problems," says Arnold of the issues such as global water shortage, global warming, pollution, poverty, and disease that are often discussed in social entrepreneurship classes. "It's up to each of us to put a multifaceted lens on these problems and create a structure that produces the optimal business, social, and environmental outcomes. What is necessary is not a new 'hot' area of study or practice that branches out, but rather that the rest of business adapts by developing this lens."

Amen.

ANCHOR

Company	Purpose	Wisdom
Wainwright	"Providing equality and financial empowerment."	Stand for something potent. Do not waver.
IKEA	"Creating a better everyday life for the many people."	Emulate the ideal results inside the company.
Patagonia	"Inspiring and implementing solutions to the environmental crisis."	Let constructive discontent be the motive for better performance.
Eileen Fisher	"Inspiring simplicity, creativity and delight through connection and great design."	Allow intuition to develop and lead business decision-making.
TerraPass	"Combating global warming by mitigating human-made environmental emissions."	Channel idealism to awaken investors, inspire consumers, and open new markets.

COLLECTIVE WISDOM: "The vision must be followed by the venture. It is not enough to stare up the steps — we must step up the stairs."
— Vance Havne

Epilogue:
From Critical Mass to Personal Best

The crisis is bringing us an opportunity to experience what few generations in history ever have the privilege of knowing: a generational mission; the exhilaration of a compelling moral purpose; a shared and unified cause; the thrill of being forced by circumstances to put aside the pettiness and conflict that so often stifle the restless human need for transcendence; the opportunity to rise.

—AL GORE, "THE FUTURE IS GREEN"

It was like cosmic clockwork. Al Gore's personal essay, largely about the collective search for higher purpose, appeared in *Vanity Fair*'s first ever "green issue" in May 2006, the week I sat down to write this epilogue. "When we *do* rise," Gore writes, "it will fill our spirits and bind us together. Those who are now suffocating in cynicism and despair will be able to breathe freely. Those who are now suffering from a loss of meaning in their lives will find hope. When we rise, we will experience an epiphany as we discover that this crisis is not really about politics at all. It is a moral and spiritual challenge."[1]

One might wonder: where was this rallying cry, this leadership, during the 2000 elections? And where was America's collective search for purpose? It seems that back then, neither had yet arrived. Revelations and mass movements are all about timing.

Today, Gore predicts an unprecedented public uprising. He posits that such an uprising will result largely from what he characterizes as the "planetary emergency" currently undermining our way of life. When the government fails to respond to global warming, Gore believes the people instinctively find the fire inside themselves to spring to action. They *deny* denial, replying to what he and various Republicans in the House of Representatives call "a blinding lack of awareness." Gore sees in global warming and other problems something of an opportunity for humankind to finally face the truth about our situation; to comprehend how we arrived in this predicament and then, to move forward; to evolve.

Apparently Gore is not alone. Activist and lawyer Robert F. Kennedy Jr.; California governor Arnold Schwarzenegger; San Francisco mayor Gavin Newsom; actors Julia Roberts, George Clooney, Edward Norton, Daryl Hannah, and scores of others with a similar vision to *deny denial* and *rise up* were prominently cast in *Vanity Fair*'s green issue. To my delight, so were corporate environmentalists who have moved against the grain in business, such as Lord John Browne of British Petroleum, Hank Paulson of Goldman Sachs, Yvon Chouinard of Patagonia—as well as eco-entrepreneurs and inventors like Dean Kamen of DEKA Research and Development, Heather Stephenson and Jennifer Boulden of IdealBite.com, Laurie David of StopGlobalWarming.org, Bill McDonough, Paul Hawken, and several others. *Vanity Fair*'s green issue presented society's new elite; the trendsetters on a silver platter. It heralded the arrival of a movement into the mainstream.

In his opening letter, editor Graydon Carter encapsulated the essence of the movement with the fashion headline: "Green is the new black." Eco-consciousness is now officially the highest form of personal expression. The most "fabulous" thing about all of this is, of course, its dire relevance. *Vanity Fair*'s "green issue" was released in sync with *Wired* magazine's issue headlined "Climate Crisis!", also featuring Gore and running a lead article titled, "The Next Green Revolution." *Time* magazine's cover story similarly warned: "Be Worried. Be Very Worried . . . The debate is over. Global warming is upon us—with a vengeance."[2] With these issues on my desk, and with *Too Hot Not to Handle* and *An Inconvenient Truth* in theaters and on HBO, it struck me that something surely *is* stirring, in people's hearts and minds and in the media. Global warming isn't the only issue that has people outraged. The myriad of environmental and social calamities presently facing humanity is increasingly covered with a vengeance. Particularly over the past year, journalists' tones have grown more acute, concurrently with global circumstances.

Some of the most effective, Pulitzer Prize–winning, or exceptionally compelling news stories—such as *New York Times* columnist Nicholas Kristof's coverage of the genocide in Darfur, the *Washington Post*'s Steve Fainaru's coverage of Iraq, CNN journalist Anderson Cooper's coverage of Hurricane Katrina, and even musician Bono's call for African debt relief during the 2005 G8 Summit at Gleneagles— provoked public outrage and, at some level at least, encouraged institutional response. From a political and cultural point of view, this might be considered a sign that things are moving in a healthier direction. Some say it means that the press corps is back—that the media finally has the tenacity to ask tough questions and to more compellingly cover world issues. I think it means that, even here in America, the scales are beginning to tip. The polls may not show it yet, but average people care more about the global agenda.

Enlightened citizens—namely, those who demand *all* the facts, the *whole* truth, followed by immediate and practical solutions—have reached a critical mass. As Gore indicates, the enlightened critical mass sees beyond party lines and understands that the stakes are as high as can be. Says Gore, they include "the survival of our civilization and the habitability of the Earth."[3]

There is a mounting global intensity, a burgeoning desire to respond to catastrophic conditions such as climate change, massive pollution, corporate corruption, global famine and poverty, the widening gap between the rich and the poor, HIV/AIDS, emerging pandemics, water deprivation, terrorism, extremism, racism, fascism, distressed communities, dysfunctional families, and a myriad of other deep-seated problems that have been brewing for decades, but that we have ignored and allowed to worsen. The present heady media coverage combined with a pattern of denial and subpar solutions from ineffective leaders and the public's sense of personal connection to the problems (either via empathy or direct experience) is likely to lead a critical mass of individuals in America and around the world to receive Gore's "epiphany."

This critical mass is now comprised of both average citizens and influencers in realms including business, world politics, media, religion, academia, and popular culture. A mission and mind-set is what distinguishes the critical mass, as at some level all members dedicate themselves to the *collective purpose* of stopping the bleeding, and of eventually reversing the damage done to the planet and society by destructive human activity. The nature and potential implications of this critical mass are fascinating and deserve further study. Theoretically, however, it is possible that the critical mass may someday form alternative political parties or governing organizations. Utopian as these prospects may sound, they are presently being imagined, even called for and configured.

New York magazine's April 24, 2006, issue announced one alternative, asking New Yorkers: "Depressed about the Democrats? Revolted by the Republicans? Introducing the Purple Party." In describing the need for this "third way," reporter Kurt Anderson presses the following points:

We are people without a party. We are open-minded, open-hearted moderates alienated from the two big parties because backward-looking ideologues and p.c. hypocrites are effectively in charge of both . . .

The simple question is this: Why can't we have a serious, innovative, truth-telling, pragmatic party without any of the baggage of the Democrats and Republicans? A real and enduring party built around a coherent set of ideas and sensibility . . . a robust new independent party of passionately practical progressives in the middle.

It's certainly time . . . Our party will enthusiastically embrace people of all religious beliefs, but we will never claim special divine virtue for our policies—we'll leave that to the Pat Robertsons and Osama bin Ladens. Where to draw the line is mostly a matter of common sense . . . Our new party will be highly moral (but never moralistic) as well as laissez-faire.[4]

How interesting, I thought. Highly moral and yet not moralistic. Driven by common sense. Passionately practical and progressive. Laissez-faire. Any of these traits sound familiar? Are these not the same ideals embodied by High-Purpose Companies?

Stepping back to consider the Purple Party alongside the high-purpose construct, I realized that the two mind-sets are really a part of the same critical mass mind-set that appears to be growing stronger all the time. Each Katrina or excessive oil CEO retirement package or crippling of stem-cell research or refusal to deal squarely with the reality of globalization serves as a catalyst for the cause, attracting more disillusioned members and further expanding the influence of the mass itself. One day, the critical mass mind-set might represent the majority of America's executives, voters, and consumers. Now, wouldn't that be something?

The psychographic nature and makeup of the enlightened critical mass appears rather remarkable, as evidence suggests that it is presently comprised of people of all political affiliations, age ranges, races, religious beliefs, creeds, and nationalities. For instance, Tony Blair and Queen Elizabeth signaled their potential membership through recent personal statements and achieved performance results. According to London's *Observer*, Queen Elizabeth for the first time expressed "grave concerns over the White House's stance on global warming," whereas England's economy has grown by about 40 percent since 1990 while its carbon emissions have been reduced by 14 percent during the same period.[5]

Equally compelling is that the people currently outside the critical mass, the people who neither identify with the need for the movement nor identify with true nature of earthly problems nor feel the innate, moral urge to swiftly respond and identify practical alternatives are fast becoming society's outcasts—representing the new *fringe*. Consider that cynics, procrastinators, and so-called fearmongers are the characters most often portrayed as foolish symbols of what caused things to go awry in the first place. The present backlash against the Bush administration is just one example of how, when the public is faced with the outcomes of serious problems, the parties (and corporations) who really or symbolically represent the root causes are mocked and dejected. Similarly, when and if used in a new optimistic context, the words *liberal* and *liberation* might finally come to hold far more positive connotations than they presently do.

In general, the public is hungry for something *worthy* of believing in—a collective purpose. And according to Abraham Maslow and others in his league, people might be preconditioned to respond to the call to rise up. At this moment, as Al Gore, Kurt Anderson, and others agree, the conditions seem ideal.

Forward-thinking leaders see that global society is experiencing a necessary shift in consciousness, along with an impending *revolt* against the mechanistic mind-set, not just a movement away from it as was laid out in the initial chapters of this book. I suspect that this inevitable turn of the emotional tides is likely to peak in intensity in the years ahead as we are faced with more of the economic, political, social, and environmental ramifications of our past and present irresponsible behavior. Additionally, the next generation (now entering their twenties and thirties) in America, Europe, and other regions possesses a mentality that is especially tuned into world problems and the need to solve them, compared with previous generations. This will likely have significant implications. On the positive front, strategists devising tactics for winning votes or selling wares may, even today, tap into a huge, new potential, as there are powerful heartstrings to be pulled. That is, if the candidates or corporations in question have the skill to reach for them and especially the tenacity to act in accordance with the viewpoints expressed.

High-Purpose Companies and the enlightened business people within them are one of the most powerful clusters within the ever more influential critical mass in that they can—and do—institute widespread change on a highly adaptive and efficient basis. High-Purpose Companies are, after all, a trend within a macro trend that is vital to humankind. It is my view that every shareholder, venture capitalist, executive, employee, activist, and consumer should immediately consider and support this group that is changing the face of business and so much more. These are the companies worth buying from, investing in, working for, and otherwise upholding—and there are *thousands* of such companies to choose from.

The High-Purpose Company is a book that gives readers a taste, a glimpse into a trend that is growing stronger every day as more enlightened businesspeople enter the fray with financially sustainable solutions that answer to fundamental, unmet environmental and human needs. Our high-purpose sample size was minuscule compared to what it could have been. This book may well have been thousands of pages long, for there is no shortage of great case stories or inspired business-people—especially when one looks to Europe, Asia, Australia, South America, and Canada for inspiration.

Personally, although it delights me to see so many exciting new ventures and "pure play" High-Purpose Companies emerging here in the United States, I am especially pleased to discover more multinational corporations legitimately investing in process change. I admit that I get a special thrill when I see McDonald's, Ford, Wal-Mart, Starbucks, DuPont, GE, or SC Johnson fundamentally shifting. I regard such change as a magnificent occurrence because what these imperfect companies do affects the lives of so many millions of people, makes such a substantial environmental difference, and creates such massive economic and market impacts. Of course, four of these companies have yet to pass the litmus test, and therefore it is also possible (although doubtful) that McDonald's, Ford, Wal-Mart, or Starbucks, the below-the-line firms, might for some reason decide that their corporate responsibility monies are better spent elsewhere. This is precisely why, for the time being, I consider it my personal purpose to help enable multinational process change. Although I realize that I will *not* fulfill this mission by praising firms unduly or overstating their accomplishments, I do think I can contribute by making crystal clear to the public the disparity between greenwashing and green growth—and by pointing executives toward sensible strategies that actually have a chance of making the necessary difference. For the sake of the planet, huge multinationals must transition in an optimal direction—as *rapidly* and *efficiently* as possible. If everyone encouraged multinationals to do this, by means of rejecting shallow gestures and embracing authentic ones, then the collective impact would be enormous.

Although I have identified my particular mode of activism (for which I am prepared to continue to be criticized by extreme CSR and environmental advocates), readers will likely favor their own. That's the great thing about this critical mass movement—its plenitude. Just as there are thousands of High-Purpose Companies to choose from, there are also countless ways to participate. No matter who we are, we can all blog; join protests or boycotts; spread word of mouth; ask the questions that deserve to be asked; promote good ideas and authentic change; reject bad ideas, lies, or overstatements; and support the companies we love through our daily purchases. We can all aggressively stand up for the leaders we believe in and stand against the leaders we believe to be wrong. This is *the* time for loud participants rather than quiet observers—and no time to follow the polite rules of society, where the topics of religion, business, politics, or the world's plight are left unspoken at social events or, heaven forbid, in the boardroom. By all means, reject old taboos. Raise a fuss. Debate serious issues and how they apply to your life, your community, and your company. Make a fool of yourself if you have to. Just do your part to get people critically thinking. This is the era when activists will seize the initiative and the day.

Al Gore is right: we *will* rise. Although knowing what to do or where we can all personally help to promote widespread change, let alone what problems to try to solve first, can be a very daunting prospect for many of us regardless of where our personal interests, affiliations, or professions reside. In such moments of perplexity, I myself turn to wiser people for guidance. I find that the most rational advice comes from political and business leaders like Robert F. Kennedy Jr. and Lord John Browne who, despite their palpable differences, talk about taking manageable steps toward making big change. (This entire book focuses on the same line of thinking.) Though radical change is mandatory, radical environmentalism, for instance, is excessively difficult to carry out and maintain in terms of business operability, governmental policy, and personal lifestyle. With respect to global warming and personal lifestyle, for instance, multiple resources like IdealBite.com, StopGlobalWarming.org, Treehugger.com, and *Plenty* and *Grist* magazines offer people useful tips about how to significantly reduce their carbon footprints without, as Jennifer Boulden from Ideal Bite puts it, "giving up on quality, style, or creature comforts."

Boulden says that once her users get the hang of how easy it is to buy locally grown organic products, switch to longer-lasting LED lightbulbs, keep their tires inflated, or escape from the clutches of junk mail, and reduce personal environmental impact by *a lot*, they grow more addicted to treading lightly. "Our users tell us that they equate reductions in eco-impact with improvements in quality of life," says Boulden. "It is a virtuous circle; a reinforcing good habit. People come at this from different entry points, and soon they understand how everything is connected and how it feels great to live in line with their values." Once people associate sustainable and quality, sustainable and convenient, or best of all, sustainable and *cool*, Boulden says, they come to think of their lives as one big earth-friendly treasure hunt and seek out commensurate experiences.

Initially, executives and consumers were turned off to the ideas behind corporate responsibility and green lifestyles because they were pitched too extremely, impractically, and judgmentally. "There was a lot of finger-pointing going on," says Boulden. Worldchanging.org's Alex Nikolai Steffen, author of *Wired* magazine's "The Next Green Revolution," agrees and portrays the movement's chief problems and future the following way:

> Green-minded activists failed to move the broader public not because they were wrong about the problems, but because the solutions they offered were unappealing to most people. They called for tightening belts and curbing appetites, turning down the thermostat and living lower on the food chain. They rejected technology, business, and prosperity in favor of returning to a simpler way of life. No wonder the movement got so little traction. . . .
>
> Business can be a vehicle for change. Prosperity can help us

build the kind of world we want. Scientific exploration, inno-
vative design, and cultural evolution are the most powerful
tools we have. . . . You don't change the world by hiding in the
woods, wearing a hair shirt, or buying indulgences in the form
of SAVE THE EARTH bumper stickers. You do it by articulat-
ing a vision for the future and pursuing it with all the ingenuity
humanity can muster.[6]

Today's green movement is about going forward versus back in time, increasing quality versus lessening quantity, living smarter *and* better. While the thinking and applications have grown more palatable and inspiring, need states have also increased as world problems worsen—causing *millions* of participants to willingly take part and, furthermore, to extend themselves. Increasingly, more people desire to achieve *personal best* through the movement itself. This desire allows participants to examine the most fundamental question in life: What am I here to do? What is my greatest potential, my higher purpose?

For me, rather than biting off more than I could chew by delving into the proverbial Why am I here? question at once, I found it helpful to first get my head around the way I had been living. There I was, recycling, buying organic, taking advice from experts on how to cut down on my personal carbon dioxide emissions. Then I visited www .myfootprint.org and learned that, irrespective of these things, my personal environmental footprint was so huge that if everyone lived the way I did, it would take 4.8 planets to support our lifestyle habits. According to this Web site, whereas it would take 6.2 acres of land just to support my personal annual mobility needs (I included flight for business travel in my calculations), there are only 4.5 biologically productive acres available worldwide per person for *all* needs—including mobility, food, shelter, and goods and services. Aside from being humbling, this experience along with others helped me to think differently about my life and what sorts of things I wanted to leave behind.

In critically viewing our past, present, and future, a lot of us might come to recognize various destructive patterns that have replayed themselves throughout the millennia. Enlightened citizens might agree that we just might be here to learn how to properly achieve balance and live constructively—even restoratively. If most every business, organization, leader, and person put *more* energy toward enabling this, then we might just save ourselves. But, one might ask, is the widespread implementation of collective purpose feasible? Could the combined force of IdealBite's user activism, *Wired* magazine's "Next Green Revolution," Gore's rise up, *New York* magazine's Purple Party, and the High-Purpose Company be tipping the global scales right now, slowly but surely? Which side—the critical mass or the resistance—will win the battle of big ideas and make our fate?

The final outcome is in our hands.

Notes

EXPLANATORY NOTE

1. Deborah Doane, "The Myth of CSR," *The Stanford Innovation Review*, Fall 2005 issue (http://www.ssireview.org/articles/entry/the_myth_of_csr/) accessed June 21, 2006.

PROLOGUE

1. Statistic taken from the Social Investment Forum's 2003 report, *Socially Responsible Investment Trends in the United States* (updated December 2003), page i.
2. Ibid.
3. Paul Hawken, "Is Your Money Where Your Heart Is?" *Common Ground,* October 2004, page 14.
4. According to the As You Sow Foundation, Pepsi has done far less than Coke on recycled content and container recovery matters. After serious resistance, the company finally agreed to match Coke's commitment to using 10 percent recycled content by 2005. Information taken from http://www.asyousow .org/sustainability/coke.shtml (accessed June 4, 2006).

   According to public records of a Form 20-F/A filed by ABB Ltd. with the Securities and Exchange Commission on April 9, 2004, the company pleaded guilty to U.S. Department of Justice and SEC complaints and paid a total of $10.5 million in fines for bribery incidents in Nigeria, Angola, and Kazakhstan that involved improper payments to government officials.

On March 7, 2003, Bristol-Myers Squibb and the Federal Trade Commission reached a proposed settlement regarding antitrust claims relating to Taxol, Platinol, and BuSpar. The FTC alleged that BMS's abuse of the patent and regulatory systems included paying a potential generic competitor $72.5 million to not challenge a BMS patent, abusing FDA regulations to stave off generic entry, making false statements to the FDA regarding patent listings in the orange book, "engaging in inequitable conduct" before the U.S. Patent and Trademark Office, and filing baseless patent infringement suits. Information taken from http://www.cptech.org/ip/health/firm/BMS/ (accessed July 27, 2005).

5. Comment posted by Pax World Funds, "Response to Paul Hawken," Letters to the Editor, *Common Ground*, December 2004, http://www.commongroundmag.com/2004/cg3112/letters3112.html (accessed July 27, 2005).

6. Quotes taken from Jeffrey MacDonald's "Has Social Investing Lost Its Way?" *Christian Science Monitor*, November 15, 2004, section 1, page 13.

7. Paul Hawken, "The Truth About Ethical Investing," AlterNet, posted April 29, 2005, at http://www.alternet.org/story/21888 (accessed July 18, 2005).

8. Terry Mollner, "Setting the Record Straight," Letters from Readers, *Whole Life Times*, February 2005, accessed at http://www.wholelifetimes.com/2005/wlt2702/letters2702.html, August 16, 2005.

9. Clive Crook, "The Good Company," *The Economist*, January 20, 2005, special insert, page 4.

10. David Vogel, "The Low Value of Virtue," *Harvard Business Review,* 83, no. 6 (June 2005): 26.

11. As of November 2005, Medtronic was under federal investigation for alleged kickbacks to physicians. Story reported by multiple sources including Emily Lambert, "First, Do No Harm," *Forbes*, June 6, 2005, http://www.forbes.com/forbes/2005/0606/170.html (accessed November 16, 2005).

12. *New England Journal of Medicine* claim reported by Diedtra Henderson, "Journal Says Vioxx Woes Suppressed; Merck Blamed; Correction Sought," *Boston Globe*, December 9, 2005, http://www.boston.com/business/healthcare/articles/2005/12/09/journal_says_vioxx_woes_suppressed (accessed December 12, 2005).

CHAPTER ONE

1. This description of Disney's purpose was derived from Jim Collins, *Built to Last* (New York: HarperBusiness, 1994) 78.

2. General Electric corporate Web site (www.ge.ecomagination.com/@

v=05272006_004@/index.html) pdf download, "Background information: I find out what the world needs, then I proceed to invent it." Accessed June 1, 2006.

3. Jeffrey Immelt, "Global Environmental Challenges," speech, George Washington University School of Business, May 9, 2005.

4. Enron, "Our Values," *Annual Report 2000*; http://www.enron.com/corp/investors/annuals/2000/ourvalues.html (accessed August 13, 2005).

CHAPTER TWO

1. Roper poll survey results as interpreted by Claudia Deutsch, "New Survey Shows That Big Business Has a PR Problem," *New York Times*, December 9, 2005, http://www.nytimes.com/2005/12/09/business/09backlash.html?adxnnl=1&adxnnlx=1134235292LnutOK+Z4TFJS1lP44PnpA&pagewanted=print (accessed March 14, 2006).

2. The Reputation Institute's 2005 corporate rankings were based on a scientifically developed instrument called the Harris-Fombrun Reputation Quotient. For more information, visit http://www.reputationinstitute.com.

3. Merck corporate Web site, http://www.merck.com/about/cr/ (accessed September 7, 2005).

4. Journal admission reported by Diedtra Henderson, "Journal Says Vioxx Woes Suppressed; Merck Blamed; Correction Sought," *Boston Globe*, December 9, 2005.

5. Quote reported by Gardner Harris, "F.D.A. Failing in Drug Safety, Official Asserts," *New York Times*, November 19, 2004, http://www.nytimes.com/2004/11/19/business/19fda.html?ei=5088&en=5192a663122d3e4b&ex=1258693200&adxnnl=1&partner=rssnyt&adxnnlx=1142110726-sOGqeiHT/T/Uw5d8n4eC6w (accessed March 11, 2006). Testimony accessible on Web: http://www.senate.gov/~finance/hearings/testimony/2004test/111804GStest.pdf.

6. Snigdha Prakash, health and science reporter, "Documents Suggest Merck Tried to Censor Vioxx Critics," National Public Radio (NPR), aired June 9, 2005.

7. Memo content reported by legal firm Specter, Specter, Evans & Manogue, P.C., http://www.ssem.com/investigations/vioxx/merck_vioxx_sales_tactics.html (accessed September 8, 2005). Memo content also appears in "Merck Hit With Multimillion Dollar Verdict in Vioxx Trial," *Brandweek*, August 19, 2005, www.brandweek.com/bw/news/recent_ display.jsp?vnu_content_id=1001018481 (accessed September 8, 2005).

8. FDA letter contents reported by *60 Minutes*, "Prescription for Trouble," aired August 28, 2005.

9. Quote reported by Beth Herskovits, "The Corporate Cure," *PRWeek*, August

29, 2005, http://prweek.com/thisweek/index.cfm?ID=240415 (accessed September 8, 2005).

10. Chevron's promotional Web site: http://www.willyoujoinus.com/vision/ (accessed September 12, 2005).

11. "Will You Join Us?" discussion board user commentary obtained from http://www.energybulletin.net/7149.html, http://jabpage.org/posts/chevron.html, and http://smirkingchimp.com/viewtopic.php?topic=36193&forum=7&start=400 (all accessed February 5, 2006).

12. Comment posted by Dr. Shepherd Bliss, message board, "What does the Chevron "Will You Join Us" campaign mean to the future of the peak oil movement?" http://www.websitetoolbox.com/tool/post/atlantabiofuels/vpost?id=612873 (accessed February 5, 2006).

13. Chevrontoxico.com, "Ecuador Trial Evidence Points to Billion-Dollar Liability for Chevron," press release, August 24, 2005, Quito, Ecuador, http://www.chevrontoxico.com/article.php?id=162 (accessed March 11, 2006).

14. Staff writer, "Monsanto Ads Censured but Safety Claims Backed," Reuters, August 11, 1999, http://www.gmfoodnews.com/re110899.txt (accessed March 11, 2006).

15. Staff writer, "GM Food Firm Rapped Over Adverts," BBC News Online Network, August 11, 1999, http://news.bbc.co.uk/1/hi/uk/416988.stm (accessed September 28, 2005).

16. Monsanto corporate Web site, http://www.monsanto.com/monsanto/layout/our_pledge/living_the_pledge/default.asp (accessed October 31, 2005).

17. Quote reported by Mark Nichols, "The Battle," *Macleans*, May 17, 1999, http://www.percyschmeiser.com/conflict.htm (accessed September 23, 2005).

18. Michael Gaworecki, "Don't Be Fooled by Corporate Greenwashing," *WireTap*, posted April 22, 2003, http://www.alternet.org/story/15699/ (accessed October 14, 2005).

19. As of 2005, Halliburton was being investigated by the U.S. Department of Justice, the U.S. Federal Bureau of Investigation and the Securities and Exchange Commission. For more information on the full extent of charges made against the company, visit http://www.corpwatch.org/article.php?id=12259.

20. Quote reported by Richard Williamson, "Under Fire, Halliburton Hails Workers' Courage," *AdWeek*, April 1, 2005, http://www.vnuemedia.com (accessed September 26, 2005).

21. Staff writer, "Halliburton: Public Relations Gaffe," *Houston Chronicle*, August 6, 2004, page B8.

22. Allstate's Web site, Advertising Campaign, http://www.allstate.com/About/pagerender.asp?page=main.htm (accessed September 29, 2005).

23. Texas Attorney General Greg Abbott, "Cease and Desist letter to Allstate,"

sent September 1, 2005. Available for download at http://www.domain04
.org/site/MessageViewer?em_id=5682.0&dlv_id=6741&JServSessionIdr01
0=b11mr5rba2.app8a (accessed March 11, 2006).

24. Staff writer, "Miss. Attorney General Hood Accuses Carriers of Cheating,"
Insurance Journal, October 3, 2005, http://www.insurancejournal.com/
magazines/southeast/2005/10/03/features/61099.htm (accessed March 11,
2006).

25. U.S. Bancorp's Web site, Corporate Governance, http://www.usbancorp.com
(accessed September 29, 2005).

CHAPTER THREE

1. Elizabeth Debold, "The Business of Saving the World," *What Is Enlighten-ment?* 28 (March–May 2005): 64.

2. Ibid., 63.

3. This UK construction industry statistic was reported by Bovis Lend Lease
Europe, http://www.bovislendlease.com/llweb/bll/main.nsf/all/news_
20050420_bll (accessed February 2, 2006).

4. Lawrence Meyers, "The Myth of Socially Responsible Investing," Motley
Fool, November 22, 2004, http://www.fool.com/news/commentary/2004/
commentary04112202.htm?source=EDNWFT (accessed October 18, 2005).

5. Nicholas Howen, Secretary-General of the International Commission of Jurists, excerpt from speech, Business and Human Rights Conference, Copenha-
gen, September 21, 2005, http://www.icj.org/news php3?id_article=3778&
lang=en (accessed October 19, 2005).

6. De Beers corporate Web site, Annual Review 2004, http://www.De Beersgroup
.com/De Beersweb/About+De+Beers/Financial+Reports/Annual+Review+
2004 (accessed October 31, 2005).

7. Greenpeace, "Environmental Groups Confront Kimberly-Clark at Annual
Meeting: Call on Kleenex Manufacturer to Stop Destroying Ancient Forests," press release, Irving, Texas, April 28, 2005.

8. Statistics referenced from Kleercut Web site, run by Greenpeace, http://
kleercut.net/en/whoiskc?PHPSESSID=a10d0e5576a9614da5b412a79cd303
0e (accessed March 14, 2006).

9. Kimberly-Clark corporate Web site, About Us, http://www.kimberly-clark.
com/aboutus/Sustainability2003/MessageFromKennethStrassner.asp (accessed
March 14, 2006), and Environment FAQ, http://www.kimberly-clark.com/
aboutus/env_qa.asp#q2 (accessed November 19, 2005).

10. Justin Fuller's quote reference from Alexandra Marks, "How One Airline Flew
Back into the Black," *Christian Science Monitor*, July 25, 2005, http://www
.csmonitor.com/2005/0725/p01s03-usec.html (accessed November 1, 2005).

11. Elizabeth Debold, "The Business of Saving the World," *What Is Enlightenment?* 28 (March–May 2005): 70.

12. Hypothesis proposed by Stanford University's Gretchen Daily, in *Nature's Services: Societal Dependence on Natural Ecosystems* (Washington, DC: Island Press, 1997) 23.

13. William McDonough and Michael Braungart, *Cradle to Cradle*, (New York: North Point Press, 2002), back cover.

14. President Hu Jintao of China, APEC CEO Summit, Santiago, Chile, speech, November 19, 2004.

CHAPTER FOUR

1. Staff writer, "Tiny Hole in Steel Pipe Led to Explosion in 2001," *New Mexico Business Weekly*, March 26, 2002, http://www.bizjournals.com/albuquerque/stories/2002/03/25/daily7.html (accessed October 14, 2005). Joseph Ditzler, "PNM Admits Mistakes Led to Blast," *Albuquerque Tribune*, March 23, 2002, page A1–A2. New Mexico Public Regulation Commission, Santa Fe, New Mexico, "Public Regulation Commission Reviews Pact that Would Commit PNM to Upgrades," news release, March 11, 2003.

2. ExxonMobil, "The Condition of Prince William Sound," news release, http://www.exxonmobil.com/corporate/Newsroom/NewsReleases/Corp_NR_Condition.asp (accessed October 21, 2005).

3. U.S. Department of Justice, "Exxon to Pay Record One Billion Dollars in Criminal Fines and Civil Damages in Connection with Alaskan Oil Spill," press release, March 13, 1991.

4. Information taken from the court order filed in the U.S. District Court for the District of Alaska, in re: The Exxon Valdez, January 28, 2004. Case number A89-0095CV.

5. Tyco, "Tyco Files Form 8-K Report On Improper Conduct of Former Management," corporate press release, September 17, 2002, Pembroke, Bermuda.

6. Ibid.

7. Marjorie Kelly, "Tyco's Ethical Makeover," *Business Ethics* (spring 2005): 14–19.

8. Quotes and references taken from BT Web site, http://www.btplc.com/Societyandenvironment, accessed November 1, 2005.

9. Verwayeen quotes come from British Telecom's CR report, *BT Social and Environmental Report: Let's Make a Better World* (London: British Telecom, May 2005), 4.

10. Statistics taken from *HSBC Corporate Social Responsibility Report 2004* (London: HSBC Holdings PLC), 2.

11. HSBC chairman Sir John Bond's quote referenced in the company's public document "HSBC Carbon Neutral Project," October, 2005, page 2.

12. *HSBC Corporate Social Responsibility Report 2004*, page 4.

13. Matthew Gitsham, "Report Reviews: An Assessment of HSBC's Corporate Social Responsibility Report 2004," *Ethical Corporation*, posted September 13, 2005, http://www.ethicalcorp.com/content.asp?ContentID=3881 (accessed October 31, 2005).

14. Gap, 2003 CR Report, *Gap Inc. Social Responsibility Report*, Paul Pressler's letter to shareholders, page 4.

15. Gap, 2004 CR Report, *Facing Challenges, Finding Opportunities,* Paul Pressler's letter to shareholders, page 4.

16. Gap corporate Web site: http://www.gapinc.com/public/SocialResponsibility/socialres.shtml (accessed October 27, 2005).

17. Gap, 2004 CR Report, *Facing Challenges, Finding Opportunities*, Paul Pressler's letter to shareholders, page 21.

18. LS&CO., "Levi Strauss & Co. Publishes List of Active Suppliers," corporate press release, October 11, 2005, San Francisco, CA.

19. Company quotes in previous two paragraphs taken from LS&CO.'s corporate Web site, http://www.levistrauss.com/responsibility (accessed October 28, 2005).

20. Wal-Mart, "Supplemental Benefits Documentation: Reviewing and Revising Wal-Mart's Benefits Strategy," memo, pages 1, 6, and 14 (accessed at http://www.nytimes.com/packages/pdf/business/26walmart.pdf, October 28, 2005).

21. Joe Garofoli, "Wal-Mart Hit Twice: Critical Film, Activism 6,800 Sites to Host DVD Premiere by 'Outfoxed' Director," *San Francisco Chronicle*, October 30, 2005, http://sfgate.com/cgi-bin/article.cgi?file=/c/a/2005/10/30/MNG4QFGE3H1.DTL (accessed October 30, 2005).

22. Wal-Mart, "Robert Greenwald to Release Another Misleading Video," press release, October 25, 2005, Bentonville, Arkansas, pages 1 and 6.

23. PNM—Quote taken from my personal interview.
    TYCO—Quote taken from my personal interview.
    BT—Quote taken from BT Web site: www. http://www.btplc.com/Societyandenvironment, (accessed November 1, 2005).
    HSBC—Quote appears in previous text with corresponding note.
    GAP—Quote appears in previous text with corresponding note.
    LS&CO.—Quote appears in text with corresponding note.

CHAPTER FIVE

1. Various quotes and references to William McDonough's thoughts and environmental leadership in preceding three paragraphs obtained from http://www.mcdonough.com/full.htm (accessed December 10, 2005).

2. Bill Ford Jr., "Remarks on Innovation," speech, September 21, 2005, Dearborn, Michigan.

3. Ford's internal dispatch reported by Bryce G. Hoffman, "Bill Ford: Get On Board or Leave," *Detroit News*, November 29, 2005, http://www.detnews.com/apps/pbcs.dll/article?AID=/20051129/AUTO01/511290350/1148 (accessed December 8, 2005).

4. Jumpstart Ford Web site, http://www.jumpstartford.com (accessed December 6, 2005).

5. Ibid.

6. Ibid.

7. Quotes reported by Florence Williams, "Prophet of Bloom," *Wired* 10.02 (February 2002), http://wired.com/wired/archive/10.02/mcdonough.html (accessed December 8, 2005).

8. Jumpstart Ford Web site, http://www.jumpstartford.com/why_ford (accessed December 7, 2005).

9. Bill McDonough's MBDC, "Cradle to Cradle Design," http://www.mbdc.com/c2c_home.htm (accessed March 9, 2006).

10. Dorinda Elliott and Joseph Szczesny, "Q & A with Bill Ford Jr.," *Time*, January 30, 2006, http://www.time.com/time/archive/preview/0,10987,1151763,00.html (accessed February 17, 2006).

11. Quote reported by Chris Isidore, "Ford to Cut Up to 30,000 Jobs," CNNMoney.com, January 23, 2006, http://money.cnn.com/2006/01/23/news/companies/ford_closings/index.htm?cnn=yes (accessed January 23, 2006).

12. Lee Scott, "Twenty First Century Leadership," speech, Bentonville, Arkansas, October 24, 2005.

13. Ibid.

14. All quotes and references taken from Lee Scott, "Twenty-First Century Leadership," speech, Bentonville, Arkansas, October 24, 2005.

15. Critic's quote reported by Lisa Roner, "Wal-Mart—An Environmental Epiphany?" *Ethical Corporation*, December 7, 2005, http://www.ethicalcorp.com/content.asp?ContentID=4009 (accessed December 27, 2005).

16. Wal-Mart corporate Web site, http://walmartstores.com/GlobalWMStoresWeb/ (accessed January 10, 2006).

17. Statistics cited by Paul Hawken, "On Corporate Responsibility: A Ronald McDonald Fantasy," *San Francisco Gate*, June 2, 2002, page D5.

18. Quote reported by Elizabeth Debold, "The Business of Saving the World," *What Is Enlightenment?* 28 (March–May 2005): 86.

19. Darcy Winslow, "Just Doing It," feature article posted on www.mbdc.com/features (accessed December 19, 2005).

20. Nike corporate Web site, http://www.nike.com/nikebiz/nikeconsidered/context.jhtml (accessed December 19, 2005).

21. "Starbucks Challenge" blog commentary featured on Green LA Girl home page, http://greenlagirl.com, (accessed January 21, 2005).

22. Starbucks, "Starbucks Annual Meeting of Shareholders Starts over a Cup of Coffee; Company's Impact Now Extends Well Beyond Stores' Four Walls," press release, Seattle, Washington, February 8, 2006.

23. Microsoft corporate Web site, http://www.microsoft.com/citizenship (accessed December 20, 2005).

24. Dell corporate Web site, http://www.dell.com/content/topics/global.aspx/corp/environment/en/prod_design_main?c=us81=en85=corp (accessed June 4, 2006).

25. Target corporate Web site, http://target.com/target_group/community_giving/index.jhtml (accessed December 30, 2005).

26. Google corporate Web site, http://www.google.com/corporate (accessed December 30, 2005).

27. Mattel corporate Web site, http://www.mattel.com/about_us/default.asp (accessed December 30, 2005).

28. Procter & Gamble corporate Web site, http://www.pg.com/company/who_we_are/ppr.jhtml:jsessionid=JG03FDBF3J4YBQFIAJ1SDHWAWAVABH MLKG (accessed June 4, 2006).

29. Both Tex Gunning quotes reported by staff writer, "I Have No Choice: An Interview With Tex Gunning," *What Is Enlightenment?* 28 (March–May 2005): 96.

CHAPTER SIX

1. Charles Holliday, *DuPont Sustainable Growth 2004 Progress Report: From the Chief Executive*, http://www2.dupont.com/Social_Commitment/en_US/SHE/usa/us1.html (accessed January 9, 2006).

2. Ibid.

3. Staff writer, "DuPont's Punt," *The Economist*, September 30, 1999, http://intranet.cseurope.org/news/csr/one-entry?entry_id=114448 (accessed January 12, 2006).

4. Gary M. Pfeiffer, DuPont senior VP and chief financial officer, "The Year 2000 Conference on Environmental Innovation: Creating Sustainable Business Assets for Today and Tomorrow," speech, The Year 2000 Conference on Environmental Innovation, Plaza Hotel, New York City, March 8, 2000, http://www2.dupont.com/Media_Center/en_US/speeches/pfeiffer_03_08_00.html (accessed January 12, 2006).

5. Charles Holliday, "Statement by Chad Holliday, Chairman and CEO, DuPont," Clinton Global Initiative Panel on Climate Change, New York City, November 17, 2005, http://www2.dupont.com/Media_Center/en_US/speeches/holliday_09_17_05.html (accessed January 12, 2006).

6. Charles Holliday, "From the Chief Executive," *DuPont Sustainable Growth 2004 Progress Report*, http://www2.dupont.com/Social_Commitment/en_US/SHE/usa/us1.html (accessed January 9, 2006).

7. Ibid.

8. Commentary obtained from DuPont's *2005 Sustainable Growth Progress Report*, http://www2.dupont.com/Social_Commitment/en_US/SHE/usa/us4.html (accessed February 6, 2006).

9. Alex Taylor, "The Birth of the Prius," *Fortune*, March 6, 2006, page 112.

10. Toyota North America, *2004 Environmental Report*, Toyota Letter to Readers, page 3.

11. Alex Taylor, "The Birth of the Prius," *Fortune*, March 6, 2006, page 113.

12. Toyota North America, *2004 Environmental Report*, Toyota Letter to Readers, page 3.

13. Aaron Robinson and Jeffrey G. Russell, "Toyota Prius: Perhaps the First Car that Runs on Guilt," *Car and Driver*, March 2000, http://www.caranddriver.com/article.asp?section_id=39&article_id=3218&page_number=1 (accessed March 9, 2006).

14. Brendan I. Koerner, "Rise of the Green Machine," *Wired* 13.04 (April 2005), http://www.wired.com/wired/archive/13.04/hybrid.html (accessed January 17, 2006).

15. Facts referenced from "Toyota Billboard Marks 100 Million Gallons of Gas Saved," Toyota press release, Torrance, California, November 28, 2005.

16. Quote reported by Alex Taylor, "The Birth of the Prius," *Fortune*, March 6, 2006, page 123.

17. Brendan I. Koerner, "Rise of the Green Machine," *Wired* 13.04 (April 2005), http://www.wired.com/wired/archive/13.04/hybrid.html (accessed January 17, 2006).

18. Jeffrey Immelt, "Global Environmental Challenges," speech, George Washington University School of Business, May 9, 2005.

19. References taken from GE corporate Web site, http://www.ge.com/en/company/news/index.htm (accessed January 19, 2006).

20. Quote reported by Daniel Fisher, "GE Turns Green," *Forbes*, August 15, 2005, http://www.forbes.com/business/free_forbes/2005/0815/080.html (accessed January 23, 2006).

21. Quote reported by Daren Fonda, "GE's Green Awakening," *Time*, (Bonus Section: Inside Business) August 2005, http://www.time.com/time/insidebiz/article/0,9171,1079496,00.html (accessed January 19, 2006).

22. Staff writer, "America's Most Admired: GE," *Fortune*, March 6, 2006, page 92.

23. Amanda Griscom Little, "It Was Just My Ecomagination," Salon.com, May 12, 2005, http://www.salon.com/opinion/feature/2005/05/12/muckraker/index_np.html (accessed January 18, 2006). Frank O'Donnell, "GE's Greenwashing," TomPaine.commonsense, May 13, 2005, http://www.tompaine

.com/articles/20050513/ges_greenwashing.php (accessed January 19, 2006). Shihoko Goto, "GE Joins Green Bandwagon," *Washington Times*, May 11, 2005, http://washingtontimes.com/upi-breaking/20050510-041031-8726r.htm (accessed January 18, 2006). Staff writer, "Green Electric? GE Unveils Eco-Strategy," MSNBC.com, May 10, 2005, http://www.msnbc.msn.com/id/7791657/ (accessed January 18, 2006).

24. Claudia Deutsch, "It's Getting Crowded on the Environmental Bandwagon," *New York Times*, December 22, 2005, page C5.

25. John Deere corporate Web site, http://www.deere.com/en_US/compinfo/envtsafety/commitment/index.html (accessed January 20, 2006).

26. Product facts and press release quote referenced from John Deere corporate Web site, http://www.deere.com/en_US/newsroom/2005/releases/corporate/2005_0728_wind.html (accessed January 21, 2006).

27. SC Johnson corporate Web site, http://www.scjohnson.com/community/default.asp (accessed January 20, 2006).

28. SC Johnson corporate Web site, http://www.dowhatsright.com/value.asp (accessed February 1, 2006).

29. Facts and quote obtained from SC Johnson corporate Web site, http://www.scjohnson.com/family/fam_pre_pre_news.asp?art_id=205 (accessed January 21, 2006).

30. JetBlue, 2004 Online Annual Report, Message to Shareholders, http://64.106.229.11/jetblue2004/letter.html (accessed February 10, 2006).

CHAPTER SEVEN

1. Robert Glassman, "The Education of a Social Activist," speech, Lawyers' Committee for Civil Rights Corporate Leadership Awards Luncheon, Boston, MA, September 14, 2004, http://www.wainwrightbank.com/site/Article-2004CRLeadershipAward-Speech.asp (accessed May 28, 2006).

2. E. Jeanne Harnois, "Bank Official Brings Financial Literacy to Inner-City Audience," *Boston Banner*, June 5, 2003; Trinity Creative Communications, "A Bank that Keeps Its Promise," *Angle e-Newsletter*, May 2002; Shawn Macomber, "Branching Out in Green," *Brookline TAB*, September 22, 2005; http://www.wainwrightbank.com/site/m2E.asp (all accessed February 15, 2006).

3. The IKEA Group publication, "IKEA Facts & Figures," 2004, page 14.

4. IKEA purpose statement referenced from "IKEA Social & Environmental Report 2004," The IKEA Group, page 4.

5. Staff writer, "The Miracle of Almhult," *The Guardian*, June 17, 2004, http://www.guardian.co.uk/retail/story/0,,1585492,00.html, accessed February 21, 2006.

6. Quote taken from Vault.com. IKEA Workplace Survey, Store Manager

Posting, March 11, 2003, http://www.vault.com/survey/employee/IKEA1_2146.html (accessed February 22, 2006).

7. References from previous three paragraphs taken from IKEA corporate Web site, http://www.ikea-group.ikea.com/work/why.html (accessed February 22, 2006).

8. Anders Dahlvig quote referenced from "IKEA Social & Environmental Report 2004," The IKEA Group, page 10.

9. Ibid.

10. "Fan" letter and subsequent passage from Patagonia, *Louder Than Words*, 1998, page 9.

11. Ibid., 2.

12. Ibid., 8.

13. Patagonia corporate Web site, http://www.patagonia.com/enviro/our_buildings.shtml (accessed February 27, 2006).

14. Patagonia, *Louder Than Words*, 1998, page 2.

15. Eileen Fisher corporate Web site, http://www.eileenfisher.com/scripts/ecatalogisapi.dll/ (accessed March 1, 2006).

16. Ibid.

17. Abraham H. Maslow, *Motivation and Personality*, 3rd Edition (New York: HarperCollins, 1987), 23.

EPILOGUE

1. Al Gore, "The Future Is Green," *Vanity Fair*, May 2006, page 197.

2. Jeffrey Kluger, "Global Warming," *Time*, April 3, 2006, cover and page 6.

3. Al Gore, "The Future Is Green," *Vanity Fair*, May 2006, page 197.

4. Kurt Anderson, "Introducing the Purple Party," *New York*, April 24, 2006, http://newyorkmetro.com/news/politics/16713/index1.html (accessed May 5, 2006).

5. Mark Hertsgaard, "While Washington Slept," *Vanity Fair,* May 2006, pages 203 and 238.

6. Alex Nikolai Steffen, "The Next Green Revolution," *Wired* 14.05 (May 2006): 139.

index